WHAT O

"I am so thrilled that Diane Cranley has written *8 Ways to Create their Fate* and I am already looking for ways to integrate it into my consulting, teaching, and advocacy work. For many years Diane has been a guest lecturer in my classes at California State University Fullerton at both the undergrad and graduate level. Based on student feedback, I can say her impact is immediate, profound, and powerful. In sharing her own story she makes people comfortable enough to open up to the idea of talking more about childhood sexual abuse. She then uses that comfort level to help her audience connect with, understand, and then fully comprehend the depth of her idea that 'we grant child molesters access to our children.' Finally, she inspires us to step up and become part of the solution with her easy to implement and virtually foolproof best practices. What I find most excellent about Diane's approach is that the best practices are designed to actually prevent child abuse before it could ever occur. We don't have to wait until after the kid is molested to act, in fact, that is much too late for prevention!"

—Dallas M. Stout, Psy.D.
Faculty, California State University Fullerton,
Dept of Counseling and Dept of Child & Adolescent Studies
Faculty, University of the Rockies,
School of Professional Psychology and School of
Organizational Leadership
Co-Owner, DoctorS Nonprofit Consulting

"As a healthy sexuality advocate, speaker, author and coach, I have seen far too many devastating impacts of childhood sexual boundary violations. The need for effective protection measures weighs heavy on my heart, but Diane Cranley is now lifting much of that weight.

8 Ways to Create their Fate stands alone! I have never seen another book that equips and empowers youth-serving organizational leaders to effectively protect the children in their care from sexual abuse. Diane imparts both extensive understanding of the topic of child sexual abuse as well as hundreds of specific recommended actions leaders can take to better protect children. Diane makes it easy to begin moving forward with changes immediately. *8 Ways to Create their Fate* has the potential to change the face of the child sexual abuse pandemic as we know it. It's simply brilliant!"

—*Shannon Ethridge, M.A.*
Million-copy best-selling author, speaker,
life coach, and creator of
B.L.A.S.T. Mentoring (Building Leaders, Authors,
Speakers and Teachers)
www.shannonethridge.com
www.blastmentoring.com

"As an advocate and educator for protecting children from predatory crimes, I am often asked for advice about creating policies that will help prevent child sexual abuse. *8 Ways to Create their Fate* is a gift to children, families, and those of us determined to keep them safe. As Diane says, 'The protection of our children is not optional.' This comprehensive guide will empower your organization's stakeholders to develop thoughtful, robust policies and practices that will deter child molesters from wanting to work for you and empower staff, parents, and most importantly, children, to understand appropriate boundaries and facilitate early reporting and communication about problematic behaviors to stop abuse before it begins. Together, we can stop crimes against children. Be Brave."

—*Erin Runnion*
Child Protection Advocate and
Founding Director of The Joyful Child Foundation
- In Memory of Samantha Runnion

"Ms. Cranley provides valuable information in *8 Ways to Create their Fate* that is presented in a clear, understandable format that can be readily applied to an organization's operations. The staggering reality of the pervasiveness of child sexual abuse not only at home, but in schools, churches, and other youth-serving organizations warrants a detailed review and implementation of the practices identified. Implementing such policies and administrative regulations, training staff, and arming those working with children with this knowledge will not only decrease an organization's risk, but more importantly will protect those children entrusted to them."

—Rafael Fernandez MPA, ARM, CSP
Former School District Risk Manager

"Diane Cranley's book - *8 Ways to Create their Fate* is an invaluable contribution to the field of sexual abuse prevention and recovery. As a treatment provider to sex offenders as well as victims, I recommend this primer as a staple for every teacher, counselor, clergyperson, coach, and parent's library. The information and practices posited herein can be helpful not only in the prevention of child sexual abuse, but also for the recovery of offenders in managing their behavioral choices; an unavoidable, albeit unpopular, component in child protection."

—Nancy B. Irwin, PsyD
Los Angeles, CA

"*8 Ways to Create their Fate* is a comprehensive road map to ending the sexual victimization of children in youth-serving organizations. If all youth professionals implemented the policies in this book, the impact would be monumental. I urge every person working with youth to be bold and put these practices to work so children are safe from sexual abuse."

—Feather Berkower, M.S.W.
Child Abuse Prevention Educator & Author
Parenting Safe Children, LLC

"Does your organization serve children and youth in any capacity? School, pre-school, church, after school programs, sports, music, or summer camps? Diane Cranley has done your homework for you! In *8 Ways to Create their Fate* you will find valuable vetted resources to build a safety plan that guards our most vulnerable community members, our children. This book is a tool to evaluate your current practices and assure that all staff and volunteers understand the issues, know when to speak up, and are prepared to take action."

—Dr. Sandra Morgan
Director Global Center for Women and Justice Vanguard
University

"*8 Ways to Create their Fate* by Diane Cranley fills an important gap for agencies serving children and teens. It is comprehensive in its scope and best of all does not shy away from describing the sexual acts perpetrated upon children that must not only be acknowledged but discussed among anyone proposing to reduce the risk of abuse. This can be used as a training guide as well as a reference book. Diane includes references and studies that are current and support her statements that abuse is a common, rather than an unusual occurrence.

Thank you, Diane, for making the time to create this book that also serves as a planning guide, for those who are serious about their agency turning from reading to action."

—Nora J. Baladerian, Ph.D.
Executive Director, The Disability and Abuse Project
Author of "A Risk Reduction Workbook for
Parents and Service Providers
to Individuals with Intellectual and
Developmental Disabilities"
www.disabilityandabuse.org

"*8 Ways to Create their Fate* references primarily U.S. statistics and laws but child molesters' behaviors are universal, making Diane Cranley's prevention recommendations applicable internationally. I am highly recommending this book to all organizations dealing with children. In fact, I will recommend it to anyone who has a child in her care. It does not mince words nor does it try to be nice. Most child protection policies are very general and do not teach how it should be implemented. This book does it and more!"

—Dr. Bernadette Madrid, Philippines
Executive Director, Child Protection Network
Foundation, Inc. Philippines.
CPN's vision is that all children in the Philippines are
protected from all forms of abuse. It is involved in the
creation of Child Protection Units in all provinces in the
Philippines.

"Diane Cranley is a leading voice in the battle cry against child sexual abuse. The personal stories shared here bring to life the realities of the need for these best practices and procedures for all youth-serving organizations. We all know that children need protecting, and now we have a step-by-step method in this useful and incredibly well organized resource. I am excited to recommend *8 Ways to Create their Fate* to my clients, and it should be required reading for anyone who has contact with our youth."

—Mary Felch MA, MFT & Survivor
Licensed Marriage and Family Therapist
& Expressive Arts Therapist
Specializing in Sexual Abuse and Trauma

"*8 Ways to Create their Fate* is a great practical guide for professionals. The book is unique as it gives an in-depth analysis of 65 specific boundaries that stop child molesters in their tracks and gives correct and in-depth insights about the way perpetrators think and act that is a fantastic guideline to identify perpetrators with certainty through their moves to groom parents and children. I found the section on cyber restrictions particularly important, explaining how child molesters often use technology to introduce sexually inappropriate discussions and even pornography to elicit sexual arousal before actually crossing the line to contact sexual abuse. Cyber restrictions that interrupt the grooming process are crucial to the safety of our children.

As a campaigner against child sexual abuse in India where every second child is sexually abused, this book can be adapted for the training of professionals including teachers, principals, children's home officials, women and child development ministry officials, as well as parents and the book is a must read for all child rights professionals working in the field of child sexual abuse.

I like and endorse Diane Cranley's statement: 'Child sexual abuse is predictable and preventable when we surround children with knowledgeable and outspoken adults. We all play a part in the solution.' I agree. It starts with you. Be a change agent."

—Sanjay K Singh, India
Founder Chuppi Todo Campaign (Break The Silence)

"In my 20 years of working as a social worker to protect children against sexual abuse, both in private practice and non-profit agencies, I have never found a book covering an area of protecting children written like this before. This organizational and systems approach to guiding our communities child focused agencies is a great start to ensuring there is one more added measure we, as providers, can implement. I would highly recommend reading *8 Ways to Create their Fate* as a guide to ensuring the safety of each child within your organization."

—Angele Morgan, M.S.W., L.C.S.W.
Author of "Healing Our Children: Surviving
the Impact of Sexual Abuse"
(A Non-Offending Parent Program)

"I sat down this morning to get a start on reading *8 Ways to Create their Fate* and found myself pulled into a clear, encouraging, in-depth flow of empowering information. Diane Cranley did a masterful job of focusing on saving our children while recognizing the challenges faced by those who care and want to make a difference. I was especially impressed with her segment on Potential Cultural Barriers, the examples she gave to support riveting statistics, and the resources she offered in 'Talk About Sex and Sexual Abuse'. This is a guide that will save lives, by a woman with heart who is committed to stopping the silence, secrets and abuse of our children."

—*Jeanne McElvaney*
Survivor of childhood sexual abuse
Amazon author of three books about childhood sexual abuse
(Books: Healing Insights, Childhood Abuse, Spirit
Unbroken: Abby's Story)
Energy Healer for survivors
GoToSpirit.com

"*8 Ways to Create their Fate* clearly illustrates how badly needed guidelines are in the fight against child sexual abuse in youth-serving organizations. As someone who has worked in this field for many years, I have been greatly concerned that so many youth organizations seem to generate and attract perpetrators and so little is being done about this problem. Ms. Cranley clearly outlines the prevalence and history of child sexual abuse; defines child molesters; and goes on to list red flags and signs of abuse in a child. The meat of her book is in the eight practices she defines and recommends. Attention to detail is her strong suit; nothing needed seems to have escaped Ms. Cranley. If every youth-serving organization complied with her suggestions the number of child abuse victims would go down dramatically. *8 Ways to Create their Fate* is thorough and highly informative and will be an enormous aid in youth-serving organizations, a must-have for anyone working in this field."

—*Marjorie McKinnon*
Founder of The Lamplighter Movement,
an international movement for recovery from
incest and childhood sexual abuse
Author of The Repair series, a program for
recovery from child sexual abuse.

"*8 Ways to Create their Fate* is a step-by step guide packed with expert guidance and invaluable information for educating youth-serving organization leaders, staff members, volunteers, and parents in understanding the multiple issues, barriers and needs for protecting children from sexual abuse. This resource is unique in that it isn't just a book--it includes free adjunct online training and educational tools to create tangible plans for sustainability in preventing child sexual abuse. As producers of documentaries related to adult survivors healing from childhood sexual abuse, we know all too well the need for comprehensive prevention resources. The simple, clear and thorough instruction, along with online training modules are practical and accessible. We have no doubt the enriching information provided in *8 Ways to Create their Fate* will empower service providers and parents to protect children, preventing thousands of children from sexual abuse each year. I only wish it were available years ago for adult survivors of childhood sexual abuse today who face such heartache as they struggle to overcome the effects of being sexually abused as children. Big Voice Pictures wholeheartedly recommends this book as a key resource for every youth-serving and child abuse prevention organization, related university programs and organizations, and public libraries. Parents need to include this book as a key resource in their home library."

—*Kathy Barbini*
Producer/Director and Founder, Big Voice Pictures

"Excellent read! *8 Ways to Create their Fate* gives a real insight into how child sexual abuse occurs and how children may be exploited at the hands of those who would harm them and how this can be prevented. The strength and resilience of Diane Cranley is overwhelming and her personal experience has helped shape and form the child protection issues that she has highlighted in this publication. Child protection is at the forefront of all that she does. This book is a must read for any parent and all organisations that surely have the interests of the child at its centre. It is well thought out and based on Diane's experiences as an advocate and her personal interest in this subject both nationally and internationally.

I have known Diane over many years and she is a seasoned campaigner and clearly knows the issues around child sexual abuse. I highly recommend this book as a survivor of child abuse and as someone who has also campaigned for many years on the issues."

—David Whelan, United Kingdom
FBGA (Former Boys and Girls Abused) in
Quarriers, campaign group.
A National Confidential Forum and
InterAction review group member in 2012,
Independent advisor to the Scottish Government,
and a committee member of
"Care Leavers Voice" UK Parliament.

"As the mother of a juvenile sex offender, who was also sexually abused without my knowledge, and stepmother of a victim, I must say that *8 Ways to Create their Fate* took any confusion out of accountability. What an accomplishment in the name of victims and non-victims to preserve our youth! This is a must read and follow for all parents, leaders and youth organization workers. Having this at our hands, allows us to put a non-complicated, yet safe and effective action plan in place, thus making a giant step in the proper direction. It gives everyone with children in their lives an actual blueprint in not failing them any further! Way to break the silence and TAALK!* I commend Diane Cranley for her amazing work and am recommending and presenting her work to the State of Nevada, so that we as a state are able to continue to move toward keeping as many of our children safe from child sexual abuse as we're possibly able!"

—Laurie Rielly-Johnson
Advocate for the Prevention of Child Sexual Abuse
and Proper Policy with Censure to One Size Fits All Laws

TAALK, Talk About Abuse to Liberate Kids, is the non-profit founded by Diane Cranley.

"As an activist and survivor of childhood sexual abuse I applaud Diane Cranley on her very important book *8 Ways to Create their Fate*. I intend to introduce it to every youth-serving organization I come in contact with. Her clarity around the set of boundaries organizations need to establish, learn and hold to is invaluable. I particularly like the clarifying questions in her 'Reflections' surveys, which will get you thinking. Diane's advice and direction to boards of directors, where the ultimate responsibility lies for maintaining children's sexual safety, is spot on. I'm certain that youth-serving organizations who employ Diane's directions will be very safe places for the children they serve."

—Donna Jenson
Founder Time To Tell
www.timetotell.org

"Intentionally creating environments where child molesters can't succeed in their work - a novel idea indeed! If you want to learn how to speak up for those who can't, read *8 Ways to Create their Fate* and learn to listen with your eyes. I was forever changed after learning about the shocking reality of the child sexual abuse pandemic. As an educator, member of several youth-serving organizations, and a mother, Diane Cranley has empowered and equipped me to be a change agent in my community!"

—Noelle Lopez, mother and educator

"As a mother and health care provider I cannot emphasize enough how important the knowledge in this book is to protect our children as they participate in youth-serving organizations. Although most of us know to teach our children not to allow anyone to touch their private area, this training is much more comprehensive. If 1 in 4 girls and 1 in 6 boys in the U.S. will be sexually abused by age 18, we are not doing a very good job of protecting them. *8 Ways to Create their Fate* will teach you how to decrease your child's vulnerability to abuse. It will train you how to recognize unsafe situations, discuss formal boundaries in youth-serving organizations and have effective conversations with the staff.

Abuse is predictable and preventable. After reading this book and completing the training you will be empowered to be a change agent. I whole heartedly recommend it to all parents and members of youth-serving organizations. Our children are counting on us, will you protect them?"

—Julie Messina
Physician Assistant and Mother, Orange County, CA

"Survivors of childhood sexual abuse often say there must be a child molester's playbook because the same tactics are seen over and over again, even across the generations. Finally someone has written the defensive playbook!!! *8 Ways to Create their Fate* is definitely a game changer in the fight to protect the sexual innocence of our children. Thanks Diane!"

—Connie Valentine M. S.
Co-founder of CA Protective Parents Association
Coordinator Safe Child Coalition.

"*8 Ways to Create their Fate* is the owner's manual that belongs in the hands of every youth-serving organization. A perfect guide on keeping the children in your care protected."

—*Mindy Uranga*
Child Advocate and Child Sexual Abuse
Prevention Facilitator

"I have worked with thousands of people who have suffered from child abuse at the hands of people who should have been safe - and I have longed for an effective book to help organizations endeavor to screen for perpetrators. Diane Cranley has analyzed the most effective ways of minimizing the possibility of abuse in the workplace.

Her knowledge is extensive and broad; her suggestions admirable and - with her online training – gives interested youth organizations the opportunity to benefit from her years of commitment to preventing child abuse.

The pandemic of child sexual abuse will only be contained if everyone, yes everyone, takes responsibility for the change. The actions provided in *8 Ways to Create their Fate* are a wonderful way for any organization to show they intend to be part of a positive change to help protect our children from the life-destroying impact of child sexual abuse."

—*Liz Mullinar AM, Australia*
Founder of the Heal For Life Foundation

"Kudos to Diane Cranley! She has utilized her expertise to craft *8 Ways to Create Their Fate*, a comprehensive guide for youth-serving organizations that will greatly benefit the fight toward child sexual abuse prevention."

—*Jill Starishevsky*
Author of My Body Belongs to Me -
A Book about Body Safety
Prosecutor, Child Abuse/Sex Crimes

8 WAYS TO
CREATE THEIR
FATE

DIANE CRANLEY

8 WAYS TO
CREATE THEIR
FATE

**PROTECTING THE SEXUAL INNOCENCE OF CHILDREN
IN YOUTH-SERVING ORGANIZATIONS**

Published in the United States of America

ISBN: 978-1-54662-892-7
1. Social Science / Sexual Abuse & Harassment
2. Family & Relationships / Abuse / Child Abuse
15.01.20

I dedicate this book to the children in your care—
past, present, and future

ACKNOWLEDGMENTS

First, I would like to thank my parents who were my strength and my comfort when my daughter first disclosed that my ex-husband was abusing her eight years ago. They have supported my vision for making a difference in the lives of children and continue to be my greatest cheerleaders.

I would like to thank my children for agreeing to go public with our story so that we could use it to educate others on how to prevent abuse. They have shown great strength and courage in the face of adversity and have never given up the belief that full healing is possible. They have always supported my calling despite the long hours, dirty house, lack of money, and my seemingly never-ending focus on the dark world of child sexual abuse. Their continued support has allowed us all to see faith and hope restored for the many survivors who cross our path. I love them dearly and look forward to supporting their callings as well.

Of course, I have to thank every survivor and parent who have had the courage to share their story with me. Without them, this book would not have been possible. I hope they will read this book and see how their courage has turned into a gift of protection for other children.

Special thanks go out to all the child sexual abuse pandemic experts who have come before me and paved the way. I have learned so much from you, and together, we are making a difference. I specifically want to thank Anne Lee, founder of Darkness to Light, who was the first expert to take me by the hand and encourage me to make a difference as she has.

I would like to thank Blaine Ung for challenging me to write this book. Though it has taken me several years to finish, I know that it is the first of many and that it will leave a lasting impact on the world. I trust that these words will come to life in many who will find the courage and confidence to intercede on behalf of kids, potentially changing the course of their lives.

Thanks to Rafael Fernandez for his time and for his invaluable feedback on the book, from the perspective of a former school administrator and as a risk management consultant. Special thanks to his wife Judy for her patience with his time away from their family.

I want to give a special call out to Jake Hart who stepped in to design the back cover of the book in record time. Jake also volunteered his expertise to film and produce the associated online training for the book and to support our on-going production needs.

Thanks to my friends and other family members who have encouraged me along the way and my deepest appreciation goes out to my fellow prayer warriors who have held me up on many occasions.

I am grateful for the provision it took to make this book possible and the life experiences which created my passion to write it.

CONTENTS

AUTHOR'S NOTE

Seven years ago, my daughter disclosed that she was being sexually abused by my ex-husband. In the process of standing up to protect and support her, I had to face my own abuse at the hands of a modeling teacher after thirty-three years of silence. You might expect that as a survivor of child sexual abuse, I would have known how to protect my daughter, but the truth is, my silence enabled abuse to repeat itself in my family, the same way that silence enables child molesters to work unimpeded in youth-serving organizations across the country and around the world.

The reason I wrote this book was to encourage you to talk and give you the words, lots of words, to get you started. Not everyone will agree with the words I have shared and that's okay. Not every organization will be able to implement each idea, even if they agree with them, because of obstacles that must be worked through over time. But if you are willing to engage in the process of debate, taking what I have written and using it to create open conversation within your organization and with the families you serve, I will have achieved my goal, and together, we will have broken the silence that enables child molesters to hurt our children.

I have spent the last seven years learning everything I could about the child sexual abuse pandemic. In addition to reading hundreds of books, research papers, and news articles, I have formally interviewed hundreds of experts, representing sixteen countries and every facet of this pandemic. I have also had the opportunity to personally support over two hundred survivors and parents of survivors through weekly support groups and I have spoken informally to thousands more. My discussions with survivors were by far the most valuable. Actually, they are invaluable because survivors are uniquely qualified to teach us how abuse happens and what adults in their lives could have done to protect them. Looking forward, that translates into a deep understanding of what *you* can do to protect the kids in your care.

I have trained adults representing every role in the community, including parents, grandparents, foster parents, educators, police officers, attorneys, pediatricians, nurses, doctors, pastors, youth leaders, coaches, dance instructors, day care staff, afterschool program staff, therapists, social workers, college students, and teens. In my experience, the vast majority of them are hungry to understand how child sexual abuse happens and what they can do to stop it. I believe people want to do the right thing, if they only knew what that was.

So I have synthesized thousands of survivor stories and validated them with research as well as the testimony of offenders through the expert work of Carla van Dam, Anna Salter, Robin Sax, and Michele Elliott to bring you this clear and concise guide on how to create an environment where child molesters virtually cannot succeed without being caught and therefore don't want to work.

We will never stop every incidence of abuse, but I do believe with all my heart that child sexual abuse is predictable and preventable when we surround children with knowledgeable and outspoken adults and we all play a part in the solution. If you are involved in a youth-serving organization and you are one of those people who would like to do the right thing if you only knew what that was, this book clearly defines your part in the resolution of this pandemic. It presents an extensive set of suggestions that each serve to better protect children. You will likely face obstacles along the way whether it is a union contract, lack of funding, or simply cultural resistance. My hope is that you keep your eyes focused on the kids and what you *can do* for them instead of letting what you can't do take the wind out of your sails. Every step forward decreases risk.

Whether you are the leader of a youth-serving organization looking to start or enhance your child sexual abuse prevention initiative, an individual staff member, or a parent, this book provides you the foundation for change and the words to break the silence that enables child molesters. I encourage you to read it thoroughly, use it diligently, and share it freely.

DEFINITIONS

Staff: I have used the term staff to refer to paid employees as well as unpaid volunteers or interns whether they work directly with children or not.

Offender: I have used the term offender to refer to anyone who:

- Has been convicted of an illegal sexual act against a child
- Has been accused of perpetrating an illegal sexual act against a child that has not yet been proven, in which case I refer to them a suspected or alleged offender

Child molester: To make the book easier to read, I have used the term child molester as an all encompassing phrase. This minimizes any confusion between legal terms, psychological terms, or industry jargon. Within this book, the term child molester refers to anyone who poses a risk to children because of underlying factors which could cause them to sexually abuse. These factors include:

- A past history of illegal sexual acts against a child, detected or undetected
- A sexual attraction to children, whether they have committed a crime or not

- Thoughts about perpetrating an illegal sexual act against a child
- Emotional, behavioral, or psychological disturbances that could cause someone to act on an unexpected opportunity to sexualize a child
- Engaging in any activity with children for the purpose of sexual gratification—theirs or others'
- Engaging in any activity which would lead to access to children for the purposes of sexual abuse or sexual exploitation
- Engaging in any activity which would serve to break down barriers to initiating sexual abuse or maintaining secrecy, such as desensitizing a child to touch or threatening a child
- Engaging in any activity which would serve to create trusting relationships with parents, caretakers, or youth-serving leaders in an effort to gain access to children for the purpose of sexual abuse or sexual exploitation

GETTING STARTED

On behalf of our children, thank you for purchasing this book and your willingness to read it. You have taken an important next step towards making kids safer.

The verbiage in this book is directed toward youth-serving organization leaders who are tasked with starting or strengthening their child sexual abuse prevention program. You may be ready to engage others in your organization. If so, this chapter outlines a step-by-step plan to put the information you learn into action as a team. On the other hand, you may be working independently to increase your knowledge and figure out how to get others involved. In that case, this chapter will provide you with a foundation that you can come back to after reading the book, when you are ready to bring others into the process.

If you are a staff member in a youth-serving organization that does not have the authority to make changes on behalf of the organization, you still have the ability to influence change from within. You can also make changes in your own personal boundaries and actions that will decrease children's vulnerability to abuse and effectively intercede on their behalf. This book will prepare you to be a change agent in your organization and in your community.

If you are a parent or other caregiver concerned about the safety of your kids when they participate in youth programs, this book will help you to understand the risks, and assess organizations' ability to provide a safe environment. It will also help you speak knowledgeably about the possible solutions where an organization's current prevention programs and policies fall short. This book will empower you to have informed and effective conversations with youth-serving organization leaders where your children participate and prepare you to be part of the solution, rather than an adversary.

This book is designed to be a long-term strategic planning tool for continuous improvement in the area of child sexual abuse prevention and support. It teaches you to create an environment where child molesters virtually cannot succeed without being caught and therefore don't want to work. I clearly define boundaries that, when followed, will significantly reduce the risk of a child being sexually abused while in your care. Most importantly, when boundaries are adopted as a formal policy, they empower management, staff, volunteers, parents, and children to be objective in their enforcement without being swayed by any individual based on trust, respect, or power. The policy applies equally to all.

Because of the comprehensive nature of the program, there is a lot of information to cover, but the process below will help you get started quickly, allowing you to produce an effective strategic plan specific to your organization. Remember this is a continuous improvement process, not a one-time event. It may take several years for your organization to implement the recommendations outlined in this book. Be patient and continue to move forward. Let's get started.

1. **Establish a team:** Create a child sexual abuse prevention team who will be responsible for developing your strategic plan. Involve a cross section of your stakeholders including those who are on the front lines with kids as well as

parents. This sets the tone from the beginning that you are all on the same side of the fight to protect kids.

2. **Read the book and complete the reflection questions:** Have each team member read the book and complete the reflection questions as directed. This process should be done independently. Give them ample time but set a deadline for completion.

3. **Schedule time to talk:** After your team members have all had a chance to review the book and answer the questions, schedule a time for everyone to talk about their response to the book and what they learned. Specifically talk through their answers to the reflection questions. Your silence enables child molesters. So, an important aspect of this process is to create opportunities to get comfortable talking about the topic.

4. **Complete the online training:** Have each team member complete module #1 and module #2 of the online training—this can be done as a group or independently.

5. **Schedule another time to talk:** Now that all of your team members have completed both training modules, create an opportunity to come back together to discuss what they learned and how it applies to your organization. If you opt to participate in the training as a group, you can just extend the session to include time for discussion.

6. **Develop a plan:** Developing an effective improvement plan is a two-part process. Part 1 is to review your current processes to see how they compare to the practices documented in this book. Areas where they fall short become opportunities for improvement. Part 2 is to review opportunities for improvement and establish priorities for closing the gaps between current processes and those documented here.

    *   *Part 1 - Complete the Assessment.* Complete the Child Sexual Abuse Prevention Assessment and Strategic

Planning Guide (assessment portion only). This assessment can be done as a group or you can assign an individual to complete the assessment portion and then schedule time to review it as a team to make necessary changes. This form is provided in the Exhibits section of this book and in electronic format at www.taalk.org on the Youth-Serving Organization Community page.

- *Part 2 - Complete the Strategic Plan.* Schedule a team meeting to complete the strategic planning portion of the Child Sexual Abuse Prevention Assessment and Strategic Planning Guide. This process will allow you to take the improvement opportunities from the assessment exercise in part 1 and develop a long term plan to close the gaps. The prioritization process should take into consideration the risk of not fixing an item immediately. It should also consider the time, skills, manpower, cost, and obstacles associated with the change. Some changes have a big bang for the buck. As an example, in the On-Site Boundaries section, you will learn about implementing volunteer rovers to provide unanticipated supervision which can make a huge impact on the safety of kids with minimal investment of both time and money. Look for these golden opportunities to tackle first.

7. **Execute the plan:** As part of the strategic planning process above, you will have identified the priority of each improvement opportunity, set target implementation dates for specific tasks, and assigned a team member to take lead responsibility. Now it's time to take action and put your specific plans into place.

8. **Review your progress:** Although individuals with responsibility for specific items will be providing regular updates as appropriate, it's important to schedule periodic

meetings to review your overall progress as a team. Make necessary adjustments to priorities, timelines, and needed resources. I recommend meeting monthly until your plan is in place and quarterly thereafter.

After you have completed these initial steps, you will simply need to continue to execute against your plan, review it, and adjust it as needed.

Remember, this is a continuous improvement process, not a one-time event. I look forward to working together to keep kids safe, so please don't hesitate to submit questions on our Web site. I have set up a Child Sexual Abuse Prevention Best Practices for Youth-Serving Organizations forum topic at www.taalk.org/forum to receive questions and create community. This will allow us to continue to learn from real-life situations and share our combined learning with others. Thank you for being proactive in the way you protect children!

INTRODUCTION

Predict: According to Merriam-Webster, predict is "to declare or indicate in advance; *especially:* foretell on the basis of observation, experience, or scientific reason."[1]

There are over 39 million survivors of child sexual abuse in America,[2, 3, 4] and from them, experts have documented time after time, behavior patterns that appear *before* abuse occurs. So with the right training, we can recognize when children are in danger and learn to put best practices in place that intercede, directly reducing the risk of abuse in our homes, neighborhoods, and youth-serving organizations.

> Child sexual abuse is predictable and preventable when we surround children with knowledgeable and outspoken adults. We all play a part in the solution.

According to Dr. Carla van Dam, the author of *Identifying Child Molesters*, if we have the right perspective that allows us to correctly identify risky behavior that might otherwise look wholesome and desirable, it will keep adults from being taken in by those whose interest in children should be cause for concern. Van Dam says, "This will protect children from situations in which child sexual abuse would otherwise predictably have occurred." She goes on to explain that, "Correctly identifying these behaviors generates opportunities to intervene long before children are at risk."[5]

As you can imagine and have probably experienced for yourself, child sexual abuse is a difficult subject for most adults to talk about, let alone the children who are its victims. Unfortunately, it is your silence that enables child molesters.

In the *Socially Skilled Child Molester*, Carla van Dam says, "Child molesters also gravitate to those people who are most likely to be too polite to fend them off, too shy and anxious to tell them to leave, too dependent to be assertive, and too impressed by rank, power, status or money to do the right thing. Child molesters deliberately associate with adults who cannot address these issues. They seek out adults who worry about hurting people's feelings. They charm adults who do not believe it could happen."[6]

The children in your care are counting on you to overcome these natural barriers, and this book is written to give you the knowledge, confidence, and courage to break the silence that puts your kids at risk. In doing so, you'll:

- Empower adults to hold each other mutually accountable;
- Teach kids the language of abuse and give them permission to tell;
- And most importantly, you'll put child molesters on notice that you're watching and your kids are off limits!

In addition to personally empowering its readers, this book clearly defines boundaries that when followed will significantly reduce the risk of children being sexually abused while in your care. Child molesters use a technique called grooming to slowly and systematically build trust with kids and adults alike, typically resulting in being granted private access to children which is when as much as 80 percent of abuse happens.[7, 8] These boundaries have been designed specifically to intercede with grooming behaviors. When adopted as a formal policy, these boundaries empower staff, parents, and children to be objective about their enforcement of the policy, without being swayed by any individual based on trust, respect, or power. The policy applies equally to all.

Not a week goes by that we don't see a headline in the newspaper or hear a lead story unfolding on the evening news about children being sexually abused.

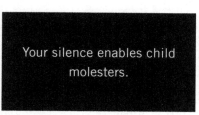

Your silence enables child molesters.

Sometimes, it's a local story of an individual child's allegations against a single offender. Sometimes, it's a snippet of the ongoing saga of a high profile case that includes a massive cover-up of years or even decades of abuse, such as the Catholic church, Boy Scouts of America, Penn State, or USA Swimming.

Child sexual abuse happens in epidemic proportions in the United States. In fact, child sexual abuse is happening in epidemic proportions around the world, making it a global pandemic. First, let's take a look at the prevalence of child sexual abuse in the general population so you can fully appreciate the gravity of the problem. Then we will dig deeper to better understand how this global problem translates into the microcosm of youth-serving organizations.

CHILD SEXUAL ABUSE
NATIONALLY AND GLOBALLY

The prevalence of child sexual abuse has been the focus of researchers for decades. The numbers have been fairly consistent over time, considering the differences in methodologies used and the specific definition of sexual abuse. Studies in the United States report:

Year	Researcher	Percent of Females Abused	Percent of Males Abused
1990	Finkelhor	27 percent	16 percent
1997	Bolen, et al.	20 percent	7 percent
1997	Gorey and Leslie	17 percent	8 percent
2003	Briere and Elliott	32 percent	14 percent
2004	Simpson, et al.	27 percent	20 percent
2005	Dube, et al.	25 percent	16 percent
2007	Albanese	20 percent	10 percent
2014	Finkelhor	26.6 percent	5.1 percent

The following international studies fall in line with the prevalence found in the United States.

Year	Researcher	Percent of Females Abused	Percent of Males Abused
2009	Pereda, et al.	19.7 percent	7.9 percent
2011	Stoltenborgh, et al.	18 percent	7.6 percent
2013	Barth	15 percent	8 percent

The bottom line is that child sexual abuse is quite prevalent. The most commonly used statistic is 1 in 4 girls and 1 in 6 boys are sexually abused before the age of 18.[9, 10] That is 20 percent of our children. To put that in perspective, the Center for Disease Control estimates that 5–20 percent of the US population will get the flu each season.[11] So this next flu season, when you hear "we can't make it, my husband has the flu" or "my son was throwing up all night" or "I really don't feel well, I think I'm coming down with the flu," imagine that they are all child sexual abuse survivors. Imagine instead that these survivors were saying "my mother was inappropriate with me my whole life" or "my uncle raped me" or "my priest molested me." Then realize that they likely represent a fraction of the people in *your* life who have been abused.

Let me get us on the same page by defining and clarifying what child sexual abuse is. Child sexual abuse is any sexual act between and adult and a minor or between two minors when there is a power differential between them. Differences in power include age, size, emotional maturity, advanced sexual knowledge, as well as forcing, threatening, bribing, or coercing.

In addition to sexually abusive behavior between minors where there is clearly a power differential, it is not uncommon for children to be touched inappropriately by other children who have been abused themselves and simply do not know that it is wrong. These interactions are often between children of similar ages. In these cases, an abused child may just be innocently reenacting what has happened to them or they may have been abused in their own home and specifically told this is how we show love for each other. So in the child's mind, sexual behaviors would be a natural extension of a good friendship. This can still be emotionally disturbing for the child being touched, even though the other child is not acting in a predatory manner. Some child-to-child sexual encounters are a normal part of a child's growth and exploration process and do not result in shame, anxiety, and secrecy.[12] For a better understanding of when sexual behaviors are healthy, concerning, or need professional attention, refer to Dr. Toni Cavanagh Johnson's pamphlet *Understanding Children's Sexual Behaviors: What's Natural and Healthy*, available at www.tcavjohn.com.

Child sexual abuse can come in several forms: contact, visual, or verbal as detailed below. The term abuse assumes that actions are taken with the intent to create sexual gratification for oneself or others. Intent is a key distinguishing factor between an action being abuse or not. As an example, it would be normal for a day care provider to touch the butt, penis, and/or vagina of an infant when cleaning them during a diaper change. However, it would be abuse if that same day care provider was touching an infant's private parts outside of diaper-changing activities or for a prolonged period of time during a diaper change with the intent of sexual gratification.

Child sexual abuse laws vary by state, but below are examples of inappropriate behaviors that may be considered sexual abuse in your state.

- **Contact Sexual Abuse**

    ○ Touching a child's private parts
    ○ Making a child touch someone else's private parts including adults or other children
    ○ Oral-genital contact in either direction
    ○ Vaginal or anal rape or any penetration with objects or body parts
    ○ Kissing: prolonged or open mouth

- **Visual Sexual Abuse**

    ○ Watching a child undress or go to the bathroom: voyeurism
    ○ Exposing private parts to a child: exhibitionism
    ○ Asking a child to play sexual games and expose themselves
    ○ Showing pornography or making a child watch sexual acts
    ○ Masturbating in front of children
    ○ Taking sexual pictures of children
    ○ Viewing, creating, buying, and selling child pornography

- **Verbal Sexual Abuse**

    ○ Using obscene or sexual language around children
    ○ Discussing sex acts or sexual gratification

Note that most children's sexual abuse training programs define "private parts" as the parts of your body that are covered by a bathing suit. However, I have worked with an endless number of adult survivors who were orally raped repeatedly, so it is important for us to teach our children that their mouth is also a private part and that they have a right to decide what goes in it, who they kiss, and who kisses them. It needs to be part of the empowerment discussion with our children. It might make it more difficult to get them to eat their peas, but that's a chance I would be willing to take! In addition, I have seen story after story of offenders rubbing the nipples of boys or the inner thighs of children. So we need to prepare our children for these types of inappropriate touches as well.

Visual sexual abuse can be just as damaging as contact sexual abuse even though there is no physical contact. As a matter of fact, I have found that survivors of visual sexual abuse often have a more difficult time healing than survivors of contact sexual abuse because it is not quite so obvious that boundaries were crossed. As an example, if a father makes a habit of walking around the house with his penis hanging out of his boxer shorts, a young child may be traumatized by the sight and the sexual energy that comes from his arousal, but it may not be clear to that child that it is wrong.

On the other hand, if a father fondles his daughter's vagina or sodomizes his son, it is much more obvious that a boundary has been crossed. While children who grew up experiencing sexual abuse in their home from a young age may not immediately know that fondling or penetration is wrong, as they get older and take sex education in school and start to talk with friends, it will become obvious. Whereas the survivor of visual sexual abuse still may not associate Dad's indecent exposure to be abusive even after they learn about sex. In these cases, survivors may suffer with the typical consequences of sexual abuse, but because they have not made a connection between their experiences and abuse, they do not have the basis to begin their healing process. Even after they realize that something was wrong and needs to be explored, it may take them years to go through all of the memories of their childhood to determine what was right and what was wrong and rewrite their boundaries.

Verbal sexual abuse is when people use obscene or sexual language around children with the intent of sexual gratification. Examples would include describing the details of sexual acts, what orgasms are and how they feel, or describing what sexually gratifies adults or how the thought of children sexually arouses them. It may include asking children about their sexual experiences such as if they ever masturbate and how it feels or asking a young boy if he has ever had a wet dream. Although the children are not engaged in a sexual act, young children are simply not developmentally capable of processing this information and it can be emotionally traumatizing.

As you can see, as we move down the scale from contact sexual abuse through visual sexual abuse to verbal sexual abuse, it is less invasive but not necessarily less damaging or easier to heal from. With the exception of pornography, as we move down the scale, it is also much more difficult to capture evidence and hold perpetrators accountable, often making it easier for child molesters to continue the abuse undetected for longer periods of time or claim it was an accident or a moment of poor judgment if they are confronted. In addition, if you flip the order of these three categories, it reflects the typical grooming process starting with verbal sexual abuse, moving to visual sexual abuse before crossing over into contact sexual abuse. Because of this, the less invasive behaviors may be a small part of a bigger picture and should definitely be considered a red flag. For that reason, I recommend that you take all of these behaviors seriously and allow the professionals to investigate and determine the full extent of the abuse.

What is most disturbing about child sexual abuse is that offenders are so successful in the grooming process that children rarely tell. Instead, they spend a good portion of their life holding on to this secret and living a lie that isolates them from friends and family. Research shows that only 33 percent of victims disclose as children;[13] one-third never disclose to anyone,[14] and a full 86 percent go unreported to authorities.[15] Protecting their secret also keeps child sexual abuse victims from getting the help they need to heal, resulting in long-term implications.

The long-term consequences of sexual abuse are staggering. Child sexual abuse is associated with a wide range of issues including low self-esteem, depression, suicide, anger and aggression, post-traumatic stress, dissociation, substance abuse, sexual dysfunction, self-injuries and self-destructive behavior, eating disorders, criminal behavior, promiscuity, teen pregnancy, contracting STDs, homelessness, increased risk of marrying an alcoholic, and marital problems.[16, 17, 18, 19, 20, 21, 22, 23]

In addition, there is a direct correlation between adverse childhood experiences (including sexual abuse) and adult health as found in the ACE Study by Kaiser Permanente in combination with the Center for Disease Control. This study looked at 17,000 Kaiser Permanente patients over a fourteen-year period and found significant increases in high risk behaviors such as smoking and substance abuse as well as direct health issues including chronic obstructive pulmonary disease, hepatitis, heart disease, fractures, diabetes, obesity, depression, and suicide. Victims also experienced occupational health issues and decreased job performance. Victims of extensive adverse childhood experiences had a life expectancy two decades shorter than the general population.[24, 25]

These issues represent the human toll of sexual abuse on its victims which eventually lead to a societal impact including increased healthcare costs, increased social services demand, prison overcrowding, need for substance rehabilitation services, the skyrocketing divorce rate, and workforce implications. Each victim who struggles with the consequences of abuse is likely to introduce dysfunction into the lives of their children, making them more vulnerable to child molesters, thus perpetuating the generational cycle of abuse.

CHILD SEXUAL ABUSE
IN YOUTH-SERVING ORGANIZATIONS

Now that you have a sense of the prevalence of child sexual abuse across the board, let's take a look at what it looks like specifically within youth-serving organizations.

Although we do not have statistics that reflect the prevalence of child sexual abuse in youth-serving organizations as a whole, research and the never-ending stream of news stories has provided us with a glimpse into some specific segments as follows:

- In 2007, the Associated Press released the results of a seven-month investigation where they found "2,570 educators whose teaching credentials were revoked, denied, surrendered or sanctioned from 2001 through 2005 following allegations of sexual misconduct. Young people were the victims in at least 1,801 of the cases, and more than 80 percent of those were students. At least half the educators who were punished by their states also were convicted of crimes related to their misconduct."[26]

- According to a 2004 report commissioned by the US Department of Education, based on data from the nationwide AAUW survey of eighth- to eleventh-grade students asking about incidents of unwanted sexual attention at school, "nearly 7 % or about 3.5 million students, report having physical sexual contact from an adult, most commonly a teacher or coach, in their school." "Reports of educator misconduct that doesn't include touching a student, but rather sharing pornography, sexual talk, sexual exhibitionism, or masturbation raised the proportion to about 10 % or nearly 4.5 million students." Settlements in teacher sexual misconduct cases in California between 2002 and 2008 had an average settlement of $2,723,000, with awards ranging from $892,000 to $6,800,000.[27, 28]

- In October 2012, the Boy Scouts of America's "ineligible volunteer files" were released. They identified 1,247 leaders and volunteers banned from the group after being accused of sexual or inappropriate conduct with boys between 1965 and 1985. "The national files are being distributed with the approval of the Oregon Supreme Court by a law firm that won an $18.5 million judgment in 2010 against the Boy Scouts in a case where a Scoutmaster sexually abused a boy."[29]

- A study conducted by John Jay College of Criminal Justice on behalf of the United States Council of Catholic Bishops, found allegations of sexual abuse against a total of 4,392 priests for the period 1950–2002 which is estimated to represent 3–6 percent of priests at that time. "A total of 10,667 individuals made allegations of child sexual abuse by priests. Of those who alleged abuse, the file contained information that 17.2% of them had siblings who were also allegedly abused." "More than 25% of the allegations were made more than 30 years after the alleged abuse began." "The total cost paid by the church exceeds $500,000,000." The abuse is alleged to have occurred in the following locations: "in the priest's home or the parish residence (40.9%), in the church (16.3%), in the victim's home (12.4%), in a vacation house (10.3%), in school (10.3%), and in a car (9.8%)."[30]

- David Finkelhor and team conducted a study of child sexual abuse in day care centers for the years 1983, 1984, and 1985. They found more than 500 day care facilities where sexual abuse occurred in this three-year period with more than 2,500 children victimized. Offenders in these cases included directors/owners of the centers (25 percent), teacher/professional (25 percent), nonprofessional child care worker (22 percent), and family of staff (36 percent). In 14 percent of the cases, the offender was a juvenile. 17 percent of the cases included multiple perpetrators—these cases were found to have the largest number of victims; be most likely to involve allegations of pornography, ritualistic practices, and extended and bizarre abuse; went on for the longest time; and the children appeared to have suffered the most serious and lasting kind of damage.[31]

- "An ABC News '20/20' investigation in April revealed that 36 swimming coaches had been banned by USA Swimming for allegations of sexual misconduct, including molestation and hidden videotaping of children in locker rooms. San Jose swim coach Andy King, 62, abused more than a dozen teen female victims over three decades and still had a clean background screening from USA Swimming in 2008, despite allegations against him and a police investigation. USA Swimming, the governing body of the sport in the U.S., is facing at least five lawsuits by swimmers who accuse the organization of failing to protect them from predatory coaches and allege cover-up at the top."[32]

- "The former director of a Big Brothers program in central Ohio has been sentenced to 10 years in prison for sexually abusing a boy." "He was one of the founders of the Big Brothers Big Sisters of Licking and Perry counties in 1969. He pleaded guilty last month to 25 sex-abuse charges involving a boy he mentored for several years. Another mentor from the same program was convicted of sex-related offenses…involving 11 boys, and was sentenced to 89 years in prison."[33]

- "On November 4, 2011, a grand jury report was released containing testimony that former Penn State defensive coordinator Jerry Sandusky sexually abused eight young boys over a period of at least 15 years. Officials at Penn State purportedly failed to notify law enforcement after learning about some of these incidents. On December 7, 2011, the number of victims was increased to 10. On June 22, 2012, Jerry Sandusky was found guilty of 45 of the 48 criminal counts related to child sexual abuse. Fourteen are first degree felonies." Jerry Sandusky gained access to his victims through a non-profit he founded called The Second Mile which served at risk kids.[34]

Clearly, the data shows that child sexual abuse at the hands of staff members is highly pervasive in every major segment of youth-serving organizations including schools, day care centers, scouting, mentoring, sports, and faith organizations.

In order to truly protect children in your care from sexual abuse, you need to be aware of four distinct risks that children face: (1) abuse by strangers who gain access to children either on your premises or during approved off-site activities, (2) abuse by family members or by acquaintances outside your program, (3) abuse at the hands of your own staff members, and (4) abuse at the hands of other children in your program. Your child sexual abuse prevention policies need to be comprehensive enough to address all four of these potential risks.[35]

The average child spends over thirty hours per week in school alone[36] and 15 percent of children spend an additional eight hours per week in after school programs.[37] On top of that, many children participate in sports and creative arts programs through youth-serving organizations. Simply by virtue of the amount of time children spend in youth-serving organizations, they play a key role in identifying signs of abuse.

States have recognized this crucial role, and "Approximately 48 states, the District of Columbia, American Samoa, Guam, the Northern Mariana Islands, Puerto Rico, and the Virgin Islands designate professions whose members are mandated by law to report child maltreatment. Individuals designated as mandatory reporters typically have frequent contact with children," according to the Child Welfare Information Gateway.[38] These professions may include youth organization staff positions such as teachers, principals, and other school personnel; directors, employees, and volunteers at entities that provide organized activities for children, such as camps, day camps, youth centers, and recreation centers; members of the clergy; and faculty, administrators, athletics staff, and other employees and volunteers at institutions of higher learning, including public and private colleges and universities and vocational and technical schools.[39]

If 20 percent of children are sexually abused before they're eighteen years old and children rarely tell, you can assume each day you serve children who are carrying the burden of abuse in silence.

If 20 percent of children are sexually abused before they're eighteen years old and children rarely tell, you can assume each day you serve children who are carrying the burden of abuse in silence. Do you know who they are? Would you recognize the signs? Are you willing to be the one they tell? Are you prepared to respond to their disclosure? Do you know how to spot a child molester? Are you willing to report a colleague you suspect of abuse?

These are just some of the pressing questions that you will have a chance to contemplate as you read this book. My hope is that by the time you have finished the book and the associated online training, you will be comfortable and confident in answering all of these questions with a resounding yes!

Let's take a deeper look at the four key risks children face. In past generations, child sexual abuse prevention was focused on "stranger danger" based on an assumption that strangers posed the highest risk to our children. However, in the last several decades, leading researchers have helped us to understand that less than 10 percent of abuse is by strangers.[40, 41] You will need to have strict boundaries in place that protect strangers from accessing children in your care, but this is not your biggest worry.

Study after study has shown that children are at significant risk of abuse within the walls of their own home. Yes, 35–45 percent of abuse happens at the hands of a family member[42, 43]— this includes immediate and extended family members. These offenders derive long-term private access to children through their family relationships and control their victims through inherent family authority. Children are often at their mercy because they depend on them to provide basic necessities such as food, shelter, clothing, and even love and attention.[44] In order to prepare yourself to help a child who is being abused at home, you will need to recognize not only the signs of abuse in children but also the behaviors that are indicative of familial abuse. However, this still isn't your biggest concern.

Your biggest concern should be the other 55–60 percent of abuse that is perpetrated by acquaintances that the child knows well such as teachers, coaches, and faith leaders.[45] Yes, these are the abusers who are likely your colleagues. Acquaintance molesters often seek careers or volunteer work with organizations where they can meet children. As a matter of fact, researchers Kenneth Lanning and Parker Dietz even refer to youth-serving organizations as a "well populated hunting ground."[46, 47] They go on to say that "acquaintance child molesters usually need repeated access to cultivate relationships with their victims."[48] This is your biggest concern because *you* are the ones responsible for protecting children while they are in your care.

The overwhelming hurdle here is that a recent study of educator misconduct found that only 11 percent of teachers would report abuse of a student by a fellow teacher.[49] From what we have seen in cover-ups across large youth-serving organizations, it seems clear that this collegial loyalty is widespread. Where does this leave our children? Who is protecting them if not you? The majority of this book is focused on empowering you to create an environment where child molesters virtually cannot succeed without being caught and therefore don't want to work.

The last risk that children face is abuse at the hands of older children. This body of sexual offenders crosses over the other three categories in that youth offenders can be strangers, family members, or acquaintances who work, volunteer, or participate in youth-serving organizations. Juvenile offenders perpetrate 30–40 percent of abuse against minors.[50, 51]

It is important to know that male offenders are responsible for about 90 percent of all abuse against children,[52, 53] but in the case of male victims, females are the perpetrators around 40 percent of the time.[54, 55, 56] So don't let the stereotypical profile of a child molester keep you from seeing that women and children can abuse as well as men, and that for the most part, abusers are people the child knows and trusts.

In so many of the cases of abuse within youth-serving organizations, the institution itself is being found culpable because of demonstrable negligence. This is typically due to lack of appropriate screening, lack of supervision, weak or non-existent policies and practices, and/or failure to report. As adult survivors stand up for justice and the protection of future generations, we will continue to see an increased demand for accountability. You have an opportunity to get ahead of the curve and be proactive in creating an environment of accountability before you're slapped with a lawsuit and public demand for change. This book provides a step-by-step guide to get you started.

Many youth-serving organization leaders have concerns that stop them from acknowledging the risk of child sexual abuse within their own organizations and taking steps to protect the children in their care. One of the greatest concerns is that past and current cases of abuse will come to light and the individuals and the organization as a whole will have to face the consequences accordingly. I can understand this concern because quite honestly, it could happen. However, allowing incidences of abuse against children to stay hidden doesn't serve anyone's best interest—certainly not the children, but honestly, the longer cases stay concealed (inadvertently or purposefully), the greater your organization's potential liability.

If cases do come to light, it simply reconfirms the need for the prevention program you are putting in place. Face the abuse that has happened in the past, stop the abuse that is currently happening, and create an environment that will keep it from happening in the future.

I'm sure you could come up with a long list of excuses for not moving forward with a proactive child sexual abuse prevention program because deep down inside, you don't believe you can actually stop it. John Eldredge said it well: "People also have a tendency to intentionally cloud the issue so that we don't have to take immediate action. High standards have a way of being ignored, because we feel as though we haven't the slightest chance of meeting them. Why bother? So we let moral issues remain cloudy as a way of excusing ourselves from ever really facing them."[57] I challenge you today to look at child sexual abuse through the eyes of a child being abused—the confusion, terror, shame, guilt, anger, and isolation they feel—and choose to do right by them, no matter how uncomfortable you are or how difficult it may seem.

Before we go any further, I want to acclimate you to what child sexual abuse looks like both from a perspective of the child molester as well as the signs in children who are being abused.

Many researches segregate child molesters into two categories such as fixated and opportunistic,[58] chronic and episodic,[59] groomers and grabbers,[60] and coercive exploiter or intimate exploiter.[61]Although their definitions differ slightly, they all seek to give us an overall vision of how child molesters interact with children. In order to create that vision for you, I would like to share the definitions of Charol Shakeshaft, a leading researcher on educator misconduct:

> Fixated Abusers—"most often found in elementary schools and the early middle school grades. This person is more likely to be male than female and is likely to be judged a good teacher by parents, students, other teachers, and administrators. Fixated abusers have a disproportionate number of teaching awards."[62]

This doesn't mean that outstanding teachers are child molesters, but it does imply that child molesters go out of their way to become outstanding teachers in an effort to gain the respect and trust of adults and children alike. Although Shakeshaft specifically refers to schools and the role of teacher, this definition also applies to child molesters in other youth-serving organization segments that target this age range of children. The same applies to the mode of opportunistic abusers, regardless of whether they are in a school setting or another type of youth-serving organization.

> Opportunistic Abuser—"These adults tend to be emotionally arrested and operate at a teenage level. They are adults who have boundary and judgment problems and aren't difficult to identify once their patterns are familiar to others in the school." "The opportunistic abusers tend to spend a lot of time around groups of students, talking with them, going to the same places they go, and trying to blend in. They are the teachers who want to be seen as hip or cool and who want the students to think they are part of the student peer group. They are adults who comment on the attractiveness of the students, talking about a student as hot or sexy. Their conversations about students are often inappropriately personal. They also know a great deal about the personal lives of individual students, more than would be available to an adult whose interactions were academic or appropriately friendly."[63]

It is important to note that these are general profiles and their associated target age ranges are not absolute. Some child molesters may show signs of both profiles and some child molesters that fit one profile may apply these tactics to a different age group. These definitions simply serve as a starting point for your education about child molesters. You will learn more about specific behavior patterns that allow you to more accurately determine if there is cause for concern.

I have talked with so many parents who say they teach their children not to let anyone touch their private parts, and while this is an essential step to empowering children, it is months too late and it is simply not enough. In order to keep our kids safe, we need to realize that by the time a child molester actually tries to touch a child's private parts, they have already created a relationship and an environment that makes it almost impossible for the child to stand up to them and say no, and it is unlikely that the child will tell someone afterward. A few months after my daughter disclosed her abuse, I asked her, "What made you finally tell?" She said, "Because I realized you already knew." Our kids are counting on us to figure it out, and more importantly, they need us to recognize signs of grooming and intercede long before a child molester tries to cross the line to abuse.

Child molesters will typically groom children and their families for months, sometimes even years, before violating sexual boundaries. Yes, I said "*and* their families!" Even adults that are aware of how child molesters groom children often fail to recognize how child molesters need to woo adults first in order to gain access to those children, especially young children.[64] Child molesters invest an inordinate amount of time in image management and ingratiating themselves to parents and other adults in the community, especially youth-serving organizations. This not only leads to private access to children, but it also establishes a level of trust that keeps adults from accusing them and/or believing an accusation made by a child or another adult. In addition, child molesters' close relationship with adults may make a child think that they would not be believed even if they did tell. According to Lanning and Dietz, parents may even encourage their children to spend time with an offender because they believe he is good for their child.[65] As you learn more about these grooming behaviors in the pages ahead, you will be empowered to intercede on behalf of the kids in your care.

As mentioned earlier, grooming is a technique child molesters use to build trusting relationships with children. In the process, they strive to break down social and emotional barriers, desensitize children to touch, test their willingness to keep secrets, and draw children into believing they are a willing participant in the activities, making them less likely to tell. If recognized, these grooming behaviors present an incredible opportunity to intercede before abuse occurs.

Okay, let's take a look at some of the common grooming behaviors that child molesters use. Note that just because someone displays one of these behaviors does not mean that they are a child molester. We are looking for a pattern which includes several of these behaviors. Any one of these behaviors should be considered a red flag that causes you to pay attention to see if there are additional behaviors that raise concern.

- Is overly helpful to adults
- Makes you or children feel uncomfortable with lack of boundaries
- Engages in excessive physical contact with children
- Spends more time with children than adults his own age
- Spends excessive time interacting with children via e-mail, text messaging, and social media
- Is unusually aware of kid's trends, terminology, computer games, and music
- Signs of other abuse, neglect, domestic violence, or substance abuse
- Exploits actual or implied authority and idolatry
- Overly interested in the sexuality or developing body of pre-teens and teens
- Arranges to spend uninterrupted time with kids
- Is great with the kids or too good to be true

- Showers kids with gifts, treats, and special outings
- Lets kids break the rules or get away with inappropriate behavior
- Asks kids to keep secrets
- Insists on bathing with or washing children who are old enough to do it themselves
- Goes into the bathroom when independent children are showering or using the toilet
- Walks in on children when they are dressing
- Creates an intimate emotional relationship with kids
- Significantly favors one child over another or one age range over another
- Watches pornography or has sex in front of kids
- Is always singing children's praises to their parents
- Gives gifts to parents
- Insists on private behind closed doors time with kids
- Administers regular enemas or medical checks (more common in incest abuse and group homes)
- Leaves the bedroom during the night or insists on kids sleeping in their bed (incest abuse, group homes, or overnights)

Now that you have a feel for the grooming behaviors of child molesters, let's turn our attention to the children. As you can imagine, most children do not know how to tell someone that they are being sexually abused. Young children may not even know what's happening or that it is wrong. Even if they do, they rarely have the vocabulary or the courage to describe what they have experienced.

I have talked in detail with hundreds of survivors who share how they were "screaming" for help, but no one came to the rescue. As they describe how they were screaming for help, they typically list the signs that were overlooked and the ways that they acted out emotionally, behaviorally, and sexually in an effort to get someone's attention. Our children are counting on us to figure it out. In the absence of words, we need to see the signs; we need to learn to "listen with our eyes."

> We need to listen with our eyes.

Let's take a look at the three main categories of signs of abuse which include physical signs, emotional and behavioral signs, and sexual signs. Don't expect obvious physical signs when a child is being sexually abused. Much of abuse is perpetrated without leaving any physical evidence of the interaction.

Physical Signs

- Evidence of physical trauma: blood, swelling, or tears in the skin around the vagina, penis, or anus (children exhibiting these signs should be taken to a hospital immediately for a forensic exam)
- Complaints of pain during urination or bowel movements
- Exhibiting symptoms of genital or urinary tract infections or STDs: offensive odor, itching, redness, rashes, blisters, or discharge in the genital area or the mouth and throat
- Stress-related illnesses: chronic stomachaches or recurring migraine headaches
- Self-mutilation: pinching themselves, burning themselves, puncturing themselves with pins, or cutting their bodies with knives or razor blades without intending to commit suicide

Emotional or Behavioral Signs

- Anxiety, panic attacks, phobias, and signs of post-traumatic stress disorder
- Extreme fear
- Aggressive behavior toward friends and family
- Withdrawal from friends, family, or activities they previously enjoyed

- Fear of certain people, places, or activities
- Excessive sadness, depression, or suicide attempts
- Decreased school performance
- Eating disorders, loss of appetite, gagging
- Sleep disturbances, nightmares, and screaming
- Regressive behaviors, bedwetting, separation anxiety
- Numbing their pain with alcohol, drugs, or cutting
- Perfection and signs of obsessive-compulsive disorder
- Loss of memory of certain years or large blocks of time

Sexual Signs

- Increased questions about human sexuality
- Excessive masturbation or masturbating in public
- Increased sexual play with friends, pets, or toys
- Talking about or acting out specific sexual acts
- Increased choice of sexually revealing clothing or covering up
- Signs of promiscuity
- Teen pregnancy
- Depicting people in a sexual way in pictures

Most child sexual abuse advocates will tell you what you are looking for is a change in behavior. It's very common for survivors to tell me that if you laid their report cards out on the table, you could easily pinpoint when the abuse happened as reflected by a sudden change in their school performance. That change was usually a drop in performance, but some actually became obsessed with school because it was the only thing they could control and it kept their mind busy so they didn't have to think about the abuse. So I would agree with this logic about change in behavior, but we also have to remember that if abuse has been happening at home since a young age, you may see these signs, but the signs of distress have always been there so you would not notice a *change* in behavior.

Please take the time to understand these signs and learn to listen with your eyes. It could make all the difference in a child's future. The following story is a great example of a mom who listened with her eyes and rescued her child from the hands of a child molester!

As a naïve fifteen-year-old, I didn't know what Gerry, an esteemed leader in our church, was up to when he enlisted me to clean his already immaculate home on a weekly basis. He would have me alone in his home during those times. His comments about my developing body made me very uncomfortable and his asking me to keep our relationship secret from other church members was confusing. The day he made me sit on his bed and told me I needed to relax while he would use a vibrator to rub my back frightened me immensely. I didn't know what a vibrator was! I was terrified to allow him to touch me. I demanded he take me home, claiming I felt sick. Actually, he had made me sick. The minute I got home, my mom took one look at my face and noted something wasn't right. She asked questions and I told her what I wouldn't have if she hadn't queried. She took a big stand for me and protected me by never allowing me to be alone with him again.

Gerry had ingratiated himself to our tiny struggling church with generous donations and a sad story of nearly dying in a hotel fire that left him toting an oxygen tank around. He had presented me with an expensive study Bible as a gift. My parents trusted him. Our concerns voiced to the board went unheard and unheeded. Sadly, Gerry went on to fully molest the pastor's twin daughters. The truth came out when one of the girls attempted suicide. Their victimization could have been avoided or cut short had the board listened and preceded in a logical manner to protect kids.

Now that we have covered the basics of the problem of child sexual abuse nationally and in youth-serving organizations, let us switch gears and begin to talk about the solution which will be the focus of the rest of the book.

THE SOLUTION

Child sexual abuse is predictable and preventable when we surround children with knowledgeable and outspoken adults. We *all* play a part in the solution. I am calling on all adults in communities across the country and around the world to become knowledgeable about the child sexual abuse pandemic. I have made my core prevention training available on our Web site (www.taalk.org/training) at no cost. So there is no reason not to get educated and begin to understand your role in the resolution of this pandemic. The online training delves deeper into understanding the signs of abuse in children and the grooming behaviors of child molesters, but most importantly, it helps you take a big problem and turn it into a set of actionable steps to help just the kids in your life.

It reminds me of a story often told about a little boy on the beach: a man came across a young boy who was throwing starfish back into the ocean one at a time; it seems thousands of them had washed up on to shore in a storm. The man said to the boy, "Why bother, it won't make a difference, there are too many of them?" As the little boy picked up another starfish and threw it back into the water, he said, "It made a difference to that one!" I encourage you to look at the child sexual abuse pandemic in this way. Don't be overwhelmed by the gravity of the situation: just focus on the kids in your life and what you can do to protect them. If we each do that, I'm confident we can all "make a difference to that one!"

The rest of the information in this book is categorized into eight practices that are focused on policy recommendations and actionable steps you can follow which will have a direct and positive impact on your ability to protect the children in your care. My hope is that as you implement these recommendations, they become more than just a policy to follow, instead they become a way of thinking and a way of being which will make the protection of children's sexual innocence second nature. This new way of *being* will indeed empower you to impact the fate of the children you serve.

I would like to say that the recommendations in this book are based on the best practices that are currently implemented in a wide variety of youth-serving organizations but the truth is, the industry as a whole lacks in-depth child sexual abuse prevention policies. Lanning and Dietz said, "We believe that the standard to which organizations should aspire should be based on informed best practice, not merely what most similar organizations do."[66] I have written this book in an effort to bring those informed best practices from a wide variety of survivors, researchers and other experts into a single easy to use training and reference guide, placing a stake in the ground on informed best practices we can all aspire to. The eight informed best practices are as follows:

- #1 Determine Your Starting Point
- #2 Manage Access to Children
- #3 Set, Document, and Enforce Boundaries
- #4 Regularly and Actively Assess Behaviors
- #5 Create an Accountability Team
- #6 Educate and Empower Children
- #7 Pre-Establish Your Response and Take Bold Action
- #8 Provide Support and Resource Referrals

The best practices are the same for every adult in the community, though they may implement them differently based on their role(s). As an example, a therapist would support victims and their families in a very different manner than a basketball coach would. The eight best practices are designed to help people easily grasp and remember a wealth of information by quickly correlating it back to these eight basic concepts. The best practices are also designed to create a common language across the community. A parent can easily talk with their child's teacher about how the school manages access to children through interviews, references, and background checks of potential staff and turn around the next day and talk with a neighbor about who will be in the house (have access) during a proposed play date.

So let's move on and look at how these eight best practices apply to youth-serving organizations.

BEST PRACTICE #1

DETERMINE
YOUR STARTING POINT

Although each organization has a culture of its own, organizations are made up of individuals who create that culture—some cultures are created from the top down by leaders of the organization and others are organically created by the masses within the organization. Effectively protecting the children in your care must stem from understanding both the organizational culture as well as the individuals who have created it.

Some of your staff may have participated in extensive training on child sexual abuse prevention in the past and be completely comfortable talking about it. However, as mentioned in the introduction, child sexual abuse is a difficult subject for most people to talk about, and quite honestly, most people haven't had much experience doing it.

I talk with people on a regular basis that are mandated reporters and obligated by law to report suspected abuse. They typically tell me that although they know they are obligated to report suspected sexual abuse, they've never been trained on what would make them *suspect* abuse is occurring. In addition, most of them have not been afforded the opportunity to practice talking about it which would create confidence and comfort with the topic.

Sexually abused children grow up and become adult survivors. That means it's likely that 20 percent of your staff have personally experienced sexual abuse.[1, 2, 3, 4, 5, 6, 7] This experience may have left them in a state of hypervigilance or it may have resulted in dissociation which could keep them from seeing abuse happening right in front of them. Still others may have been proactive in their healing and be in a good position to effectively protect children.

> Some of your staff may be child molesters.

Some of your staff may be child molesters who are seeking opportunities to groom, engage, and abuse the kids in your care. What better opportunity than to work in an organization where they have regular access to kids? Research has found that child molesters often seek careers or volunteer work with organizations where they can meet children.[8, 9] Youth-serving organizations are a magnet for child molesters.

As in any navigational exercise, you must know where you are and where you're going in order to chart your course. This first best practice is to engage in an open and proactive evaluation and discussion with your staff about where you are as an organization and where you all are as individuals. For larger organizations, this discussion may have to be limited to the executive or management level staff members or facilitated by location.

Even if the interactive discussion is limited to executives or managers, we recommend that you ask all staff members to do a self-assessment so they are aware of their own starting point. This request can simply be part of an introductory letter or e-mail to your staff which includes the reflection questions from this chapter.

You don't need to specifically ask people to disclose if they've experienced abuse, and certainly, perpetrators won't be readily offering their stories, but you can ask each person to do a self-assessment of their values, beliefs, experiences, feelings, and past training that contribute to or hinder their ability to protect children and let them share what they wish. Some may share experiences of their own abuse or experiences of the aftermath of others in their lives that have experienced abuse. Still, others may take time to get comfortable with the idea and share experiences in the months to come.

If you really want the truth, I encourage you to ask staff members to complete the questionnaire anonymously. You could create an easy online template in a program like Survey Monkey to capture the data confidentially which would give you more truthful insight both about people's personal barriers as well as what they perceive the organizational barriers to be.

It's not fair to ask people to talk about this difficult subject if we're not willing to provide them a safe place to work through personal issues that may arise. So we encourage you to either provide direct support if you have mental health professionals on staff or provide a list of local mental health professionals and support groups they can reach out to for help. Be proactive with this information by providing it upfront and making it easily accessible at any time. You want people to be able to get the help they need without the embarrassment of telling other staff members that they are struggling.

Now, let's meet people where they're at in preparation for charting the course to where you're going.

Reflection:

Complete the following questions as a basis for both personal reflection and as possible input to your interactive staff discussion.

➢ Every organization has a unique culture when it comes to communication. Describe the culture within your organization when it comes to talking about child sexual abuse or other difficult topics.

_____

_____

_____

_____

_____

_____

_____

_____

_____

_____

➤ What are your organization's formal policies regarding child sexual abuse?

_____

_____

_____

_____

_____

_____

_____

_____

_____

_____

➢ What are your organization's and your informal practices regarding child sexual abuse?

_____

_____

_____

_____

_____

_____

_____

_____

_____

➢ Everyone has some level of discomfort when talking about sexual abuse, but if it goes unresolved, it can keep you from seeing abuse that's happening right in front of you. Describe your personal level of comfort with talking about it. Describe your discomfort.

_____

_____

_____

_____

_____

_____

_____

_____

➤ How does your level of comfort differ when talking with children about sexual abuse versus adults?

_____

_____

_____

_____

_____

_____

_____

_____

_____

➤ What are your values, beliefs, experiences, and feelings that contribute to or hinder your ability to protect children?

_____

_____

_____

_____

_____

_____

_____

_____

_____

➢ What formal or informal training have you had regarding the child sexual abuse pandemic?

_____

_____

_____

_____

_____

_____

_____

_____

_____

➢ Rate your level of knowledge regarding child sexual abuse on a scale of 1 to 10, with one being minimal knowledge, 10 being extensive knowledge. Consider prevalence; medical, emotional, behavioral, relational, social, criminal, and economic impact as well as what you know about prevention.

_____

_____

_____

_____

_____

_____

_____

_____

➢ What are some of the most important aspects that you know about the pandemic?

_____

_____

_____

_____

_____

_____

_____

_____

_____

_____

Now let's take a look at a list of cultural barriers that youth-serving organizations may face when making a decision to implement a child sexual abuse prevention program or in getting their staff members to report suspected abuse. When you have finished reading this list, go back and re-answer the questionnaire, providing additional information that may have been revealed in the process of reading the list.

Potential Cultural Barriers[10, 11, 12, 13, 14, 15, 16, 17, 18]

- Fear that you will lose a valued employee who is critical to your operation
- Fear that you will open a can of worms if you report a suspected offender
- Fear that the accused will find out who reported
- Fear that you will unearth unknown cases of abuse if you implement a prevention program

- Fear that your insurance rates will go up if reported abuse is substantiated by the authorities
- Fear of being sued by the victim's family and having to pay a settlement fee
- Fear of being sued by the accused for defamation of character
- Fear that the families you serve and the community will perceive you have a child sexual abuse problem in the organization if you implement a prevention program
- Fear of breaking existing confidentiality agreements with previously accused former staff members
- Focused on the negative impact on the organization's reputation if word of an allegation gets out—damage control
- Organization leaders intimidate you into not reporting abuse
- Denial: the attitude that it can't happen or doesn't happen in our organization
- A belief that you can and/or should handle allegations internally, maybe with campus police but not outside authorities
- Cognitive dissonance: the inability to believe that something outside of your current view could actually be happening[19]
- Mandated reporting is an obligation to report cases where we suspect children are being abused at home but doesn't apply to suspected abuse within the organization
- Ignorance or incompetence due to lack the knowledge and training
- No time and/or no money to implement a prevention program
- Child sexual abuse prevention is not part of our core competencies or program charter. It is not our responsibility.
- Culture of silence or secrecy

- Philosophy of forgiveness (particularly present in faith organizations)
- Good old boy network
- Following legal advice to be less than forthright
- Protecting family members or friends who you suspect have broken boundaries
- Outright cover-up of known sexual abuse
- Culture of doing the minimum the law requires rather than the maximum the law allows[20]
- Focused on preparing your legal defense rather than on uncovering the truth and supporting the victim
- Taking the side of the accused when allegations arise— being a character witness for them, wearing armbands or t-shirts that show support for the accused, raising money for the defense of the accused
- It is faster or cheaper to remove an accused staff member through internal agreements than through the legal route
- Disbelief
- Accusing the child of lying or assuming children often lie about sexual abuse
- It is so hard to get a conviction and we'll be stuck with him. If we transfer him, at least our kids will be safe.[21]
- Institutional loyalty[22]
- Collegial loyalty: a research study found that only 11 percent of teachers surveyed would report a colleague![23]
- Potential for the state licensing board to suspend or revoke the organization's license
- The burden of having to negotiate with the union
- Putting the rights of adults before the rights of kids: innocent until proven guilty instead of true until proven false
- Attitude or history of threatening parents for making accusations or asking them to leave the program

- You think the abuse will stop now that the offender has been confronted. Maybe he even tells you he is sorry for his bad judgment and will never do it again.
- And my favorite, as shared by Shakeshaft: "'If I reported and I was wrong, I would have ruined the life of another teacher.' I have never heard a colleague say, 'If I didn't report and this person had abused, I'd have ruined the life of a student.'"[24]

Next Steps:

- Schedule a staff meeting to discuss responses to the reflection questions. Make an effort to document your organization's enablers and create an open dialogue about the barriers that may keep your organization from effectively protecting the children in your care.
- What is revealed will help you determine changes, beyond my recommendations, that need to be made in order to create change in the culture of the organization. You will need to consider what you learn as you create your strategic plan.

The remaining best practices will not only provide a roadmap for specific actions your organization can take to better protect kids, but in the process of implementing each best practice, you will gently move each of your staff members toward a higher level of knowledge, understanding, and comfort with the topic of child sexual abuse. More importantly, the future chapters will empower you and your staff to put what you learn into action!

> You must know where you are in order to chart a course to where you're going.

BEST PRACTICE #2

MANAGE ACCESS TO CHILDREN

Disclaimer: This chapter is intended to provide basic guidelines that will help your organization integrate a child protection focus into your existing applicant screening process. I assume your organization already has an established human resources practice which reflects the needs of your organization and complies with governing federal, state and local laws, and licensing requirements. This section is intended for informational purposes only and is not meant to replace professional and/or legal advice.

A research study by the National Center for Juvenile Justice found that more than half of all juvenile victims of sexual assault were under age twelve. For those victims, four-year-olds were at greatest risk of being the victim. As a matter of fact, a full 14 percent of all sexual assault victims, including adults, were five or under.[1] These are preschool and kindergarten aged children who are virtually defenseless against their perpetrators. Leading child sexual abuse expert, Anna Salter, said, "Offenders were rarely stupid. They weren't slow to realize that if they restricted themselves to preschoolers, then their chances of a conviction were virtually zero."[2] It is your responsibility to proactively manage access to the kids in your care and do everything possible to minimize the potential of sexual abuse.

It is also crucial to understand the mind-set of fixated child molesters. In *The Socially Skilled Child Molester*, van Dam wrote about how important it is to view child molesters' compulsive behavior as an addiction. She said, "Those familiar with addictions recognize that the addiction drives the behavior because every act is directed at obtaining greater access to the drug of choice. For that reason, addicts primarily associate with people who can help them facilitate that goal, and do not tolerate those who interfere with that goal."[3] In our case, the drug of choice is children and child molesters will not tolerate working with people who cannot deliver victims.

> In our case, the drug of choice is children and child molesters will not tolerate working with people who cannot deliver victims.

This best practice is specifically designed to create boundaries within your screening process that serve to identify "addicted" child molesters and let child molesters know up front that your organization will not support their goal of greater access to children. You may be surprised how quickly they disappear.

ESTABLISH RESPONSIBILITY

Responsibility for the protection of children needs to come from the top down and someone needs to be accountable for ensuring the safety of the children in your care. For non-profits and for-profit corporations, the highest authority is the board of directors. The board is responsible for managing the overall activities of the organization and their duties are defined in a legal document called bylaws which are required when an organization submits their request to the state to become a corporation. The bylaws should be amended to include the board's responsibility for your child sexual abuse prevention program, if it is not already included. Most public school districts are also managed by a board of directors or board of supervisors whose oversight responsibilities and authority are clearly defined and documented and should be amended accordingly.

Since the majority of youth-serving organizations are managed by a board, I will focus on this model. The processes I outline may need to be altered if your organization is not structured as a corporation but formal responsibility should still be established at the highest level in the organization and documented.

This declaration is crucial because we need complete clarity about who is responsible for the protection of children, and although some of the day-to-day activities may be delegated, the ultimate responsibility cannot be delegated if it's established in the bylaws.

The board of directors should maintain active oversight of your child sexual abuse prevention program and program updates should be incorporated in the standard reporting process for routine board meetings. Incorporation into the board reporting process allows board members to monitor specific aspects of the program including training of staff, parents, and children; reporting and resolution of boundary violations; reporting and resolution of observed, disclosed, or suspected abuse and the organization's plans for and progress toward full implementation of the best practices detailed in this book.

INTEGRATE CHILD PROTECTION INTO THE APPLICANT SCREENING PROCESS

As a leader of a youth-serving organization, you may grant child molesters access to your kids. It's tough to hear, but it is a reality.

Every time you hire an employee or bring on a volunteer, you have potentially given a child molester access to the precious children you serve. You have potentially put your children in extreme danger that could change the course of their lives and they may never tell. Your kids are counting on you to make conscious choices about who you allow to be with them.

Child molesters seek opportunity, and what better way to gain access to kids than to choose a career (or community service role) where it is your job to spend time with them?[4, 5] More importantly staff who go above and beyond their assigned duties to develop strong relationships with kids and their families, are typically well respected by their management, peers, parents, and kids. This is the exact image that child molesters attempt to hide behind and use to their advantage.

> As a leader of a youth-serving organization, you may grant child molesters access to your kids.

This section is designed to transform the way you think during the application screening process so your screening process becomes focused on the protection of children, rather than just on finding the most qualified applicant.

It's important that you take everything you will learn in this book and use it as a filter during the applicant screening process. You are not just looking for a new staff member; you are looking for child molesters so you can keep them out!

> You are not just looking for a new staff member; you are looking for child molesters so you can keep them out!

Child sexual abuse is predictable and preventable when we surround children with knowledgeable and outspoken adults and we all play a part in the solution. Your part is to study and embrace the behaviors of child molesters. They are masters of deception, but if you have done your homework and understand how they work, you'll begin to see them appear before you as they apply for positions in your organization. More importantly, they will see you. They will see you as someone who will indeed intercede on behalf of the children in your care.

Once you give yourself permission to see the truth, you'll find that the knowledge you have learned about child molesters will create a new way of thinking. This new way of thinking manifests itself as intuition, an instinct you can rely on.

It's all too easy to overlook or dismiss your intuition when you are under pressure to fill a particular position on your staff or your organization's services are highly dependent on volunteers. However, every person who will have access to kids in your care should go through a child protection focused screening process. This includes paid staff, unpaid volunteers, student helpers and interns, as well as any partners that will have access to your kids such as contracted cafeteria staff, bus drivers, janitorial workers, or a guest instructor. The process also applies to people you know well, that you have worked with before, or who are being promoted or transferred within your organization.[6] Let's look at some ways to turn your existing applicant screening process into a child protection focused screening process.

An effective child protection focused screening process is designed to achieve two key objectives:

1. To ensure that you are not unknowingly staffing someone with a criminal record or pending charges of a sexual offense, violent offense, or other offenses against children; and

2. To deter child molesters from wanting to work for you.

Objective #1

This first objective is crucial to protecting children. You would never want to allow someone with a background of sexual assault, violence, or crimes against children to have access to kids in your care as it would put the kids at increased risk. In addition, this due diligence serves to mitigate financial risk to the organization in the unfortunate event that abuse does occur and you're sued.

> In 2000, Alex Dale Thomas was sentenced to death for the rape and murder of a high school student. Thomas had worked at the school as a janitor for just three days before his arrest. He was on parole for manslaughter at the time of the crime.[7]

Although Alex Dale Thomas was on parole, he was allowed to start the job before his background check was complete. This case prompted the California legislature to pass new laws banning the hiring of felons and requiring background checks to be completed for school employees *before* they begin work.[8] Even if laws in your state do not specify these same guidelines, I encourage you to use them. It is crucial that you know the criminal record of all staff members before granting them direct or indirect access to children in your care. So take your time in the screening process and wait for the results of the background check.

Objective #2

The second objective is just as important because according to Robin Sax, former Los Angeles Deputy District Attorney, Dr. Gene Abel's research in the late 1980s found that there is only a 3 percent chance of an offender getting caught for a sexual offense. Sax went on to say, in her 2009 book, "Dr. Abel's statistic hasn't changed significantly over the past twenty eight years—a damning testimonial to the continuing problem facing everyone who wants to prevent and solve these crimes."[9] Only 14 percent of sexual assaults are reported to authorities[10] and only a small percentage of those cases have sufficient evidence to go to trial and result in a conviction. This leaves a large population of child molesters who have never been detected or convicted. Since you have no surefire way of determining who they are, it's important that they know your organization is focused on and committed to preventing private access to kids, the access that they're specifically looking for.

Let's take the time to explore your current policies and procedures related to managing access to children.

Reflection:

Complete the following questions before continuing.

➢ Who in your organization is ultimately responsible for protecting children from sexual abuse? Is it in writing? Where is it documented? What does it say? How is it communicated to parents and staff?

_____

_____

_____

_____

_____

_____

_____

_____

➢ What are the components of your existing screening process that focus on child protection?

_____

_____

_____

_____

_____

_____

_____

_____

_____

➤ How do these components specifically address Objective #1?

_____

_____

_____

_____

_____

_____

_____

_____

➤ How do these components specifically address Objective #2?

_____

_____

_____

_____

_____

_____

_____

_____

_____

_____

➤ Do you have a standard application form? Does it ask specific questions about past criminal convictions? Does it ask if they have ever been accused of sexual misconduct?

_____

_____

_____

_____

_____

_____

_____

➤ How attuned are you with your intuition? Do you tend to override uncomfortable feelings or do you allow yourself to acknowledge them and make them part of the decision criteria?

_____

_____

_____

_____

_____

_____

_____

_____

_____

_____

➤ What are the specific objectives of your interview process? How many people interview a prospective staff member before a decision is made? How about for volunteers? How does the interview process differ for minors?

_____

_____

_____

_____

_____

_____

_____

_____

_____

➤ How do you proactively assess a candidate's character? How do you determine if they have healthy boundaries with the kids and families they serve?

_____

_____

_____

_____

_____

_____

_____

_____

_____

_____

➢ Do you have a probationary period for all staff and volunteers? How long?

_____

_____

_____

_____

_____

_____

_____

_____

➢ Do you discuss your child sexual abuse prevention policies and practices with candidates? If so, what level of detail do you share and for what purpose?

_____

_____

_____

_____

_____

_____

_____

_____

_____

_____

➤ Do you do reference checks for staff and volunteers? How do you conduct those checks in a way that brings forth critical information on the candidate's ability to work safely with children? Do you check other sources than what was provided on the candidate's application?

_____

_____

_____

_____

_____

_____

_____

_____

➤ Do you do criminal background checks for staff and volunteers? Are these checks done based on name, social security number or fingerprints? Are the checks done against state or national databases? Do you wait for the results before hiring? Do you do recurring background checks? If so, how often?

_____

_____

_____

_____

_____

_____

_____

_____

_____

A study conducted by the Government Accountability Office (GAO) in 2010 specifically looked at select cases in public and private schools that hired or retained individuals with histories of sexual misconduct. They found that:

"At least 11 of these 15 cases involve offenders who previously targeted children. Even more disturbing, in at least 6 cases, offenders used their new positions as school employees or volunteers to abuse more children. GAO found that the following factors contributed to hiring or retention: (1) school officials allowed teachers who had engaged in sexual misconduct toward students to resign rather than face disciplinary action, often providing subsequent employers with positive references; (2) schools did not perform pre-employment criminal history checks; (3) even if schools did perform these checks, they may have been inadequate in that they were not national, fingerprint-based, or recurring; and (4) schools failed to inquire into troubling information regarding criminal histories on employment applications."[11] These same issues have been raised in other segments of youth-serving organizations as well, not just schools and are directly related to objective #1 identified above. These issues should be used as a basis of learning for all youth-serving organization leaders.

In order to effectively address the two aforementioned objectives, I recommend the following key components as part of a child protection focused applicant screening process:

- A standardized application form
- Incorporate personal interviews

    ○ Respect your intuition
    ○ Conduct multiple interviews
    ○ Include character focused interview questions
    ○ Include boundary focused interview questions and what if? scenarios
    ○ Discuss your child sexual abuse best practices program
    ○ Formalize the feedback process from interviewers

- Conduct a thorough reference check process
- Require criminal background checks
- Thoroughly investigate red flags
- Institute a thirty-day probationary period

As you move through these key screening processes, you may uncover that your candidate has a criminal record or pending charges of a sexual offense, violent offense, or other offenses against children, which should immediately disqualify them from working with children. On the other hand, you may find a history of accusations of sexual misconduct against your candidate or enough unexplainable red flags that cause you to decide the risk is too high and you pass. However, there is a third possible result of your screening process: you may not find anything to substantiate concern, but the sheer fact that you diligently followed this child protection focused screening process, you have likely deterred any undetected child molester from wanting to work for you.

So let's take a look at the individual steps of the recommended process to better understand how they work together to achieve the end result of managing child molesters' access to the children you serve.

A STANDARDIZED APPLICATION FORM

Regardless of the size of your organization, you should use a standardized application form for all candidates whether they are applying for paid positions, volunteer positions, internships, or contractor positions. You should use them for adults and adolescents alike.[12, 13]

The form should include basic profile questions such as name, address, and phone number but should also ask for maiden name, any aliases, previous addresses, and social security number. This additional information will be used when completing their background check. All social security numbers should be verified.[14, 15]

Include questions on education and certifications or licensing applicable to the position. Ask if their credentials have ever been suspended or revoked and if so, why. Also ask questions on previous employment and volunteer positions on the application including dates and locations of each position. This is very important so that you are able to identify any gaps in employment as well as candidates who have moved repeatedly within the same community and even across communities or states. You should ask the reason for leaving each position.[16]

It is important to ask direct questions that will identify red flags that should be further researched. Researcher Sandy Wurtele suggests, "asking about candidate's experiences and interests, asking applicants if they have ever been convicted of a misdemeanor or felony, accused of sexual misconduct, or resigned or dismissed from a youth-serving position due to complaint(s) of sexual abuse of a minor."[17] A publication by the Center for Disease Control and Prevention (CDC) also recommends such questions, expanding them to include crimes of violence or any crimes against children.[18] The answers to criminal conviction questions will then be validated during your background check process, but the other questions are not quite as easy to verify though your reference check process can help. These direct questions will show your candidate from the start that you are serious about protecting the children in your care.

The CDC also recommends that you ask some open-ended questions that encourage broad answers so you can follow up on them in the interview portion of your screening process. They include suggestions such as: "What age/sex of youth do you want to work with?" "How would you feel about working with a different age/sex?" and "What other hobbies or activities do you enjoy?" See their publication for further examples.[19] Another good question is, "What do you like to do during your break time at work?"

The application should include a certification clause stating that all information is true and correct and require a signature and a date. Lying on the application should be considered an automatic disqualifier.

After you receive the completed application from a candidate, you should review it thoroughly; take your time. You are looking for red flags that need to be researched further during your interview, reference, and background check process. I recommend using a checklist that helps to ensure your process is complete and helps you to identify red flags. Here are some questions I would include on your checklist:

- Did the candidate answer all the questions on the application?
- Was the candidate able to provide their social security card for verification?
- Did the candidate indicate that they have a criminal record or that they have been accused of sexual misconduct?
- Does the candidate seem to have a fixation on an age range or gender of children they want to work with?

- Does the candidate seem to spend an unusually significant portion of his/her time with kids or doing activities that are childlike in lieu of healthy adult relationships and activities?
- Has the candidate had gaps in employment? Have they changed jobs regularly? Have they moved from one location to another? Have they left jobs midway through the year or program duration?
- Has the candidate ever had their credentials suspended or revoked?

The GAO published a report that referenced cases where candidates either didn't answer the questions on criminal background or answered them affirming they had a record and no one in the hiring process noticed.[20] Make a checklist and use it to prompt you to stop and look at these critical data points and document red flags that could pose a real risk to the children in your care.

> Note: All applications are confidential. They should be secured under lock and key and shared only on a need to know basis with other staff members involved in the hiring process.

INCORPORATE PERSONAL INTERVIEWS

Interviews can be one of the most important steps in your screening process. This is a time when you are validating specific information from the application including the education, licensing credentials, past experience, and specific skills of your perspective candidates as well as their passion for working with children. Interviews are also a time for you to follow up on red flags that may have been raised in reviewing their application. Most importantly though, this is a time when you get to know your applicant and begin to develop a gut feel about them.

Respect Your Intuition

> Intuition is always right in at least two ways; it is always in response to something; it always has your best interest at heart.
>
> —Gavin de Becker, author of The Gift of Fear: Survival Signals that Protect Us from Violence[21]

A comprehensive applicant screening process is important. However, sometimes the formality of the process makes us focus solely on the intellectual analysis of an applicant's background, education, and skills, and we fail to recognize how we "feel" when we're interacting with the applicant. Some might say that making a hiring decision based on "feelings" is unprofessional, but those feelings are our intuition, which is sometimes telling us that something is wrong.

Gavin de Becker, the author of *The Gift of Fear: Survival Signals That Protect Us from Violence*, said, "Intuition is always right in at least two important ways; it is always in response to something; it always has your best interest at heart."[22]

So throughout your screening process, make a concerted effort to focus on your intuition or that gut feeling and know that it is in response to something. If you have an uneasy feeling about a candidate, even if you can't pinpoint why, make a commitment to respect "*The Gift of Fear*" and pass on that applicant.

Conduct Multiple Interviews

Candidates should be interviewed by at least two people, preferably three in larger organizations. This provides an opportunity to gather input on a broader set of discussion points, receive feedback on gut feel from multiple people, and have another set of eyes looking to be sure your process is complete and nothing has been overlooked.

Include Character-Focused Interview Questions

> It's easy to fall into the trap of being skills focused instead of character focused when conducting interviews. We tend to focus our interview questions on "what they have done" instead of "who they have become."

It's easy to fall into the trap of being skills focused instead of character focused when conducting interviews. We tend to focus on "what they have done" in their life instead of "who they have become." Although your candidate's education and past experience are very important and the information they have provided on their application should be validated, the interview process is about getting to know *the person* behind the credentials. As such, I recommend that you incorporate questions that provide the opportunity for dialogue about the candidate's character.

One of the easiest ways to do this is to focus on the Six Pillars of Character® by the Josephson Institute Center for Youth Ethics and incorporate character questions *that are relevant to your organization's services and the candidate's background.* Your questions should be open ended so you get a glimpse of how your candidate is likely to handle themselves while on the job. Here are a few sample questions based on The Six Pillars of Character which are listed below for your reference:

- Tell me about a time when you were faced with having to make a choice between doing the right thing and taking the easy or comfortable way out?

- Respect is earned. How would your colleagues say you have earned their respect?
- What standards do you use when setting a good example for the children in your care?

Six Pillars of Character
Josephson Institute Center for Youth Ethics[23]

Trustworthiness

Be honest • Don't deceive, cheat, or steal • Be reliable—do what you say you'll do • Have the courage to do the right thing • Build a good reputation • Be loyal—stand by your family, friends, and country

Respect

Treat others with respect; follow the Golden Rule • Be tolerant and accepting of differences • Use good manners, not bad language • Be considerate of the feelings of others • Don't threaten, hit, or hurt anyone • Deal peacefully with anger, insults, and disagreements

Responsibility

Do what you are supposed to do • Plan ahead • Persevere: keep on trying! • Always do your best • Use self-control • Be self-disciplined • Think before you act—consider the consequences • Be accountable for your words, actions, and attitudes • Set a good example for others

Fairness

Play by the rules • Take turns and share • Be open-minded; listen to others • Don't take advantage of others • Don't blame others carelessly • Treat all people fairly

Caring

Be kind • Be compassionate and show you care • Express gratitude • Forgive others • Help people in need

Citizenship

Do your share to make your school and community better • Cooperate • Get involved in community affairs • Stay informed; vote • Be a good neighbor • Obey laws and rules • Respect authority • Protect the environment • Volunteer

> Disclaimer: Conduct interviews and reference checks in compliance with all federal and state laws and regulations. The Americans with Disabilities Act prohibits asking non-job-related information. Avoid questions regarding marital status, religion, age, race, health-related issues, child care, transportation, worker compensation claims, and any other non-job-related questions. All questions, including character questions and boundary questions, should be directly related to the applicant's previous work or volunteer positions and/or the position they are applying for.

Include Boundary-Focused Interview Questions

Boundaries are a protective shield that helps us keep kids safe. They are of utmost importance in any child sexual abuse prevention program. However, formal boundaries can feel very controlling and can be seen by some as an obstacle to building a strong rapport with kids. Your candidates will come to you with differing levels of experience working with boundaries.

The value and purpose of including boundary questions in your interview process is to engage your candidate in discussion so you have a feel for where they fall on the spectrum, both in terms of experience and in terms of attitude. This will serve to bring any potential boundary concerns to the surface as well as allow you to identify and close the gap between their experience and attitude and that of your organization, if indeed you select them to fill the position.

A discussion about boundaries also lets your candidate know that boundaries are important to your organization and are specifically an area of focus.

Below are some sample questions you can choose from to engage your candidate in a discussion regarding boundaries:

- How do you build trust and rapport with the kids in your care?
- What kind of relationship would you like to foster with the parents of the kids in your care?
- Explain how your past experience will help you manage kids' behavior in this position?
- What kind of tangible and intangible rewards do you use to promote good behavior?
- What is your philosophy on "respect for authority?"
- Were there specific boundaries in place at your previous employers to minimize the risk of child abuse? What were they?
- How did the boundaries impact the staff's ability to serve kids?
- Have you ever suspected a child in your care was being sexually abused by a colleague? What happened?
- What personal boundaries do you enforce that help protect kids and mitigate your risk of being falsely accused of sexual abuse?
- Tell me about your level of awareness regarding the prevalence and risk of child sexual abuse.
- Tell me about any formal or informal training you have had specific to preventing child sexual abuse.
- Tell me about any formal child sexual abuse prevention programs in place at your previous employers (or volunteer organizations)?

As you create a discussion about boundaries with your candidate through these open-ended questions, it is important to respond to apparent boundary concerns in a "nonjudgmental, nonthreatening and receptive manner," as recommended by Lanning and Dietz.[24] This will put your candidate at ease, allowing you to more fully engage in conversation and understand their rationalization for lack of boundaries.

According to Lanning and Dietz, "offenders will generally try to conceal their sexual interests and behavior from anyone they believe will not accept their rationalizations for it, but often disclose, at least in part, their sexual interests—or at least their excessive interest in other people's children—to those they believe will accept their rationalizations."[25]

As you talk with candidates about boundaries, listen for indicators that they may lack empathy for other people's needs and feelings, especially children's. This may become particularly apparent as a candidate is rationalizing bad boundaries. In *Identifying Child Molesters*, van Dam says, "Watch out for the charmer who as no empathy." She goes on to reference this as a "common thread in a study of over 300 interviewed sex molesters."[26] Lack of empathy is one of the signs of narcissism along with a sense of entitlement, grand sense of self-importance, exploitive behavior, and the belief that they are worshipped and adored by others. Short of costly specialized personality tests which must be administered by mental health professionals, your interviewers may be the first and only line of defense in recognizing these traits common to child molesters.

Several experts recommend including what-if scenarios in your interview process.[27] This provides an additional opportunity to learn about your candidate's view on boundaries and how they will potentially handle difficult situations in real life. Robert Shoop's book on sexual exploitation in schools includes several very good scenarios along with discussion questions.[28] It would behoove you to incorporate one of these into the interview process with each candidate.

Discuss Your Organization's Child Sexual Abuse Prevention Program

Your child sexual abuse prevention program should be discussed within the interview process including (1) boundaries that limit private access to kids and inappropriate behavior, (2) your assessment and communication process, (3) mandatory child sexual abuse prevention training for staff members, (4) the creation of an accountability team with parents and children, (5) mandatory reporting of suspected abuse, and (6) pre-established consequences for boundary violations. Experts agree that this type of discussion in the interview process sends a clear message that you are serious about protecting kids and your kids are off limits. Some go on to suggest that you have all candidates read your full policy, ask if they have any concerns with it, and ask them to sign an acceptance of the policy, should you choose to hire them.[29, 30] This is consistent with my recommendations in Best Practice #5.

> Child molesters will quickly realize that they will not have their desired access to children and will want to work somewhere else that is still consumed by silence.

Child molesters will quickly realize that they will not have their desired access to children and it is highly probable that they will be caught if they try. Remember, the drug of choice is children and child molesters will not tolerate working with people who cannot deliver victims. Child molesters will likely want to work somewhere else that is still consumed by silence.

Formalize the Feedback Process from Interviewers

People's opinions can be easily and unconsciously swayed by a phenomenon called Groupthink. This concept was first proposed by Dr. Irving Janis in the early 1970s and describes the process in which group members seek unanimous agreement despite their own individual doubts. I will not go into this phenomenon in depth but instead focus on one key element that helps to mitigate the effect of Groupthink, acceptance of and promoting opportunities for divergent thinking.[31, 32]

It's not uncommon for a first line interviewer to ask another member of the team to interview a candidate and typically the request comes with a narrative that may highlight the positive qualities of the candidate that have caused them to move the candidate on to a second interview and/or a list of concerns that the manager would like the second interviewer to explore further. On the surface, this sounds like a valuable introduction and strategy, but it immediately focuses the second interview on the topics that have already been explored and the concerns that have already been surfaced, leaving the second interviewer to consciously or perhaps unconsciously gather additional data points to justify or rationalize the conclusion of the first interviewer. Looking at the flipside, this process stifles the natural critical thinking process of the second interviewer who is then unable to provide valuable *independent* input on this candidate.

In order to create an environment that promotes independent input, I recommend organizations use a formal process to gather feedback which includes the following key elements:

- *Interviewer's feedback on candidates should be kept private until all interviews have been completed.* This allows each interview to start from a clean slate and the interviewers to come to independent conclusions regarding the qualifications of each candidate, concerning red flags, and their gut feel about the candidate's passion and interest in working with children.

- *Initial feedback should be provided in writing, using a standard Candidate Feedback Form.* This ensures that each interviewer has a chance to completely formulate and take a stand on their own opinion, alleviating the natural tendency to agree with others which is especially common when feedback is only verbal.

- *Candidate Feedback Forms should include sections that draw out input on the skills and experience of the candidate as well as their gut feel about the candidate.* It's so important for each of us to master the process of acknowledging and embracing our intuition, even when we can't completely explain *why* we feel the way we do. If an interviewer knows they will have to write a written response about how they "felt" when talking with a candidate, it is more likely they will stay in tune with their intuition during the interview process. If they are able to stay in tune with their intuition, they are more likely to recognize the source of any concern.

- *Share and discuss interviewers' feedback after all interviews are completed.* Now that all interviews have started with a clean slate, interviewers have had a chance to formulate their own opinion and gut feelings have been elicited, feedback should be shared with the other interviewers and a meeting held to discuss input. This creates open communication and an opportunity for interviewers to elaborate on their feedback. There are many other symptoms of Groupthink that can come into play during this group discussion and final decision making process which we do not have time to elaborate on. However, I have provided recommendations that will help you develop a strong foundation for divergent thinking. I encourage you to further your understanding of the symptoms of Groupthink as well as additional strategies to overcome them.

- *Hire "the right" candidate, not "the best" candidate.* It's easy to fall into the trap of comparison hiring which sometimes leaves you selecting the lesser of two evils. In other words, you are looking for the best out of a pool of candidates of which none may be truly qualified. Although it may extend your hiring process and leave a position open for a longer period of time, if you are willing to say, "No, thank you" to all of the candidates and start over, you are much more likely to make a good hire.

INCORPORATE A THOROUGH REFERENCE CHECK PROCESS

Note: Acquire necessary permission to contact references. Some states require an organization to receive explicit permission to contact former employers, references, or someone not listed on the application. In addition, you may need a separate clause to protect the confidentiality of the information gathered so you can assure the reference the information will not be disclosed to the applicant. Contact an attorney who understands your state's employment law for guidance. If applicable, include a permission and confidentiality clause on your application.[33]

All information gathered in the reference process is confidential. It should be secured under lock and key and shared only on a need-to-know basis with other staff members involved in the hiring process.

For many organizations, checking references is a rote process that brings minimal value to selecting the right candidate. The applicant provides references they know will say good things about them, the person checking the references uses a predictable set of questions and the reference has often already agreed to provide positive feedback. In some cases, the candidate may actually have a signed confidentiality agreement with a previous employer that forbids them from telling the truth, even if the truth is that they had accusations of sexual abuse of minors! The 2010 GAO report referenced a discussion with a district superintendent stating, "The superintendent told us that sometimes the terms of a 'letter of separation' can prevent a principal from disclosing information which a representative from human resources could disclose."[34] So I highly recommend that you contact the human resources department as well as direct references listed on your candidate's application.

However, there are several concepts you can incorporate into your reference process that are more likely to drive valuable input about potential candidates as follows:

- *Indicate that feedback is confidential.* References are often uncomfortable in providing negative feedback because they fear this information will get back to the candidate. If you let them know up front that the information provided will be kept in confidence (assuming you have covered your legal requirements to do so), they will be more likely to open up and be honest.

- *Include verbal and written references.* Many employers will only give a written reference which typically consist more of an employment verification process, confirming that they indeed worked there, their dates of employment, title, and maybe their responsibilities. This precludes you from having the opportunity to ask direct questions about their performance, why they left, if they would hire them again, and of course, you do not have the opportunity to hear the "unspoken words" that come from voice inflection, hesitation, and question avoidance.[35]

- *Focus on professional references versus personal references, even for volunteers.* Personal references often find it difficult to be objective and may not have had the opportunity to see the candidate in job related activities. Even though you may not be paying volunteers, it is still important that they are able to work in a professional and safe manner with your kids, families, and other staff members and thus you should still expect professional references for them, even if the references are from volunteer positions.[36]

- *Request at least two references who were direct supervisors.* Although it may seem impressive for a candidate to provide a vice president, executive director, or district superintendent as a reference, if they were not the candidate's direct supervisor, you may receive vague responses that don't accurately reflect their competency in executing day-to-day responsibilities and interacting with children. This is also true of references from a human resources staff member.

- *Include independently identified references.* As mentioned earlier, candidates are likely to provide references that have agreed to provide positive feedback. So experts agree it is important to go beyond the references listed and find others who have worked with the candidate or for the same organization. You will likely get a more objective overall assessment of the candidate's fit for the position.[37, 38, 39, 40]

- *Match references to employment history.* It is important to compare the candidate's employment history to the references they provided to see if there are previous employers who have been left off the list of references. These may be some of those independently identified resources you want to pursue discussions with.[41]

- *Validate application and resume information.* It's not unusual, especially in a tough job market, for candidates to exaggerate their experience, skills, income, and/ or responsibilities. The reference process is a chance to ask specific questions regarding income and dates of employment as well as open-ended questions about the candidate's skills and responsibilities to see if the feedback reflects the same level of experience that was presented on their application. Identify ahead of time the information you need to validate.

- *Ask character and boundary questions.* In addition to a variety of standard questions on performance, attendance, team work, specific skills, and leadership qualities, it's important to ask character and boundary questions as you did in your interview. This allows you to get a glimpse of "the person" versus their skills and gives you a comparison to how the candidate perceives themselves. This would be a great opportunity to select a question that specifically addresses a red flag that was raised in the interview. Refer back to the "Include Character Focused Interview Questions" and the "Include Boundary Focused Interview Questions" topics earlier in this section.

- *Ask direct questions—the tough ones.* Asking tough questions may be part of the standard process for larger organizations but smaller youth-serving organizations, especially those run by volunteers, may have a tendency to avoid confrontation. However, to get a better understanding of the candidate's fit for your organization, it's important to ask direct questions that get to the root of their past employment or volunteer departures such as:[42, 43, 44, 45]

  - Why did he/she leave your organization?
  - Did his/her conduct ever require disciplinary measures? If so, what was the conduct in question?
  - Were there ever any substantiated or unsubstantiated accusations of sexual misconduct made against him/her?
  - Is there anything that would not allow you to rehire him/her? If you had the chance, would *you* recommend rehiring him/her?

- *Be alert to and make note of unusual responses.* There is often as much to be learned by what a reference does *not* say as there is from what they do say. Look for hesitations, vague, ambiguous or evasive answers, overly negative responses, or overly enthusiastic responses. Don't be afraid to ask follow up or clarifying questions to understand "why" the reference is responding the way they are.

REQUIRE CRIMINAL BACKGROUND CHECKS

Disclaimer: Legal requirements and restrictions for criminal background checks vary by state. This section is not intended to provide legal or professional advice. Contact your state attorney general's office or an attorney who understands applicable state and federal laws regarding employment practices and the protection of children.

Dr. Abel "calculated that the chance of getting caught for a sex offense is about 3 percent."[46] Therefore, you cannot depend on background checks to keep sexual predators away from your children. Do not let background checks give you a false sense of security when it comes to effectively protecting children. Unfortunately, a 2014 report from the GAO says that "Background checks were the primary tool states used to prevent sexual abuse and misconduct by school personnel."[47] Background checks simply aren't enough and need to be just a part of your overall screening process.

That said, in an effort to prevent child sexual abuse, most states require background checks to be conducted for staff members of schools and day care centers.[48, 49] However, some states have no such requirements. Even in the states that do, these same requirements do not necessarily extend to all types of youth-serving organizations, especially those that are primarily staffed by volunteers such as faith organizations and sports leagues.

Some experts call for background checks to be fingerprint based, national in scope, and recurring. While I agree this is the most comprehensive approach, this is not possible in all circumstances. According to another GAO report from 2010, "two states limit the check to state databases, while another state limits the check to state databases if the employee or applicant has been a state resident for the prior 2 years."[50] In another report published by the US Department of Education, it was noted that because of teacher unions, "In most states, teachers who are already employed are exempt from regulations such as fingerprint identification."[51] So I cannot emphasize enough that you thoroughly understand federal, state, and local laws and consult your attorney and insurance company in the development of your background screening procedures and be sure that your selected background check provider can effectively meet your specific needs. Refer to Charol Shakeshaf's report, *Educator Sexual Misconduct: A Synthesis of Existing Literature*, for more information on legal considerations.[52]

In a perfect world, background checks should:

- *Be utilized for all staff members* who have direct or indirect access to children. This includes contract workers and volunteers. It excludes adolescents as their records are not publically available.[53, 54]
- *Be fingerprint based* which ensures you are running the check on the right person just in case the candidate has provided you a false name or is fraudulently using multiple social security numbers. If there is a legal or contractual limitation on doing fingerprint-based background checks, social security number checks are better than name-only checks.[55]
- *Be nationally based;* the FBI database is the most comprehensive database available at this time.[56, 57, 58]
- *Be multi-state based,* as necessary. As an example, if a candidate has moved frequently, it is crucial for you to check state records for each location he has lived in rather than rely on just your state's database.[59, 60, 61]

- *Include a check against the Registered Sex Offender Registry.* However, the public sex offender registries (SOR) can only be searched by name, not social security number. So use this approach with caution and use available images to confirm if any matches are actually your candidate.[62, 63]

- *Include a check against the Child Abuse Registry* through your local child protective services agency to see if there are any pending investigations of abuse.[64]

- *Include additional databases as appropriate.* As an example, in the 2014 GAO survey, they found that "nearly half of all states (25) reported consulting the National Association of State Directors of Teacher Education and Certification (NASDTEC) clearinghouse—a database of information voluntarily reported by states on teachers who have lost teaching certifications due to abuse or misconduct."[65]

- *Include a check against applicable state licensing agencies* to validate that candidates currently hold the credentials they say they do and they have never been suspended or revoked.[66, 67]

- *Include a check against internal records.* The 2007 Center for Disease Control and Prevention report suggests that, "This strategy involves keeping lists of applicants who are disqualified during the screening process and employees/volunteers who are dismissed because of an offense. During the screening and selection process, your organization would then check current applicants against these lists to make sure the applicant has not been previously disqualified or dismissed."[68] You will be able to refer to your Assessment and Communication Forms for boundary violations (Best Practice #4) as well as your reports of observed, disclosed or suspected abuse (Best Practice #7) as part of your internal records review process.

- *Include an Internet search and social media search* to see if the results raise any red flags that should be further investigated. Remember that it is easy to get the wrong person when just searching on someone's name so use this avenue with caution and only as input for further research.[69, 70]

- *Be performed on a recurring basis.* They should be scheduled periodically and utilized if allegations arise. It is important to know that a person's criminal history can change in a day. Your request for written permission to do a background check should also ask for authorization to do them on a recurring basis.[71, 72, 73, 74]

- *Be completed and results received before employment begins* so that you eliminate any potential risk to children and do not run the risk of forgetting to follow up on the results after the candidate has begun work.[75]

- *Be delayed to the end of your screening process to minimize time and costs,* allowing you to provide the most comprehensive background check process to only those candidates who have successfully passed all the other screening activities.[76, 77]

- *Be compared to pre-establish disqualifiers* to determine if they are eligible to work for your organization. At minimum, violent behavior and child sexual abuse offenses should automatically disqualify candidates. Depending on your organization's mission and the specific job the candidate is applying for, other crimes such as substance abuse might also be disqualifiers.[78] Providing false information or purposely omitting requested information on the application should also be considered an automatic disqualification.

Beyond the goal of protecting the children in your care from abuse, it is also crucial that you institute background checks in an effort to lower your organization's liability. According to Wurtele,

"From a liability standpoint, criminal background and SOR checks are essential to include, because YSOs *(youth-serving organizations)* can be found liable for harm caused by unchecked staff and could be subject to civil suits and rising insurance costs should an unchecked staff member with a previous history of sexual offenses subsequently abuse a child."[79] (Italics added for clarification.)

THOROUGHLY INVESTIGATE RED FLAGS

As you move through the sequence of your screening process, there are red flags that may become apparent during each phase. It is important that you take the time to thoroughly investigate each red flag before making a final hiring decision. Some red flags may be simple misunderstandings and resolved through clarification. Others may not be able to be explained away or it may become apparent during the clarification process that the candidate is trying to justify their behavior which at the core is inappropriate or lacks good judgment. If a candidate has several red flags, especially if detected by multiple interviewers, this should be cause for concern and the risk they may present should be taken into consideration when making a final hiring decision. Here are some red flags that may appear during the process:

Application

- Questions have been left unanswered such as criminal history
- Affirmative answers to criminal background or accusations of sexual misconduct including sexual assault, violent crimes, crimes against children, violence against animals, DUI/DWI, substance abuse, domestic violence, sexual misconduct, "behavior not becoming of a teacher, etc."
- Gaps in employment
- Frequent moves within the community

- Multiple moves across different states
- Job changes midway through the year or program duration
- Credentials that have been suspended or revoked
- References that do not include direct supervisors
- Providing only personal references instead of professional references
- References that are not aligned with employment history—important references missing
- Hobbies or interests that are overly childlike in nature
- Spending excessive time with children rather than with adults
- Apparent fixation on working with a particular age range or gender
- Spending lunches or break time with kids rather than adult colleagues
- Inappropriate motives for working with kids

Interviews

- Gut feeling that something just isn't right, that you are not seeing the whole picture
- Multiple interviewers who found the same red flags
- Multiple interviewers who found as series of different red flags
- Shows lack of character: honesty, respect, integrity,
- Shows inappropriate boundaries with children, parents, or colleagues
- Has no understanding of the need for boundaries
- Considers boundaries to be an inhibitor to building good relationships with kids
- Provides inappropriate responses to what-if scenarios
- Overemphasis on building relationships with parents
- Lacks good judgment in discipline methods and/or rewards

- Seems to want to be "friends" with kids
- Has an unhealthy demand for children to respect his authority
- Shows a concerning response to your child sexual abuse prevention program. This could be an negative response or it could be an *overly* enthusiastic response. Lanning and Dietz call out candidates who offer evidence of good character including "conducting child-sex-abuse prevention programs" and "offers to assist law enforcement."[80]

Reference Checks

- Only able to provide written references, no one willing to talk with you
- References provide less than satisfactory feedback
- References have a very different impression of the candidate than he has of himself
- Reference job details do not agree with information provided on the application
- References are not willing to recommend them for rehire
- References respond to difficult questions with hesitation, ambiguity, or avoidance
- References are overly negative or overly positive
- Candidate seems too good to be true

Background Checks

- Background check turns up criminal history not disclosed on the application
- Candidate unable to provide a government ID and/or social security card for verification
- Candidate refuses to provide fingerprints
- Candidate shows up on the Sex Offender Registry
- Candidate shows up on the Child Abuse Registry
- Candidate shows up with a suspension or revocation of credentials on licensing database

- Candidate shows up with a record on a specific industry database
- Candidate has been previously dismissed or disqualified for employment by your organization
- Candidate has previously broken boundaries documented in your internal database
- Inappropriate information is found about the candidate via an Internet search
- Candidate refuses to agree to recurring background checks
- Candidate pushes for employment to start before the results of their background check is received

Note that I have included the recommended automatic disqualifiers on this list because I want them to be included in your process of looking for red flags so you are prompted to look for them. However, remember that your list of automatic disqualifiers is likely to be very short. The rest of the items on this list are just red flags that should be further researched, they are not automatic disqualifiers. As you review the possible red flags, you are looking for a pattern of behavior that would indicate increased risk for children.

When a candidate passes the application, interview, reference check and background check processes, and you indeed make a decision to hire, the individual's name should be added to your Approved Access List. No one other than the people on the list should be allowed into areas of your facility where children are, unless they are escorted by someone on the approved list at all times.

INSTITUTE A THIRTY-DAY PROBATIONARY PERIOD

Just in case all of your due diligence simply wasn't enough to uncover underlying concerns, I recommend all new staff members be hired on a provisional basis, allowing termination without cause within thirty days, just in case concerns arise. This provides an opportunity for you to closely monitor new staff members and learn much more about their character and boundaries which are more difficult to accurately assess during the screening process than the automatic disqualifiers.[81, 82, 83]

As we mentioned earlier, organizations may encounter a variety of obstacles to this "perfect world" scenario of background checks, reference checks, and interview recommendations based on local, state, and federal laws as well as existing employment contracts. The more significant the limitations are, the more important the probationary period becomes. Adjust the duration of the probationary period to reflect how much time you really need to fill in the information gaps. The probationary period should be looked at as a long-term interview where you can weed them out through character inquiries, observation, and heavy supervision.

Next Steps:

- Review your current applicant screening process and develop a plan and timeline to incorporate these key child protection best practices.

BEST PRACTICE #3

SET, DOCUMENT, AND ENFORCE BOUNDARIES

Written boundaries are at the heart of protecting children. Without them, every day is filled with a myriad of subjective choices that are far too often hindered by our emotions, opinions, relationships, and quest for personal gain (promotion, raise, etc.). When boundaries are established and documented in writing, they set clear expectations and provide a mechanism for objective decision making that applies to everyone who comes in contact with children in your care. No exceptions![1, 2]

However, you must be willing to enforce the boundaries you set. According to van Dam, "Child molesters are continuously busy with activities to gain access to children, but they focus on children only after the adults responsible for those children have signaled an unwillingness to monitor boundary violations, thereby having communicated that subtle cues of misconduct will be overlooked, ignored, or tolerated."[3] Our kids are counting on us to intercede on their behalf!

As you read these boundaries, my hope is that you will begin to see the forest through the trees, that you will see how child molesters can and do masterfully interweave grooming behaviors in a manner that seduces unsuspecting adults and children alike.

My hope is that you choose instead to be suspect of grooming behaviors which often appear as strengths but should be cause for concern. My hope is that you choose to intercede before abuse happens.

Consequences for breaking the boundaries should also be clearly established and documented as part of the planning process which removes the need for decisions about repercussions at the time of a boundary violation.

> Written boundaries set expectations and provide a mechanism for objective decision making.

You simply need to follow through with the associated consequences which have already been communicated to staff members, parents, and children during training (Best Practices #5 and 6). So the consequences should not be a surprise to anyone. This approach alleviates the potential for emotion and subjectivity to determine the course of action. There should be a direct correlation established between breaking the boundaries and continued employment and/or access to children. As a matter of fact, Shakeshaft said, "policies must stress that even acts of sexual misconduct that do not break the law will not be tolerated and can lead to termination of employment."[4]

> Establish a direct correlation between breaking boundaries and continued access to children.

Effective boundaries for youth-serving organizations fall into seven key categories which I will cover in-depth:

1. Legal Boundaries
2. On-Site Boundaries
3. Off-Site Boundaries
4. Off-Hours Boundaries
5. Electronic Communication and Social Media Boundaries

6. Child-to-Child Boundaries
7. Gift Boundaries

Boundary categories 2 through 7 are what I refer to as organizational boundaries which are specifically designed to intercede with grooming behaviors. These are boundaries that are determined by the organization and breaking them is not against the law, but it is against organizational policy and predetermined consequences will be enforced.

Sometimes, children's boundaries are being violated elsewhere. Setting and enforcing boundaries within your program serves not only to protect children while they're with you but also teaches healthy boundaries that children should expect no matter where they are. Even if inappropriate behavior or situations are initiated by children, it is your responsibility to quickly but gently correct the situation, letting them know in an age-appropriate manner, that it's inappropriate. If an adult doesn't say no to child-initiated inappropriate behavior, the child is still the victim![5] Effective boundaries also serve to protect you and your organization from false allegations.

BEST PRACTICE #3

LEGAL BOUNDARIES

Reflection:

Before continuing, complete the questions below regarding legal boundaries. It is important to answer these questions from your current knowledge. Now is not the time to go and look for the answers.

➤ Do you know what constitutes child sexual abuse in your state? What are the laws regarding rape, statutory rape, rape in concert, incest, sodomy, lewd or lascivious acts, oral copulation, sexual penetration, and child molestation?

_____

_____

_____

_____

_____

_____

_____

➢ What are your state's laws regarding child pornography possession and production? What are your formal and/or informal policies regarding the possession of adult pornography on organization property (on premises, computers, phones, etc.)?

_____

_____

_____

_____

_____

_____

_____

➢ What are your state's laws regarding voyeurism and exhibitionism?

_____

_____

_____

_____

_____

_____

_____

_____

➤ Are there additional state laws that apply to people in positions of power and authority over children?

_____

_____

_____

_____

_____

_____

_____

_____

_____

➤ What body parts are considered off-limits by law?

_____

_____

_____

_____

_____

_____

_____

_____

_____

➤ Are all staff members in your organization aware of the state laws regarding child sexual abuse? How and when are they communicated to staff? Are they communicated to parents and youth? If so, how and when?

_____

_____

_____

_____

_____

_____

_____

_____

➤ What is the age of consent in your state? Does your organization have any formal policies that extend the state laws beyond the age of consent? How about beyond the age of eighteen?

_____

_____

_____

_____

_____

_____

_____

_____

➤ What are your organization's immediate consequences of allegations of breaking one of these state laws? What are the long-term consequences if these allegations are substantiated? How about if the allegations are not substantiated?

_____

_____

_____

_____

_____

_____

_____

_____

_____

➤ What is the statute of limitations on sexual abuse in your state for criminal cases? How about for civil cases?

_____

_____

_____

_____

_____

_____

_____

_____

_____

Though illegal sexual behavior may be obvious to the majority of people who work for your organization, it is still critically important to document it as part of your formal policy. I am not talking about the gray areas or grooming behaviors that are covered in the rest of Best Practice #3, but the behaviors that are absolutely wrong, black and white, without question. The best source for these non-negotiable inappropriate behaviors is your state's penal code. These are the behaviors that are illegal and your policy should state that when any suspicion arises that these boundaries have been crossed, alleged offenders will be reported to local authorities for investigation. In every boundary area, we want to set clear expectations and we cannot overlook this basic expectation to abide by the law, even though it may seem obvious that these behaviors would be considered unacceptable.

All states have laws that clearly define what is considered child sexual abuse, often referred to as sexual assault of a minor. Though laws vary by state, sexual assault laws typically prohibit vaginal or anal intercourse, oral copulation, vaginal penetration with an object, sodomy, touching a child's private parts or having the child touch yours or someone else's, and masturbation in the presence of a child. State laws also include penalties for voyeurism and exhibitionism as well as laws addressing sexual exploitation which is using a child in a sexual manner for personal and/or monetary gain.

Many states recognize that children are more vulnerable at the hands of people who have power or authority over them and have therefore established additional penalties for anyone in a position of authority who sexually abuses a child.[1] Check to see if your state has an overriding statute regarding sexual abuse at the hands of people in positions of authority.

The details of these laws vary so it is important for you to find out what your state's laws are and document them as part of your child sexual abuse prevention policy. As an example, in California, it is illegal to touch a child's intimate parts, which by the law's definition includes the inner thighs. This is not something that most people would know or even expect to be illegal, even if they thought it was inappropriate. By documenting this level of specificity in your policy, you set clear expectations of all staff members and empower your staff, parents, and children to hold everyone accountable to the law.

Each state has established an age of consent of 16, 17, or 18. Beyond this age, it is legal for minors to engage in sexual activities, with the exception of states that also have age-gap provisions that legalize teen sexuality as long as the two parties are within a certain age range.[2] However, because of the differential in power and authority between a youth and a staff member, your formal policy should prohibit sexual relations of any type with children until they have reached the age of eighteen or are no longer under the care of your organization, whichever comes later.[3]

Below is an excerpt from a case study referenced in a recent report published by the GAO which serves as a good example of the need for this extended policy provision. Even if offenders are not held criminally accountable based on your state law, it is important that you have the ability to protect the children in your care from further risk. By extending your boundaries for sexual activity beyond the age of consent, you have the ability to enforce the associated consequences for breaking the boundaries as set forth in your policy which should call for termination under such circumstances.

LEGAL BOUNDARIES

"...the police initiated an investigation that found that the relationship between the teacher and the student had progressed to a sexual relationship. Although the teacher was prosecuted and convicted of sexual assault, the state Supreme Court later overturned the teacher's criminal conviction because the student had reached the state's age of consent at the time of the sexual relationship. Following this case, the state changed its law to provide that consensual sex between a student and teacher, who has supervisory or disciplinary authority over the student, constitutes sexual assault even if the student is at or past the age of consent. The student was not in the teacher's class, but the court recognized that, on occasion, the student was subject to the teacher's authority while she was assigned to cafeteria duty and, as a student in the school, is expected to obey teachers because they are faculty members."[4]

Please note that possession of child pornography is directly correlated to contact sexual abuse. One study showed that 85 percent of offenders who were convicted of child pornography eventually disclosed hands-on sexual abuse as part of an intensive, residential, sex offender-specific treatment program (SOTP). When analyzed, the 40 offenders who had known histories of hands-on sexual abuse at the time of sentencing disclosed an average of 19.4 victims during their treatment period. In comparison, the 115 subjects with no known histories of these crimes ultimately disclosed an average of 8.7 victims. If any staff member is suspected of possessing child pornography, it is highly likely they are also abusing children in your care and should be reported to authorities immediately.[5]

I have included a subset of the California Penal Code below as an example for you to review. This section references other penal

127126

code sections which I have not included for the sake of space. However, you should review all referenced sections in your state code and include all pertinent sections in your written policy.

CALIFORNIA PENAL CODE[6]

Section 11164

(a) This article shall be known and may be cited as the Child Abuse and Neglect Reporting Act.

(b) The intent and purpose of this article is to protect children from abuse and neglect. In any investigation of suspected child abuse or neglect, all persons participating in the investigation of the case shall consider the needs of the child victim and shall do whatever is necessary to prevent psychological harm to the child victim.

11165 As used in this article "child" means a person under the age of 18 years.

11165.1 As used in this article, "sexual abuse" means sexual assault or sexual exploitation as defined by the following:

(a) "Sexual assault" means conduct in violation of one or more of the following sections: Section 261 (rape), subdivision (d) of Section 261.5 (statutory rape), 264.1 (rape in concert), 285 (incest), 286 (sodomy), subdivision (a) or (b), or paragraph (1) of subdivision (c) of Section 288 (lewd or lascivious acts upon a child), 288a (oral copulation), 289 (sexual penetration), or 647.6 (child molestation).

(b) Conduct described as "sexual assault" includes, but is not limited to, all of the following:

(1) Any penetration, however slight, of the vagina or anal opening of one person by the penis of another person, whether or not there is the emission of semen.

(2) Any sexual contact between the genitals or anal opening of one person and the mouth or tongue of another person.

(3) Any intrusion by one person into the genitals or anal opening of another person, including the use of any object for this purpose, except that, it does not include acts performed for a valid medical purpose.

(4) The intentional touching of the genitals or intimate parts (including the breasts, genital area, groin, inner thighs, and buttocks) or the clothing covering them, of a child, or of the perpetrator by a child, for purposes of sexual arousal or gratification, except that, it does not include acts which may reasonably be construed to be normal caretaker responsibilities; interactions with, or demonstrations of affection for, the child; or acts performed for a valid medical purpose.

(5) The intentional masturbation of the perpetrator's genitals in the presence of a child.

(c) "Sexual exploitation" refers to any of the following:

(1) Conduct involving matter depicting a minor engaged in obscene acts in violation of Section 311.2 (preparing, selling, or distributing obscene matter) or subdivision (a) of Section 311.4 (employment of minor to perform obscene acts).

(2) Any person who knowingly promotes, aids, or assists, employs, uses, persuades, induces, or coerces a child, or any person responsible for a child's welfare, who knowingly permits or encourages a child to engage in, or assist others to engage in, prostitution or a live performance involving obscene sexual conduct, or to either pose or model alone or with others for purposes of preparing a film, photograph, negative, slide, drawing, painting, or other pictorial depiction, involving obscene sexual conduct. For the purpose of this section, "person

responsible for a child's welfare" means a parent, guardian, foster parent, or a licensed administrator or employee of a public or private residential home, residential school, or other residential institution.

(3) Any person who depicts a child in, or who knowingly develops, duplicates, prints, or exchanges, any film, photograph, video tape, negative, or slide in which a child is engaged in an act of obscene sexual conduct, except for those activities by law enforcement and prosecution agencies and other persons described in subdivisions (c) and (e) of Section 311.3.

Section 288

(a) Except as provided in subdivision (i), any person who willfully and lewdly commits any lewd or lascivious act, including any of the acts constituting other crimes provided for in Part 1, upon or with the body, or any part or member thereof, of a child who is under the age of 14 years, with the intent of arousing, appealing to, or gratifying the lust, passions, or sexual desires of that person or the child, is guilty of a felony and shall be punished by imprisonment in the state prison for three, six, or eight years.

Section 311.11

(a) Every person who knowingly possesses or controls any matter, representation of information, data, or image, including, but not limited to, any film, filmstrip, photograph, negative, slide, photocopy, videotape, video laser disc, computer hardware, computer software, computer floppy disc, data storage media, CD-ROM, or computer-generated equipment or any other computer-generated image that contains or incorporates in any manner, any film or filmstrip, the production of which involves the use of a person under 18 years of age, knowing that the matter depicts a person under 18 years of age personally engaging in or simulating sexual conduct, as defined in subdivision (d) of Section 311.4, is guilty of a felony and shall be punished by imprisonment in the state prison, or a county jail for up to one year, or by a fine not exceeding two thousand five hundred dollars ($2,500), or by both the fine and imprisonment.

Section 314

Every person who willfully and lewdly, either:

1. Exposes his person, or the private parts thereof, in any public place, or in any place where there are present other persons to be offended or annoyed thereby; or,
2. Procures, counsels, or assists any person so to expose himself or take part in any model artist exhibition, or to make any other exhibition of himself to public view, or the view of any number of persons, such as is offensive to decency, or is adapted to excite to vicious or lewd thoughts or acts, is guilty of a misdemeanor.

Section 647

(j) (1) Any person who looks through a hole or opening, into, or otherwise views, by means of any instrumentality, including, but not limited to, a periscope, telescope, binoculars, camera, motion picture camera, camcorder, or mobile phone, the interior of a bedroom, bathroom, changing room, fitting room, dressing room, or tanning booth, or the interior of any other area in which the occupant has a reasonable expectation of privacy, with the intent to invade the privacy of a person or persons inside. This subdivision shall not apply to those areas of a private business used to count currency or other negotiable instruments.

(2) Any person who uses a concealed camcorder, motion picture camera, or photographic camera of any type, to secretly videotape, film, photograph, or record by electronic means, another, identifiable person under or through the clothing being worn by that other person, for the purpose of viewing the body of, or the undergarments worn by, that other person, without the consent or knowledge of that other person, with the intent to arouse, appeal to, or gratify the lust, passions, or sexual desires of that person and invade the privacy of that other person, under circumstances in which the other person has a reasonable expectation of privacy.

(3) (A) Any person who uses a concealed camcorder, motion picture camera, or photographic camera of any type, to secretly videotape, film, photograph, or record by electronic means, another, identifiable person who may be in a state of full or partial undress, for the purpose of viewing the body of, or the undergarments worn by, that other person, without the consent or knowledge of that other person, in the interior of a bedroom, bathroom, changing room, fitting room, dressing room, or tanning booth, or the interior of any other area in which that other person has a reasonable expectation of privacy, with the intent to invade the privacy of that other person.

Section 647.6

(a) (1) Every person who annoys or molests any child under 18 years of age shall be punished by a fine not exceeding five thousand dollars ($5,000), by imprisonment in a county jail not exceeding one year, or by both the fine and imprisonment.

Now that we have covered boundaries that reflect illegal behaviors, let's move on to boundaries that intercede with known grooming behaviors child molesters use to build trusting relationships with children and their families. According to former deputy district attorney and author, Sax, "This seemingly innocent behavior is intended to make a child feel comfortable before any hint of sexual inappropriateness begins."[7] These behaviors serve to create access, identify the vulnerable, desensitize children to touch, illicit complicity and test a child's ability to keep a secret.[8]

Next Steps:

- Review, document, and distribute new Legal Boundaries to staff, parents and children.

BEST PRACTICE #3

ON-SITE BOUNDARIES: INTRODUCTION

Reflection:

Before continuing, complete the questions below regarding on-site boundaries. As in the previous section, it is important to answer these questions from your current knowledge. Now is not the time to go and look for the answers because honestly, if you don't know what your organization's boundaries are, then they don't really exist in a manner that effectively protects kids and that is important to recognize.

➤ What boundaries does your organization currently have in place to protect kids from sexual abuse?

_____

_____

_____

_____

_____

_____

_____

_____

_____

_____

➤ What boundaries does your organization have in place to limit physical access to children while in your care?

_____

_____

_____

_____

_____

_____

_____

_____

➤ If the children in your care have access to computers as part of your program, what boundaries do you have in place to protect them from Internet predators and viewing inappropriate material?

_____

_____

_____

_____

_____

_____

_____

_____

_____

➤ How do you communicate to your staff that there are no truly private times with children?

_____

_____

_____

_____

_____

_____

_____

_____

_____

➤ Are there any areas on the grounds that are off-limits to staff and/or children? If so, what are they? How are these off-limits locations communicated to staff and children? Are there areas that are isolated and *should* be off-limits but are not currently?

_____

_____

_____

_____

_____

_____

_____

_____

_____

_____

➤ What are your formal policies and informal practices regarding pulling children out of their regularly scheduled program activities?

_____

_____

_____

_____

_____

_____

_____

_____

_____

➤ What are your formal policies and informal practices for children helping before and after normally scheduled program hours?

_____

_____

_____

_____

_____

_____

_____

_____

_____

_____

> What additional boundaries do you have in place to protect vulnerable populations such as infants, toddlers, and children with disabilities?

_____

_____

_____

_____

_____

_____

_____

_____

> What boundaries do you have in place that limit family members working or volunteering together?

_____

_____

_____

_____
_____
_____
_____
_____
_____
_____

➢ What is your policy for supervision during nap time?

_____
_____
_____
_____
_____
_____
_____
_____

➢ How do you provide protection for children during lights-out activities, such as movies?

_____
_____
_____
_____

_____

_____

_____

_____

_____

_____

➢ What policies or boundaries are in place for diapering and/or monitoring bathroom activities?

_____

_____

_____

_____

_____

_____

_____

_____

➢ Do you have regular unexpected supervision of all program activities? How do you accomplish this?

_____

_____

_____

_____

_____

_____

_____

_____

_____

➤ What is your policy on parents' supervision and involvement in your program?

_____

_____

_____

_____

_____

_____

_____

➤ What guidelines do you have in place regarding appropriate and inappropriate topics of conversation between staff and children?

_____

_____

_____

_____

_____

_____
_____
_____
_____
_____

➤ What boundaries do you have in place regarding the use of intimidation by staff?

_____
_____
_____
_____
_____
_____
_____
_____

➤ What boundaries do you have in place regarding discussions of or exchange of sexually explicit material?

_____
_____
_____
_____
_____

_____

_____

_____

_____

➤ What are the organization's boundaries regarding personal body space? Do you have boundaries that specifically limit physical touch of children by staff and vice versa? How are those boundaries communicated to staff, parents, and children?

_____

_____

_____

_____

_____

_____

_____

➤ What boundaries do you have in place regarding children changing clothes in front of staff or vice versa? If you have locker rooms, what are your boundaries regarding showering?

_____

_____

_____

_____

_____

_____

_____

_____

_____

➤ What is your policy regarding staff dispensing drugs to children?

_____

_____

_____

_____

_____

_____

_____

_____

_____

➤ What is your current policy regarding taking photographs during program activities?

_____

_____

_____

_____

_____

_____

_____

_____

_____

I have created three subcategories for On-Site Boundaries to help facilitate easy retrieval in the future. These categories are Access Boundaries, Isolation Boundaries, and Behavioral Boundaries. We will look at these in the following three chapters.

BEST PRACTICE #3

ON-SITE BOUNDARIES: ACCESS

SECURE THE FACILITY AND LIMIT ACCESS TO CHILDREN[1, 2]

Organizations that offer their programs in a physical building or campus should ensure that visitors, including strangers, contractors, parents, etc., are required to go through a centralized entry point where they are asked to identify themselves. This entry point should be staffed at all times when children are on the premises, allowing the staff member to determine if visitors have a legitimate reason to be there. If so, they should be asked to sign in and given a temporary identification badge showing that they have been properly screened and granted access to the facility. Anyone who has a legitimate reason to be on the premises will have gone through the applicable screening process as outlined in Best Practices #2 and have been added to your Approved Access List. If a staff member sees someone roaming around without an identification badge, they should intercede and escort the person back to the entry point to go through the appropriate process. Of course, anyone requesting entry that does not have a legitimate reason to be on the premises or has not gone through the applicable screening process and been added to the Approved Access List should not be granted access but instead referred to an appropriate staff member to assist them.

Another important aspect of securing the facility is discussed by Shakeshaft in her paper *Know the Warning Signs of Educator Sexual Misconduct* where she writes, "Locked classrooms, storerooms, and teacher offices are all places where sexual misconduct occurs, often before or after school. They need to be secured. A staff person should be assigned to check classrooms at the end of each school day to ensure that they're empty and that students have left the building unless they are in approved activities."[3] I wholeheartedly agree that each area of your facility, whether it is a school or other organization, should be secured at the end of the program schedule.

For those organizations such as sports leagues that use unsecured public facilities as their primary activity location, it is even more important for you to have clear guidelines for securing access to the children in your care. Document and communicate to parents, how and when children are transferred into your care and back to the parents. During the time they are with you, there should be established guidelines for supervision of children, ensuring that none of them leave the area without an approved adult's company. This includes children going to use a public bathroom. Volunteer coverage such as Team Moms can help to make this boundary manageable, but don't forget that volunteers need to be fully screened and held accountable for all boundaries!

There are convicted child molesters in every community and it's important for you to know who they are so you can keep them away from the children you serve. Whether you deliver programs at your own facility or a public venue, you should check the national sex offender registry by location and identify all registered sex offenders who live within a five- to ten-mile radius of where you are (http://www.nsopw.gov/en). Their profiles should be printed, including photographs, and made available to your staff so that you would all recognize them if they were hanging around. Someone on your staff should reach out to their parole officers and ask if there are any terms of parole that restrict them from being within the vicinity of where children gather. This process should be completed for your primary site as well as any approved off-site locations. I want to emphasize that anyone who uses registered sex offender information to threaten, intimidate, or harass any individual, including registrants or family members may be subject to criminal prosecution or civil liability under federal and/or state law. I am recommending you use the information only to be able to visually identify if a registered sex offender is within an illegal range of your children.

Lastly, you will need to have documented guidelines for how to control access to children during off-site activities as well. You can look into those as part of the off-site location approval process later in this chapter.

RESTRICT ACCESS AND/OR MONITOR REGISTERED SEX OFFENDERS

It is extraordinarily dangerous to allow registered sex offenders access to children and the best way to ensure they do not have access to the children you serve is to keep them off of your premises. However, this can be a challenge for faith organizations as their mission is typically to love everyone, especially the lost and this would certainly include sex offenders. So what do you do when a registered sex offender wants to come to weekly services where children are present?

There are a few possible solutions that should be considered. The first and safest in my opinion is to not allow registered sex offenders on your premises. If possible, collaborate with other like faith organizations that do not have children's ministries and refer sex offenders to those sites instead.

The second option is to collaborate with like faith organizations and create a separate set of services (sermons, bible study, etc.) for sex offenders that is open to a broader geographic community, perhaps a single location within the county. However, this could pose problems for some registered sex offenders as they may have terms of probation that restrict them from communing with other registered sex offenders.

The third option is to direct registered sex offenders to pre-recorded services available on your website which would provide them the message for the week but it would certainly not provide them with the valuable opportunity to be involved in the faith community.

The fourth option is to allow registered sex offenders on your campus only if they are accompanied by an approved escort at all times. This provides them the opportunity to partake in a variety of services and be an active part of the faith community. However, there is a significant risk involved because if members of the congregation are used to seeing a particular person on campus, they would assume they are safe. If the registered sex offender arrives on your campus and does not make previous arrangements to be with an approved escort, the congregation members would not be aware of the potential danger which would be a significant risk to the children in your care. One option to overcome this risk would be to notify the adults within your congregation of who the registered sex offender is and engage them in holding that offender accountable for being with an approved escort. The challenge with this approach is that congregation members may not be comfortable with the sex offender's presence and therefore choose to attend a different faith organization as a result.

Allowing registered sex offenders on your premises is by far the riskiest option I have offered you for consideration and I would personally not recommend it because I believe the risk far outweighs the benefit. However, I do know faith organizations who have adopted this approach and you may do so as well. I would like to be perfectly clear though, you must go into this type of scenario with your eyes wide open and leave your religious trust behind. You must involve a broad enough group of people to ensure accountability for constant supervision of registered sex offenders. You should also be acutely aware of the increased liability you have if a registered sex offender you have allowed on your premises abuses a child in your care. This is especially true if you do not notify parents in advance. Check with your insurance company to determine if this option would be in compliance with your terms of coverage.

RESTRICT AND MONITOR INTERNET ACCESS

The previous boundary addresses securing physical access to children, but it is also crucial for you to control electronic access to the children in your care. We are living in the age of technology and computer skills are required for employment as well as basic social interaction. In an effort to support this requirement, many children's programs provide access to computers and organizations such as schools, after-school programs, and boys and girls clubs often have computer labs with training built into their core curriculum. However, computer access poses an additional risk of students accessing external sites that are inappropriate and possibly dangerous. It is essential that youth-serving organizations that provide computer access for kids have a strict usage policy, but we cannot rely on policy alone to protect our kids. Organizations must also install software that restricts access and monitors activity on the computers. Organization leaders should work closely with their IT department to select the most suitable program for their environment, but here are a few considerations to keep in mind when making your selection:

- Select a software program that determines what they can access versus what they cannot. The Internet is vast and ever changing and it would be impossible to keep up on the possible dangers. We recommend that the list of acceptable sites is developed by using a formal process with input from stakeholders that is approved by the board. The list should not be made by individual teachers or group leaders.

- Social media sites should *not* be included in programs that are accessible as they provide access to build relationships that cannot be effectively monitored. These sites include but are not limited to Facebook, Twitter, Pinterest, Skype, chat, and instant message applications, etc.

- You are looking to limit not only what the children access but what your staff can access. If you have a staff member who is a child molester, they can use the Internet to show children pornographic pictures or even establish a video chat with someone who exposes themselves live. Video chat also lends itself to child molesters "producing" child pornography by getting a child to expose themselves or participate in sexual acts for someone else to view.

- The software you select should also monitor activity on the computer including files that have been uploaded or downloaded, what applications have been used and what Web sites have been accessed. Preferably you should have software that sends automatic alerts to key personnel when unapproved activity is spotted. If you do not have that level of sophistication available, you should at least have someone monitoring reports on a regular basis to ensure there is no unexpected and/or unapproved activity.

- Computers on the grounds of a youth-serving organization should be limited to computers which are owned and controlled by the organization so that they can be properly restricted and monitored. Staff and volunteers should not be allowed to bring personal computers onto the premises. They not only have the ability to view pornographic images on the computer, but almost all laptops have built in webcams now which could be used to take inappropriate pictures of children undetected.

- Computers owned by the organization should not have webcams installed unless there is a specific reason, in which case it must be secured for that purpose only and tightly controlled. Not only can staff members misuse webcams on computers owned by the organization, hackers can turn on a webcam remotely, providing unauthorized visual access.

• If you do not have the skills or funding to properly manage electronic access to the children in your care, I would recommend that you do not provide computer access in areas where children are permitted.

• If you don't have these skills but still need to provide computer access for staff use, you can provide computers in secure locations and manually monitor their usage. Basic information on manually monitoring Internet access can be found in a book called *Catch Me if You: Discover Internet Habits, Dangers and Abusers, A Step by Step Guide Anyone Can Do* by Travis Morgan.

> In one case, Kimberly Crain, who was a third-grade schoolteacher in Oklahoma, was accused and eventually convicted of exploiting children in her class. One of the ways that she accomplished her exploitation was by luring the kids into using Skype to talk with an older man she referred to as "Uncle G" and then having them watch as this man exposed himself. The video chat program was accessed through a district-owned computer the teacher had in her classroom.[4, 5, 6]

Next Steps:

• Review, document, and distribute new On-Site: Access Boundaries to staff, parents and children.

BEST PRACTICE #3

ON-SITE BOUNDARIES: ISOLATION

In the foreword to Salter's book *Predators, Pedophiles, Rapists & Other Sex Offenders*, Gavin de Becker made child molesters' need to isolate children extraordinarily clear. He said, "Just as with animals, human predators must separate their targets from the flock."[1] With this in mind, let's look at boundaries that will intercede with child molesters' intentional attempts to separate and isolate children.

NO ONE ADULT–ONE CHILD SITUATIONS[2, 3, 4, 5, 6]

Eighty percent of childhood sexual abuse happens in one perpetrator–one child situations. So simply by restricting private access to children in your care, you can significantly lower the risk of abuse.

When my daughter was in sixth grade, she hurt her ankle and had a doctor's note to excuse her from PE until further notice. Because there was no specific end date, the school removed her from the class and enrolled her in study hall where she was to go to the library during that period to study. Teachers were assigned specific periods when they were to bring their classes into the library, but for some reason on the first day of my daughter's enrollment in study hall, the assigned teacher did not bring her class to the library. This resulted in my daughter spending forty-five minutes in a closed library alone with a male librarian. When I expressed my concern to the assistant principal and asked for the school's policy on child sexual abuse prevention, she began desperately searching the district Web site to find it. I told her that if as a leader of this school, she could not articulate the policy to me, they don't have one, even if she found it. I later confirmed they did not. This one adult–one child situation put my daughter at risk of being abused and created exposure for the librarian to be accused of inappropriate behavior even if it didn't happen. If the school had a no one adult–one child policy in place, the librarian simply would have walked my daughter to the office and let them know she couldn't stay in the library today and mitigated the risk.

While a no one adult–one child policy could be achieved with one adult and two children, my recommendation is to have at least two adults present at all times. I understand that this may be difficult in some circumstances such as classrooms, but this should be the goal and volunteers should be used to augment your staff to make it possible.

> Shakeshaft shared one case that she reviewed and said, "In one class, boys reported that the teacher would call them up to his desk at the front of the room and, one at a time, while discussing homework, would fondle each boy's penis. Every child in the room knew what was happening and students talked about it among themselves. The teacher repeated this behavior for 15 years before one student finally reported to an official who would act upon the information that everyone knew."[30]

We have seen more and more high profile cases of abuse with groups of children. As a matter of fact, 19 percent of juvenile sexual assault victimizations involved another individual.[7] The Boy Scouts of America have adopted a two-deep policy where "Two registered adult leaders, or one registered leader and a parent of a participating Scout or other adult, one of whom must be 21 years of age or older, are required for all trips and outings."[8] This approach significantly decreases the likelihood of sexual abuse.

Because of the risk of abuse by other minors, teen employees or volunteers should always be accompanied by an adult.

Depending on your current practices, this boundary could increase the cost of your program. As an example, if a before/after school care program staffs according to their state licensing board's mandated staff/child ratio, they may find that they only need one staff member during the first and last hour of the day. However, this would leave the potential of that staff member being alone for some period of time with the first child who arrives in the morning or the last child to leave in the evening. Therefore, this ratio-based

The protection of our children is not optional.

staffing model would not meet this recommended safety measure and would need to be modified to have at least two staff members on-site during these low attendance hours.

Some organizations say that it's not in the budget and they can't possibly afford to have this level of coverage. My response is that the protection of our children is not optional.

You have other options such as raising your program fees across the board or charging a premium for services during those hours, but discarding best practices is simply too risky. If you cannot establish a viable business model to staff appropriately during those hours, then those hours of coverage should be cut from the program.

If a staff member finds they are unexpectedly alone with a child, they should attempt to remove themselves from that situation right away, by either asking another staff member to join them or moving to another area of the facility where there are people. If there are no other adults left in the facility, the staff member should notify a supervisor immediately, and if safe, move to a publically observable situation such as going outside to play ball or for a stroll, etc.

With all that said about one adult–one child situations, we also have to realize that 20 percent of the time, abuse happens with other children or other adults present. It never ceases to amaze me how brazen child molesters can be whether it is a coach inappropriately touching a child in the front seat of a car with other children in the backseat,[9] a day care owner digitally penetrating a little girl in the back corner of the room while other children watched television[10] or a teacher fondling the genitals of each male student when he invited them to his desk to review their homework while the other children continued with their assignment, knowing all the while what was happening.[11]

Because of the statistical prevalence of abuse in one perpetrator–one child situations, this is one of the most important boundaries you could implement. I encourage you to make it a top priority. Start the process today!

APPROVED AND OFF-LIMITS LOCATIONS[12, 13, 14]

Knowing that our intention is to keep kids safe by ensuring staff's interactions with them are observable by others, it is important to consciously assess the facility design and determine if there are on-site locations that should be deemed off-limits. Specifically, we suggest any location that is visibly isolated should be off-limits for children—they shouldn't be there alone, they shouldn't be there with other kids, and they shouldn't be there with any staff members. This could include outside locations such as behind buildings or dumpsters or inside locations such as offices, closets, or supply cabinets. Assess the landscape for private areas as well and cut back or remove plants that create private areas.

> One adult victim shared that they were molested regularly during nap time at an in-home day care center. The room where the kids slept during nap time wasn't quite large enough for all the kids enrolled, so this child's assigned napping location was in a hallway off of the main room. Unfortunately, it was out of sight and directly in front of the bedroom door of the owner's teenage son, who proceeded to come out and molest the child every day.

Even though locations may be deemed off-limits, that doesn't actually keep a staff member from taking a child there if their intent is to be alone with the child. So as an extra precaution, I recommend that all inside doors include a large window, making it possible to see anyone inside and that your policy clearly states that the windows cannot be covered.[15, 16]

Covering the only window in his office with a bulletin board was one of the many steps that Highland Park Baptist Church children's pastor took to create a secluded place where he abused his victims. He was eventually arrested, pleaded guilty to "16 counts of sodomy for oral sex, three counts of sexual abuse of a child under 12 and one count of possession of child pornography" and was sentenced to thirty years in prison. The district attorney said the number of his victims was in the double-digits.[17]

NO PULLING CHILDREN OUT OF THEIR REGULARLY SCHEDULED PROGRAM[18, 19]

The option for a staff member to pull children out of their regularly scheduled program activities should be eliminated where possible and highly scrutinized and managed where needed. This ensures that staff members, administrators, and parents know exactly where their children are and who they are with at any given time of day and that they are protected by the other safety precautions you have in place within your policy.

> Your programs are thoughtfully designed to effectively deliver program materials in a safe and healthy manner. As soon as you deviate from that thoughtful process, you introduce risk.

Your programs are thoughtfully designed to effectively deliver program materials in a safe and healthy manner. As soon as you deviate from that thoughtful process, you introduce risk. It's not uncommon to hear about child sexual abuse cases where a staff member has pulled a child or small group of children out of the regular program to work on a special project or meet with them individually.

Unfortunately, it became apparent after the fact, that this is exactly how these child molesters gained private access to the kids.

Please note that even lunchtime and recess are part of your regularly scheduled program. Children should not be called into a staff member's office, classroom, or any other location during break time.

If for some reason, your organization has specific circumstances that would require a child to be pulled out of their program (i.e., student council meetings or an event committee meeting), then there should be a formalized process developed and documented ahead of time. An individual staff member should not have the authority to take such action independently.

Formalizing the process should include the following steps:

- The board of directors should:

  o Develop and approve a list of "acceptable reasons" a child can be pulled from their regularly scheduled program and who is eligible to make such a request.

  o Designate and approve specific locations where "out-of-program" activities can take place, ensuring that other boundaries such as "No one adult–one child situations" are respected.

  o Define the frequency and duration of out-of-program activity requests that will be approved for individual children and for individual staff members. Out-of-program activities should be the exception, not the norm. Frequent requests should be considered a red flag.

  o Define and approve a designated list of individuals (or titles) that are authorized to approve individual requests.

- A written request should be submitted at least two days prior to the expected event.

- Written approval should be obtained by at least two previously authorized individuals.
- Approval notification should be sent to the parents.
- Arrangements should be made for another staff member or volunteer to "drop in" on approved out-of-program exceptions to ensure they are not being used as a means to gain inappropriate access to kids.

Formalizing the process slows everything down which helps to eliminate informal subjective decisions about how children spend their time while in your care. Children stay on the regular program schedule unless an exception is fully documented and only for reasons that are pre-approved.

We understand there may be people on staff whose job it is to pull kids out of regularly scheduled program activities for private meetings such as school guidance counselors. If this is the case with your organization, the facility should be set-up so that those meetings happen in a centralized location where other staff members are present with either doors open or windows in the doors. The people who have this level of authority should be extremely limited and closely monitored. Outside of this exceptional circumstance, staff members should not be able to pull a child from their regularly scheduled activities. The process applies equally to all staff members—no exceptions!

> According to the Grand Jury Report, Jerry Sandusky from Penn State routinely had contact with Victim 1 at a Clinton County high school where the administration would call him "out of activity period/study hall in the late afternoon to meet with Sandusky in a conference room."[20]

Please understand that the restriction on pulling children from their regularly scheduled programs applies to everyone— staff, volunteers, and even people outside of your organization.

The only exception would be if the person is on the child's emergency list and authorized by the parents to remove the child from school. Even then, if it is done on a regular basis without a specific reason (i.e., doctor's appointment, etc.), this should be considered a red flag and discussed with the child's parents.

NO BEFORE OR AFTER PROGRAM HELP[21]

I regularly hear about kids who stay after school to "help in the classroom" or arrive early to "help coach set-up." While staff members may need and appreciate the help, it's risky for children to arrive early or stay after regularly scheduled program activities without their parents present. Even though most staff members would engage in this activity innocently, if any staff member is allowed to do this, it sets a precedent that child molesters will exploit to gain access to children. This boundary should apply even if there are multiple children staying as a group. Child molesters often select small groups of vulnerable and impressionable children and engage them in inappropriate activities as a group. If help is needed, ask for another fully screened staff member or parent volunteer to be present as well.

TWO ADULTS WITH INFANTS, TODDLERS, AND NONVERBAL CHILDREN

Caring for kids who are nonverbal, whether due to age or disability, requires some additional protections be in place. Clearly, infants, toddlers, and children with cognitive or verbal deficiencies are not in a position to recognize and/or hold adults accountable for inappropriate behavior. This is where two adults are absolutely necessary, even

> Nearly 80 percent of childhood sexual abuse happens in one perpetrator–one child situations.[22, 23]

with multiple children present because it is the perfect scenario for child molesters to work uninhibited, with minimal chance of disclosure. The risk is just too high!

VIDEO CAMERAS IN LOCATIONS THAT SERVE CHILDREN WITH DISABILITIES AND OTHER HIGH-RISK AREAS[24]

There are specific disabilities that significantly raise the level of risk of sexual abuse. Some physical disabilities make it impossible for children to remove themselves from an abusive situation; cognitive disabilities can make it virtually impossible to educate and empower children about inappropriate touching; while verbal disabilities practically ensure that silence will be kept. For these reasons, it is imperative that video cameras are installed in any location where children with disabilities are being served. In addition, it is not enough to just install the cameras and refer back to the footage if someone raises an issue, it is crucial that the video be monitored to ensure compliance with safe pre-established boundaries. This monitoring function does not require any formalized training so it can be staffed by screened volunteers.

Cameras should also be used in other high-risk areas as needed such as buses that transport students with disabilities.

A forty-six–year-old former New Hampshire school bus driver was sentenced to 160 years in federal prison for sexually abusing special-needs children and recording some of the attacks. John Wright, of Milton, New Hampshire, was indicted in October 2011 and pleaded guilty to five counts of sexual exploitation of children and one count of possession of child pornography. He worked for the Provider bus service in Strafford County, Rockingham County, and Kittery, Maine, since 2008. Before that, he drove a bus for the Milton schools for four years.

"Wright was arrested in September 2011 during an undercover investigation of people trading child pornography on file-sharing networks. Authorities found several videos showing Wright sexually assaulting children who 'suffered a variety of disabilities,' some of whom were 'completely nonverbal.' Wright recorded some attacks using a camera attached to his glasses. Police also found and estimated 10,000 images of child pornography on Wright's computer."[25]

NO FAMILY MEMBERS WORKING TOGETHER[26]

It is not uncommon for husbands and wives to offer to volunteer together, whether it is to coach a softball team or to teach on Sundays in the children's ministry at their church. It is important to understand that spouses hold special privileges within some states that protect their personal communications from being divulged in civil and criminal cases as well as the right to refuse to testify against their spouse and/or not to be called as a witness in a case against their spouse. Some of these privileges are available under US Federal Common Law as well. Laws differ by state and are subject to change so it is not my intention to provide any guidance on state or federal laws. It is my intention, however, to make you aware of the possibility of these privileges and how they could adversely affect your ability to provide a safe environment for the children in your care. So at minimum, if you allow husband/wife teams to volunteer or work for you, it is essential that you do not treat them as two individual adults when it comes to boundaries such as one adult–one child situations. You would need a third adult in the room if they are going to be alone with a child. Your risk would be further minimized by simply not allowing spouses to serve together. I have included the section from California's Penal Code below as a reference.

Section 970–973[27]

970. Except as otherwise provided by statute, a married person has a privilege not to testify against his spouse in any proceeding.
971. Except as otherwise provided by statute, a married person whose spouse is a party to a proceeding has a privilege not to be called as a witness by an adverse party to that proceeding without the prior express consent of the spouse having the privilege under this section unless the party calling the spouse does so in good faith without knowledge of the marital relationship.

While other family members are not afforded the same protections regarding testifying in court, it is still much less likely that a staff member would report inappropriate behaviors of a family member, so I recommend following the same guidelines as we outlined for spouses. In an extensive research study of day care centers documented in *Nursery Crimes*, David Finkelhor and his team found that "The mother-son abuser combination is particularly common" in multiple perpetrator cases.[28]

TWO ADULTS MONITORING NAP TIME

Since kids do not require much supervision during nap time, it's not uncommon for organizations to leave a single adult in the room with the kids. However, this creates an opportune time for child molesters to move close enough to abuse under the guise that a child was having problems sleeping and needed soothing. With the room dark and all the other children asleep, it has a similar risk level of a one adult–one child situation. The research represented in the book *Nursery Crimes*, indicates that "Almost a third of all abuse occurred during nap time."[29] Our kids are counting on us to protect them and in this case to stand guard over them. So it is crucial for two adults to be present in the room during nap time.

MULTIPLE ADULTS DURING MOVIES OR OTHER LIGHTS-OUT ACTIVITIES[30]

Generally speaking, I recommend that you minimize the types of activities that require the lights to be out and have those activities pre-approved similar to the process you'll use for approving who and when a child can be pulled from their regular program. Whenever lights are out, it increases the risk of children being sexually abused. So it is important to know ahead of time when these activities will take place so you can make arrangements for an additional staff member or volunteer to be present. We have seen cases of teachers fondling their students during a movie in their classroom as well as turning the lights off at lunch to make people think no one is in the classroom, all the while molesting a child in the dark. It is important to take precautions and minimize lights-out activities.

OBSERVABLE DIAPERING AND BATHROOM MONITORING

No matter what age children your organization cares for, diapering and bathroom activities are part of the daily routine. Unfortunately, these activities can be a very vulnerable time for children because of the inherent exposure of the genitals. As a matter of fact, Finkelhor's study found that the bathroom is the most common location for abuse within day care centers with almost two-thirds of all abuse happening there.[31]

Below is a simple list of guidelines to follow. I understand they may need to be adjusted to fit the design of your facility. If that's the case, focus on the *intent* of the boundary (*in italics below*) and come up with the best possible solution you can provide under the circumstances. But as we discussed earlier, the protection of our children is not an option. So if your facility or staffing does not allow you to provide safety during diapering and bathroom activities, then it needs to be escalated to the board of directors as a significant risk to be addressed by an increase in staff or facility remodeling which may require additional program funding.

> Diapering and bathroom activities are the most vulnerable time for children because of the inherent exposure of the genitals.

- Diapering should be done in an observable area. If you're unable to achieve this based on the design of your facility, you should create a process where diapers are changed at intervals with two staff members present. *No one adult–one child situations, especially when genitals are exposed.*
- For *older* children, stalls in bathrooms should have doors and the kids should be instructed to close them as soon as they are potty-trained and able to handle this activity by themselves. *This is an opportunity to establish privacy boundaries, not only to protect kids in your care, but also to establish boundaries they can call upon when they're elsewhere.*
- For *young* children, bathrooms should be designed with low partitions and open entrances. *This provides for more supervision, but it is still crucial that children's privacy is honored so you are modeling appropriate boundaries.*

- When kids are using outside bathrooms such as on a playground, a staff member should check the bathroom to ensure it is empty before sending kids inside. *This helps to protect kids from strangers or other adults who may be inside without your knowledge.*
- When sending kids to the bathroom, there should be a staff member present to monitor the interaction between kids. However, the staff member should be in the doorway where they are observable by others versus being inside the bathroom with the kids. *Kids who have been abused sometimes touch other kids inappropriately because it's what they've grown up with and they don't know it's wrong.*
- Although I do not recommend sending kids to the bathroom using the buddy system without a staff monitor, if you must, the bathroom visits should be with kids of similar age and developmental level. *30–40 percent of child sexual abuse happens at the hands of other juveniles,*[32, 33, 34] *so sending kids to the bathroom with older children could pose a real and present danger.*
- Also if you must use the buddy system, send three kids rather than two. *Just the presence of a third child can help to minimize the potential of children touching children, even in an innocent manner.*

I understand these guidelines may be stricter than you are used to, but it is important that you provide extra precautions during the most vulnerable moments of a child's day with you.

Recently, I was talking with a professor at a local college who had his young daughter in the day care center at the college. It was a new facility that was designed for child safety so there were no doors in the bathroom area. Instead, there was a short pony wall with the toilet and sink behind it, which provided privacy while also allowing the teacher to check on the child from the classroom side of the wall if necessary. This sounds like a good setup, but the center also had a policy that required parents to take their children into the bathroom area to wash their hands when they arrived for the day, to minimize the spread of germs. Unfortunately, it was not unusual for a child to be using the toilet when another parent arrived and had to take their child to wash their hands. So the children who were using the bathroom had their privacy invaded on a regular basis by complete strangers, teaching them that they do not have the right to privacy while going to the bathroom. As you are designing your boundaries, remember that we are always modeling for our children and that they will take these learned behaviors and expectations into all other circumstances including those where child molesters work and live.

DESIGNATE AND SCHEDULE ROVERS

One of the most important concepts your organization should embrace and communicate is that there is no time with children that is completely private. It's important to designate one or two staff members who are responsible for walking the premises and dropping in on activities "unannounced." The organization should schedule rovers throughout the day, preferably two at any given time with no agreed upon declaration of where each of them will appear. This random schedule helps to minimize the possibility of child molesters "working around" the rovers' schedules or even that a rover would knowingly enable inappropriate behavior by coordinating their schedule with a child molester. The intent of the rover position is simply to create a presence which deters inappropriate behavior with children by increasing the likelihood of being caught. There are no specific skills required for this position other than the willingness and commitment to report inappropriate behavior they encounter, so it can be easily staffed by volunteers (fully screened, of course!) at no cost.

Be sure that rovers regularly check designated off-limits locations. I also highly encourage you to use rovers to spot-check field trips and after-school activities as well.

> In one case reviewed by researchers of day care center abuse, "children were taken from the center for a field trip, but went instead to the home of one of the perpetrators, where they were abused."[35]

PROVIDE PARENTAL ACCESS AND SUPERVISION

It is important for parents to play an active role in the lives of their children, and ultimately, it is their responsibility to protect their children. Giving parents open access to their children when participating in youth-serving activities is an important step in ensuring the safety of the children in your care. In Finkelhor's study of day care facilities, he found that "Although only 19% of the cases in our in-depth sample involved multiple perpetrators, 57% of the cases at facilities that limited parental access involved multiple perpetrators."[36]

Providing parental access and supervision may look different depending on the programs you offer. As an example, a day care center should have an open-door policy where parents can enter at any time, even if it is a home day care facility. Indoor sports centers, dance studios, and the like could be designed to provide parents visual access to their children via an observation area. Even music studios that provide one-on-one drum lessons that need to be behind closed doors for noise abatement purposes can allow parents to either sit in on the session or at minimum observe through a window in the door or wall.

Providing parents access to supervise their children gets a bit more difficult in the case of schools where learning and focus is critically important and children would not get anything done if parents were walking in and out of the classroom all the time. However, if we focus on the intent of the boundary, we should be able to arrive at an acceptable alternative. In the case of schools, you could implement a parent classroom volunteer program which not only serves to better protect kids but also gives teachers an extra set of hands. You could present the program to parents emphasizing the need to have one of the parents in the classroom at all times. Of course, as parent volunteers, they should be fully screened.

Next Steps:

- Review, document, and distribute new On-Site: Isolation Boundaries to staff, parents and children.

BEST PRACTICE #3

ON-SITE BOUNDARIES: BEHAVIORAL

So far, you have set boundaries that are very clear about what is illegal and will be immediately reported to law enforcement for investigation. You have set boundaries that control who has physical and cyber access to children in your care. You have also established boundaries that directly intercede with child molesters' attempts to isolate children. Now let's take a look at the boundaries that delineate inappropriate behavior of those who you grant access to the children in your care.

NO UNPROFESSIONAL BEHAVIOR[1, 2, 3]

The relationship between a youth-serving organization staff member and a child they care for is strictly professional and a staff member's behavior should reflect that. Unprofessional behavior would include inappropriate comments, stories, or jokes, being flirtatious, snapping bra straps, comments about hair, clothing or make-up, talking about the staff member's personal struggles or sex life, giving preferential treatment to a specific child, or hanging out with teens in your care. These are examples but feel free to add any other specific behaviors that reflect a relationship is getting too close or too casual. Keep in mind that when child molesters are grooming children, it is a seduction process, much like that of adults dating. So if you see signs that look as though there is an intimate emotional relationship developing, that is the time to step in.

> In 2014, the "daughter-in-law of Nike co-founder Bill Bowerman was arrested for sexually abusing a 17-year-old boy she coached for an Oregon high school track and field team." In May 2012, she had been dismissed as a volunteer coach from another high school after she escorted a seventeen-year-old boy who was on her team to the prom.[4]

Though these behaviors may not seem directly sexual, when it comes to youth-serving organizations, it is best to be overly inclusive in concerning behavior. Researchers, Lanning and Dietz, suggest that when determining what is sexual misconduct, youth-serving organizations should include (1) "any action toward a child motivated by sexual desire" or (2) "any sexual act toward a child, regardless of motivation."[5]

NO INTIMIDATION: SECRETS, LIES, THREATS, COERCION, OR VIOLENCE[6, 7, 8]

Child molesters use a variety of tactics to intimidate children and keep them from disclosing abuse. They may play to the child's friendship and respect for them and simply ask the child to keep it a secret. They may lie and tell a child that their parents know and approve of their activities. They may coerce children with gifts or threats of punishment. They may manipulate them with an offer of a higher grade or a spot on the starting team. They may threaten to kill the child, their parents, or their pets and even use violence or weapons to make their threats seem real. Child molesters often start with small secrets, lies, and acts of coercion to see if the child will be complicit before they move into contact sexual abuse.

One of the most disturbing uses of intimidation is when clergy use their role as a representative of God to abuse a child, often directly linking sexual events to their religious beliefs and traditions. This form of sexual abuse takes on an additional twist referred to as spiritual abuse. A friend and fellow child advocate shared her story of spiritual abuse, which I hope will give you a glimpse of how sexual abuse can start with and be interwoven into the religious beliefs of a child.

> I felt anger and hatred toward my grandpa because of what he did to me and I prayed that he would go away so he couldn't hurt me anymore. When he became paralyzed and eventually died, I experienced an overwhelming sense of guilt and shame that my prayers had come true. As a child I was taught that if I had a question or concern about anything spiritual, I should go to the priest—he was like God on earth and he would give me guidance. I was seven and had just received the sacrament of penance, so I went to confession to ask the priest for his help.
>
> With a kind smile and gentle pat on my shoulder, Father assured me that everything would be fine and I would be forgiven if I followed his direction and "God's Plan." He began by telling me that "forgiveness often requires pain and suffering" and then he told me the things God wanted me to do. In my determination to relieve my guilt and regain God's love, I was ready to do whatever was required. I dutifully followed the priest's guidance, and when he finally assured me my soul was cleansed and I was freed from my sins, I experienced a sense of joy that I had never known! God loved me again! A great burden had been lifted from my heart.
>
> For the next four years, Father would take that joyful, grace-filled spirit which he had cultivated in me and use it for his benefit. He had made me dependent on him for my salvation and established himself as my conduit to heaven. Even now, as I write these words, I feel a piercing of my soul and great sadness at this realization (continued on next page)...

> I dutifully followed Father's "guidance," and as a result, I was put into situations which provided the opportunity for the abuse to occur. What began in the confessional, continued in the sacristy, parish house, and school basement until I was eleven. Over time, I had reservations about what was happening, but I never doubted what Father was telling me—he was speaking for God. So obediently and without question, I continued to follow the "pathway to heaven" he set out for me.

Having a boundary focused on intimidation provides a means for children to recognize the early signs of manipulation. It also provides a chance for youth organization leaders to take action and intercede on behalf of kids, potentially before abuse even occurs.

NO SEXUAL DISCUSSION, EXPOSING CHILDREN TO PORNOGRAPHY OR SEXUALLY EXPLICIT MATERIAL[9, 10, 11]

Child molesters slowly and systematically desensitize children to sexual acts and talking about sex and the use of pornography is particularly effective with adolescents and teens that are or have already gone through puberty. Child molesters may start by talking about sexual things such as body changes during puberty, wet dreams, masturbation, or the sensuality of other students in the program. The child molester may turn the discussion around and share details of their own sex life in an effort to educate kids about sex.

As the discussions proceed, the child molester is looking to see how the child responds and if they tell. If they do tell, the child molester will likely just apologize for his bad boundaries and insist that he will never do it again because he really hasn't gone too far—yet. If the child doesn't tell, he is now complicit with the inappropriate discussion which allows the child molester to take it to the next level and use the child's complicity to create shame and guilt, virtually ensuring the child will continue to keep the secret and comply with future overtures. The child molester will often introduce pornography at this point to elicit sexual arousal and more complicity before actually crossing the line to contact sexual abuse.

In Best Practices #6 when I discuss empowering children, there are recommendations to educate children about sex and sexual abuse in an age-appropriate manner. On the surface, that recommendation may seem to contradict this boundary, but our recommendation is for formalized training for children that is done in a group setting. Follow-up questions regarding the training should be directed to a specific individual who has job responsibilities and skills to handle such a discussion in a safe and appropriate manner. Examples would be a school nurse or counselor. If a child approaches a staff member for clarification about the training or guidance on sexual topics of any sort, the staff member should immediately refer them to the appropriate individual who is responsible.

LIMIT PHYSICAL TOUCHING[12, 13]

Children, like adults, long to be loved and shown affection. Unfortunately, this is a child molester's dream and kids are at risk of child molesters exploiting this very natural need. Kids who live in dysfunctional family situations where they lack attention and healthy loving relationships are at even higher risk. Child molesters are looking to fill just this type of void in a child's life. According to van Dam, "The molesters all agreed that more than any one single visible behavior, the touching, roughhousing and tickling games served the purpose of desensitizing the child to touch. They also helped establish parental approval of such activities, which were initially at least partially done in full view of adults."[14]

When you establish clear and limiting physical boundaries with kids in your care, you not only protect them from potential abuse when they're with you, you also empower them to expect the same of others in their lives. They carry the benefit of your protection with them.

> Child molesters establish parental approval to touch their children through tickle games, piggy back rides, and roughhousing in full view of adults.

Personal space is important in the protection of children. Child molesters use seemingly innocent forms of touching such as hugs and touches on the shoulder, arms, or legs to desensitize children to the shock of being touched. Over time, as a child seems to be comfortable with the current level of touch, they'll begin to escalate it in steps, lingering longer and/or getting closer to the child's private parts.

Child molesters may also use seemingly innocent forms of touching such as horseplay or sitting on laps as an opportunity to "slip" and touch the child's private parts. This provides the child molester with a quick and easy explanation if the child or another adult raises concern about their inappropriate touch—they can simply claim it was an accident.

Therefore, physical touching between staff and children in your care should be kept to an absolute minimum. Below is a list of specific guidelines to help you establish protective boundaries:

- No kissing, not even on the cheek
- No massage (In some sports environments, massage is necessary as a form of rehabilitation of injuries. If massage is necessary, it should be done only by personnel who are trained and have job responsibility for this practice such as a physical therapist. In addition, massage should never be done in a one-on-one setting, regardless if it is an approved staff member.)
- No stroking of hair or any other part of the body

- No front-to-front or front-to-back hugs, only side hugs
- No sitting on laps
- No physical horseplay, piggy back rides, or tickle games
- No assisted instruction that includes body-to-body touching (batting, musical instruments, etc.)
- No excessive touching of any type

These limits on physical touching go in both directions (i.e., children should not be massaging staff members or stroking their hair.) We understand it's sad that our world has come to a place where we can't give a child a hug to comfort them or let them know we care, but unfortunately, that's exactly where we find ourselves and it's our responsibility to recognize the risk and respond appropriately.

NO SHOWERING WITH CHILDREN OR CHANGING CLOTHES IN FRONT OF EACH OTHER[15, 16, 17, 18, 19]

Similar to bathrooms, locker rooms pose a high level of risk for children to be sexually abused because of the nature of physical exposure. To minimize the risk of exposure, youth-serving staff should not change clothes in front of the kids, nor should kids change in front of staff members. Under no circumstances should a staff member shower with a child! We saw the horrific results of this behavior in the Jerry Sandusky case at Penn State.[20] To provide a level of protection against child-on-child abuse, make every effort for kids to be in the locker room in groups, rather than one-on-one and keep the groups of similar ages. Another option suggested in the Center for Disease Control report is "adopting a policy that requires more than one adult to be present at all times" in locker rooms.[21]

If the children in your program live at your facility such as orphanages, group homes, or boarding schools, this boundary needs to be expanded even further, stating that caretakers are not allowed to bathe children who are capable of bathing themselves.

Even when children are toddlers, they should be taught and empowered to wash their own private parts and as soon as they are beyond the risk of drowning, they should be given privacy during baths and showers. I cannot begin to tell you the number of incest survivors whose parents were still bathing them when they were 10, 11, and 12 years old. When children live in your facility, you have to include boundaries that are typically only seen in incest situations because of the close physical proximity between the potential offenders and victims.

NO ENTERING CHILDREN'S ROOMS AT NIGHT

When I am teaching parents about boundaries within their homes, I recommend a strict boundary around one of the parents leaving the bedroom in the middle of the night. If this happens, the other parent has a right to know where they are going and what they are doing. In fact, the other parent has a responsibility to find out. A vast number of incest survivors are abused in their own bedrooms at night when the rest of the household is asleep. So for orphanages, group homes, and boarding schools that have Directors, Headmasters, or Headmistresses who live on premises, there must be a strict boundary around going into children's rooms at night unless it is medically necessary and even then it should be on rare occasions and best accompanied by another adult. Since a Director may not have another adult sleeping in the room with them that would notice if they got up in the middle of the night, it is essential to tell children about this boundary and empower them to expect it to be honored.

LIMIT MEDICAL EXAMS/TREATMENT BY STAFF MEMBERS

Another common behavior found in incest abuse, particularly with female offenders, is disguising sexual abuse behind the need for medical examinations such as vaginal, penile or anal examinations as well as medical treatment including enemas and the application of ointments to the private parts. There may be a time or two in a particular child's life when this type of exam or treatment is required by someone other than a medical professional, but it is not common and most certainly outside the norm to require these treatments repeatedly. It is also extraordinarily uncommon for more than one child to require such treatment. Again because of the proximity of staff, this boundary should be included in your policy if you have children living on premises. Staff members should only be allowed to provide this type of treatment if it is at the direction of a medical professional with another adult present and it should be the exception. Any repeated requests should be denied.

NO SHARING ALCOHOL, PRESCRIPTION DRUGS, OR STREET DRUGS[22, 23]

Child molesters often use drugs and alcohol to lower their own inhibitions as well as the inhibitions of children. According to Finkelhor, substances may be used to get children to comply with sexual activity or to confuse them, making any disclosure less credible. Child molesters may even use drugs to sedate other children so they can focus on the abuse of a smaller number of victims.[24]

Therefore, it is important to have a clear boundary that prohibits staff members from sharing drugs or alcohol with children. The boundary should also prohibit the staff member from participating in such behavior with children even if they were not the one providing the substances. The boundary should specifically call out prescription drugs as well as illegal street drugs.

Staff members who provide drugs or alcohol to minors could also be charged criminally for contributing to the delinquency of a minor based on current state law. It is important to know the law in your state and report violations of those laws to authorities.

The National Minimum Drinking Age Act of 1984 was established by Congress and penalizes states for allowing people under the age of twenty-one to purchase or publically possess alcoholic beverages. However, the minimum drinking age remains in state control and forty-five states have exceptions to the national guideline which allow people under twenty-one to drink under specific circumstances. Because the intent of this boundary is to protect children from child molesters who are trying to lower a child's inhibition to allow sexual activity and lure them into complicity by agreeing to break the law, it is important to set your boundary to preclude staff from providing or using alcohol with any child that is in your care, regardless of age and regardless of your state's minimum legal requirement.

NO PHOTOGRAPHS OF KIDS[25]

Although it may seem innocent, I recommend a strict policy of no photographs by staff members. I also recommend that no devices that have the capability of taking photos or video be allowed in areas with an expectation of privacy such as bathrooms, changing areas, locker rooms, etc. This includes not only cameras and video recorders but also cell phones, laptops, iPads, and the like.

When we eliminate all photographs, we empower children with a black and white boundary. Kids no longer need to be prepared to effectively debate their position over what may or may not be inappropriate.

Many organizations include in their registration package a written authorization to take pictures of the kids in the program and where these pictures can be displayed or posted as well as whether the child's name may be included. These precautions are primarily to protect the privacy of the children and serve to protect children from potential stranger danger scenarios such as a predator figuring out where a child goes to school, approaching the child, and calling the child by name, saying their parents had an emergency and asked them to pick the child up.

What is not typically addressed in organization's photograph policy is the fact that many child molesters build their pornography collections by taking pictures of children. When an authority figure tells a child what to do or presents it as a game, it's difficult for the child to discern what is okay and what is inappropriate unless the boundaries are extremely clear.

There have been several high profile cases of child pornography being taken in the classroom including these:

"A Clovis teacher used his darkened empty classroom to take video of a blindfolded second-grade girl giving him oral sex in what he called 'the lollipop game,' a federal investigator says."[26]

"Police have found 200 more student bondage photos allegedly taken by Los Angeles school teacher Mark Brendt, who is accused of sexually abusing elementary school students. Los Angeles Sheriff's Department Sgt. Dan Scott said today that the pictures were much like the first 200 collected by authorities in the year-long investigation into Berndt, but at least 25 more students from Miramonte Elementary School are depicted in the pictures." "The initial batch of photos showed children blindfolded, with cockroaches on their faces and spoons full of semen in front of their mouths."[27]

One student in Kimberly Crain's class (a third grade teacher from Oklahoma) said that "three to four times a week she would take photos of particular girls in the class posing on the desk and chairs using her personal cell phone."[28]

Some organizations may want to consider just limiting photos in bathing suits but allow photos of general program activities. However, the demand for child pornography continues to grow and it's difficult to stay abreast of what types of images are in demand—bondage, torture, blindfolding, etc. The images are not always of exposed private parts. When we eliminate all photographs, we empower children with a black-and-white boundary. Kids no longer need to be prepared to effectively debate their position with an authority figure over what may or may not be inappropriate.

There are different guidelines for program activities that are open to parent participation or observation. There's not much you can do about parents taking pictures of their own kids and the group as a whole, but if you, as an organization, designate a specific person to be responsible for pictures of a public event, that person should be considered a formal part of your staff (even if they're a parent volunteer) and subjected to the full screening process.

> I talked with a parent whose son was on the swim team at school, and through the coach, the school asked for specific volunteer positions to be filled by parents, including the role of historian. A father of one of the boys stepped up to this position, but the problem was he was a registered sex offender. When the parents found out about it, they requested that the school intervene, but they would not, even after being escalated to the school district. The district had no policy in place that would allow them to take action. The parents had to make a choice between allowing a registered sex offender to take pictures of their child in their bathing suit or to leave the team.

NO HANDS IN OTHER PEOPLE'S POCKETS

Child molesters often attempt to disguise their sexual behaviors as games. One of the games child molesters use is to put candy or money in their pockets and get the kids to reach in and get the prize and the kids get to keep whatever they come out with. Of course, the child molester is receiving sexual gratification by children grabbing at his genital area. He is also desensitizing them to touching him. Although this may start out as a game, it may cross the line and become sexual touch as the children encounter his erect penis.[29] This game can be played in reverse as well so it is important to have a clear boundary that no one on campus is to put their hands in anyone else's pockets for any reason.

KEEP HANDS WHERE THEY CAN BE SEEN

In *The Socially Skilled Child Molester*, van Dam states that "many child molesters enjoy the added challenge of molesting children in the presence of adults." She goes on to share a story of a child molester who abused a six-year-old boy while in the living room watching a movie with his parents. The little boy was sitting on his lap under a blanket.[30] In *Nursery Crimes*, Finkelhor shared another example, "At the Big Blue Bird day care facility, 'Grampa' would hold children in his lap while playing cards. With the view of the table slightly obscured by a bookcase, he could put his hands in the children's pants and fondle them."[31]

It is so important to set a boundary that ensures you can see the hands of your staff when they are with kids. If you didn't have this boundary, what would stop a child molester from sitting on the floor next to a child (since we have a boundary that prohibits sitting on their lap) with a blanket draped over their laps, all the while fondling the child?

NO MASKS, BLINDFOLDS, BONDAGE, SCATTING, FETISHISMS, OR RITUALS[32, 33]

There is no limit to the sexual fetishes and fantasies that exist in our society and if you are not interested in that kind of thing, it's pretty easy to ignore. Unfortunately, we have seen it make its way into our classrooms, day care centers, and churches across the country including the use of masks and blindfolds, spanking, biting, bondage, playing dead, scatting (defecating), urinating, fetishes, and even spiritual and ritual abuse. While it may be one of the most uncomfortable things I address in this book, I need you to stay with me here.

If you are not willing to acknowledge the possibility of these activities happening within your organization, you are likely to miss the signs if it does. Needless to say, that is what child molesters are counting on.

While you can't possibly list all of the potential signs, I do recommend you have a boundary that specifically calls out this type of behavior so it raises the awareness of your staff and parents. We have seen cases in the past where parents, staff members, and authorities alike had a hard time believing children's disclosures because their stories were so outlandish. If we are not aware of the possibility, we are likely to dismiss children's allegations of a teacher's obsession with boy's nipples, day care workers urinating and defecating on toddlers or digging up graves, staff cutting open animals and drinking their blood, teachers blindfolding children and forcing them to eat cookies laced with semen or play the lollipop game (oral copulation).

> Follow up with a simple statement, "That's interesting, tell me more about that."

Finkelhor's research of day care center sexual abuse found that "An allegation of ritualism was present in 66% of all multiple-perpetrator cases, compared to only 5% of single perpetrator cases." Finkelhor goes on to say that "The ritualistic cases generally involved more children of both sexes, went on for longer periods of time, and included more serious types of sexual activity."[34] These cases likely represent the worst abuse that is happening in our youth-serving organizations so please don't disregard bizarre comments by children, instead follow up with a simple statement, "That's interesting, tell me more about that."

> There was a mother I was working with whose son had disclosed sexual abuse at the hands of his father on multiple occasions but would never disclose to a professional. One day, during a routine medical exam, her son disclosed his sexual abuse to the pediatrician, but after telling about his father's sexual behavior, her son went on to share about how his father poops on his stomach. The pediatrician informed the mother that he would have to report the disclosure to child protective services. The mother was so relieved that her son finally told someone other than her as the authorities had been unable to substantiate the abuse. Unfortunately, when the pediatrician filed the report, he was so shocked by the story of the father pooping on this little boy, it was all he could remember and he failed to report the disclosure of sexual abuse, the social worker disregarded the poop disclosure, and once again, the authorities were unable to substantiate the sexual abuse.

My hope is that by making you aware of the possibility for serious abuse happening under seemingly bizarre circumstances, I can minimize your shock and prepare you to be fully present to see, hear, and act on signs that may not even seem to be related to sexual activity on the surface.

Next Steps:

- Review, document, and distribute new On-Site: Behavioral Boundaries to staff, parents and children.

BEST PRACTICE #3

OFF-SITE BOUNDARIES

Reflection:

Before continuing, complete the questions below regarding off-site boundaries.

➢ How do you control physical access to children during off-site visits?

_____

_____

_____

_____

_____

_____

_____

_____

_____

➤ Are there times when you take kids off the main grounds of the organization? If so, what kind of activities would qualify to be off-site? What locations are approved and who approves them?

_____

_____

_____

_____

_____

_____

_____

_____

➤ What's the process of gaining permission to take kids off the main grounds?

_____

_____

_____

_____

_____

_____

_____

_____

➤ How do you address the need for increased supervision during off-site visits? Do you use parent chaperones? If so, what is your policy for screening them?

_____

_____

_____

_____

_____

_____

_____

_____

➤ When you leave the grounds, what type of transportation is used and what boundaries apply during transportation? Do you provide transportation for kids as part of your regular programs?

_____

_____

_____

_____

_____

_____

_____

_____

_____

➤ What similar, different, or additional boundaries apply once you arrive at the other location?

_____

_____

_____

_____

_____

_____

_____

_____

➤ Does your program include opportunities for out-of-town travel? If so, what additional boundaries are in place to protect children during these trips?

_____

_____

_____

_____

_____

_____

_____

_____

> ➤ Do you allow or require parent chaperones on out-of-town trips? If so, what is the process of ensuring they are safe to be with kids? Are they held to the same standards of behavior as your staff? How are standards of behavior communicated to parent chaperones?

_____

_____

_____

_____

_____

_____

_____

_____

All off-site locations pose an additional level of risk simply because it's an environment you do not control. A formal pre-approval process slows everything down to ensure decisions for off-site trips are not taken lightly but rather handled with an active engaged evaluation of the need for the trip as well as the associated risk. It also ensures that off-site decisions are made on behalf of the children as a whole and not to substantiate access to an individual or small group of children.

> Off-site locations pose an additional level of risk simply because it's an environment you do not control.

> Many years ago, there was an end-of-year party for my daughter's softball team that was held at a park by the beach. The parents had reserved a BBQ site, and as the parents prepared food, the girls were playing in the grass nearby. Then one of the parents noticed the girls sitting in a circle in the grass, playing clapping hand games. Not an unusual sight for a group of ten-year-old girls except for the fact that there was a young man about thirty years old sitting in the circle playing with them. The other parents seemed uncomfortable with what they saw, but they seemed more uncomfortable with taking action. So they brought it to my attention and asked what we should do. I didn't hesitate telling the young man and the kids that it wasn't appropriate for the kids to be playing with strangers and insisted he leave.

Van Dam described a similar scenario in *Identifying Child Molesters* and said, "Asking someone to leave under such circumstances is extremely difficult, which is why most people passively watch events unfold instead."[1] It's important to be very conscious about access to the children in your care during off-site activities and be willing to intercede when appropriate.

WRITTEN AUTHORIZATION FOR OFF-SITE LOCATIONS

Children should never be taken off the organization's premises without prior written authorization, signed by the parent and predetermined organization managers. There are to be no exceptions to this boundary—it doesn't matter if the person requesting to take a child off-site is the director, founder, or largest donor, the process must still be followed.

A formal approval process should be predetermined and in writing so no one in the organization has to make a subjective decision. I recommend the following off-site activity approval process.

- The board of directors should:

  ○ Develop and approve a list of acceptable off-site "activities" (such as education trips to museums, a summer picnic, or sports event) and who is eligible to take children off-site.

  ○ Designate and approve a list of specific "locations" where these off-site activities can take place. There should be a formal assessment of each location to determine any potential risks based on the location and/or facility. All on-site boundaries still apply, so it's important to view the facility from a perspective of isolated areas, staff coverage for bathroom visits, stranger access to the kids, etc.

  ○ Define the frequency and duration of off-site activities to ensure this opportunity is not exploited by any particular staff member.

  ○ Define and approve a designated list of individuals (or titles) that are authorized to approve requests for off-site visits.

- A written request should be submitted at least three weeks prior to the requested activity. Requests should only be approved if they are for pre-approved activities at pre-approved locations and the opportunity is available equally to all children in the program, ensuring no individual or small groups of children are being singled out for off-site access.

- Increased supervision is also required so staff ratios will need to be determined for each location, as appropriate. The request should document how the increased supervision will be provided.

- Written approval should be obtained by at least two previously authorized organization leaders.

- A detailed permission slip should be sent to the parents and returned with written approval prior to the activity.

PARENT CHAPERONES

Because off-site field trips naturally require a higher level of supervision to keep

> A formal pre-approval process slows everything down to ensure decisions for off-site trips are not taken lightly.

children safe, youth-serving organizations often use parent chaperones to augment their staff. All parent volunteers should go through the full screening process and be held to the same boundaries and standards set forth in your child sexual abuse prevention policy. However, some youth-serving organization leaders say that it is cost- and time-prohibitive to screen volunteers that will only be with them for the day. Though I disagree with allowing the children in your care to be with people who have not been screened, if this is the situation you find yourself in, you should at minimum pair unscreened volunteers with a staff member who is with them at all times. You need to stand firm with a policy that all repeat volunteers or volunteers used for overnight trips must be fully screened. Remember that child molesters are looking for access to children and acquaintance molesters typically require repeated access to build trusting relationships. So you need to intercede in that part of the grooming process.

CONTROL TRANSPORTATION TO OFF-SITE LOCATIONS

We will not delve deeply into transportation options including contract busing services, organization-owned vehicles, and/or use of staff's personal vehicles. There are many liability issues to consider which are beyond the scope of this book.

What is pertinent to protecting children from sexual abuse is that at no time should a child ride alone in a car with an individual staff member, since our on-site boundaries call for no one adult-one child situations and those on-site boundaries carry over to off-site activities. So when planning off-site activities, transportation should begin and end at a centralized site where multiple kids get in and out of the car at the same time. Kids should not be picked up or dropped off at home resulting in one child in the car with a staff member or even worse, the opportunity for a staff member to enter a child's house.

We've seen this rule easily set aside when an organization's participants are young teens, but as long as the children are in your care, even over the age of eighteen, these boundaries should apply.

This boundary applies to children riding alone in cars with staff members whether it is approved by your organization or not. Staff members should not give the children in your care a ride to your program facility or event or a ride home. In Michele Elliott's study of offenders, she found that 46 percent of the offenders offered to give kids a ride home specifically as a strategy to gain access.[2]

To decrease the risk even further, we would recommend that all children sit in the backseat outside of reach of your staff member who's driving, even when there are multiple kids in the car.

There was a case I supported a few years back that was family abuse rather than abuse within a youth-serving organization, but it illustrates the importance of managing access within the confines of a car. In this particular case, the parents were in the front seat driving and their daughter was in the backseat with her uncle. Her uncle was bold enough to fondle the young girl in the backseat of the car while her parents were right there. I share this because I want you to understand that for many child molesters, it is an addiction that they cannot control, which often leads to them getting caught if we're paying attention.

ADDITIONAL BOUNDARIES FOR OUT-OF-TOWN TRAVEL

> Jesse Stovall, a USA swim coach, was sentenced to "four years probation on a second degree felony charge of sexual activity with a 16 or 17 year-old and will be required to register permanently as a sex offender." "The crime occurred when Stovall, then a coach for the Berkeley, CA, Bear Swimming team, took the 16–year-old swimmer to Orlando for a week-long swim meet in March 2008. 'He provided her alcohol and then sexually battered her' in the hotel, according to the police report, including oral sex and penetration."
>
> "Stovall 'obviously used his trust with the victim to do something illegal and used his trust with the family to help facilitate that.'" "According to the police report, while the girl's parents usually accompanied her to out of town meets, 'Stovall convinced her parents to let her go alone, using the argument that [the girl] could use the opportunity to mature.'"[3]

When taking kids out of town such as traveling to a sports tournament or missions trip, there are several additional boundaries that should be in place.

Adequate Supervision: All trips should require multiple staff members to be in attendance and parent chaperones as well. Do not be fooled into believing that older children require less supervision—their independence is likely to present an even higher risk.

Hotel Rooms: Staff members should not share a hotel room with a child that is not theirs, nor should they be permitted to enter a child's hotel room—for *any* reason and vice versa.[4] Formal meetings and informal discussions should transpire in a public setting such as the lobby or restaurant.

Alcohol Use: Staff members should not consume alcohol at any time during the trip. This is not just when staff members are with the kids but even in the privacy of their own hotel room. When you're traveling with kids, you are "on" 24/7—you never know when a situation may arise that will require you to be with the kids unexpectedly or an emergency situation where you will need to think clearly, to potentially save a child's life. Specifically as it relates to child sexual abuse, drug and alcohol use can alter a staff member's judgment, leaving children more susceptible to inappropriate behavior.

If you have parent chaperones traveling with you on overnight trips, they should go through the complete screening process and be held to the same boundaries as the staff. They should be trained on the boundaries prior to departure and sign a copy of your policy acknowledging their understanding of the boundaries and agreement to be held accountable to follow them.

All other on-site and off-site boundaries apply when traveling.

> If parent chaperones travel with the kids, they should go through the complete screening process and be held accountable to follow the same boundaries as the staff.

Next Steps:

- Review, document, and distribute new Off-Site Boundaries to staff, parents and children.

BEST PRACTICE #3

OFF-HOURS BOUNDARIES

Reflection:

Before continuing, complete the questions below regarding off-hours boundaries.

➤ What formal policy does your organization have in place regarding how staff communicate and interact with the kids you serve during their off-hours?

_____

_____

_____

_____

_____

_____

_____

_____

_____

➢ What informal practices do you or your organization have in place regarding how staff communicate and interact with the kids you serve during their off-hours?

_____

_____

_____

_____

_____

_____

_____

_____

➢ Do your staff members babysit or tutor children in your program on their own time? How about siblings of the children in your care? Do you have any policies in place that limit this type of access?

_____

_____

_____

_____

_____

_____

_____

_____

➤ Do you have any boundaries that restrict your staff members from visiting the homes of the children in your care or vice versa?

_____

_____

_____

_____

_____

_____

_____

_____

➤ Does your organization host sleepovers either on-site or off? Can a sleepover be hosted by just one staff member? Do you allow sleepovers at staff member's homes?

_____

_____

_____

_____

_____

_____

_____

_____

_____

➤ What specific boundaries are in place to provide adequate protection from sexual abuse during organization approved sleepovers? How are these additional boundaries communicated to staff, parents, and children?

_____

_____

_____

_____

_____

_____

_____

_____

➤ Does your organization serve teenagers? If so, what is your formal policy regarding those teens dating staff members? What are your informal practices in this area?

_____

_____

_____

_____

_____

_____

_____

_____

Once again, we would like to remind you that child molesters seek opportunity to gain access to kids and youth-serving organizations inherently provide that opportunity within their programs. What some organizations and parents don't realize is that child molesters are not only looking for access *within* the organization's programs, but often the biggest benefit of working or volunteering for the organization is the additional access gained *through* the program.[1]

> Families and organization leaders are often unsuspecting, but if it seems too good to be true, it probably is.

When a child molester has worked with kids within your program and gained their trust and friendship, they are now in a position to push the limits and work toward gaining access to the kids during their off-hours. Families are often unsuspecting, and since staff members likely already have a great relationship with their child, it seems like a natural extension of the relationship to have staff involved in their kid's and even the parent's lives in other ways.

As documented in Lanning and Dietz' paper titled *Acquaintance Molestation and Youth-Serving Organizations*:

"One camp counselor with many victims on several continents so thoroughly seduced parents of his child victims that he was permitted to sleep in the rooms of the children at their family homes during his off-season travels. Restrictions on out-of-program contact—which should be publicized to parents and other caretakers—would reduce the opportunity for personnel to circumvent organizational safeguards by becoming involved with the children outside of the organizational setting."[2]

Child molesters use grooming to establish trust with kids *and* their families. They may show a particular interest in a child who is struggling with their school work and offer to tutor them. They may offer to babysit for single parents who need free time or for families who are struggling financially and need to work extra hours. They may even offer to babysit for free because they know the family can't afford to hire someone. Again, child molesters are looking for opportunities, and the more vulnerable the child or family is, the more likely that family is to accept their help. If it seems too good to be true, it probably is!

Your organization can play a key role in helping to protect kids by having boundaries in place that limit the access your staff has to kids during their off-hours.[3] Of course, there's the added benefit of reducing your organization's risk in case abuse does occur and a parent tries to blame the organization for having "represented" this staff member as a safe person. Later in the book, I will cover how you engage parents to help you enforce the boundaries that you've established.

There are a variety of opportunities that may arise and it's impossible to document them all. So your boundaries should be written to be all inclusive—stating that staff members should have no communication or planned interactions with the children or families your organization serves during their off-hours, including but not limited to the following activities:

WHEN IN PUBLIC, LEGAL, ON-SITE, AND OFF-SITE BOUNDARIES APPLY

If staff members run into kids during their off-hours, they should follow all the same boundaries previously established in the on-site and off-site boundaries section, but especially the following:

- No one adult–one child situations
- Limit physical touching
- Avoid isolated locations

- No photographs of kids
- No driving with individual kids or kids in the front seat

NO BABYSITTING[4]

Staff members should not be permitted to babysit for the families of children in your care. This applies not only to a child who is in your program but also to any other siblings in the family as well. This includes paid babysitting or offers to watch the kids at no cost. The exchange of money is not the determining factor; the intent of this boundary is to limit access to the kids in your care during your staff's off-hours, thereby limiting the interest of a child molester wanting to work for your organization. In a 1995 study by Elliott, 48 percent of the molesters interviewed obtained access to their victims through babysitting.[5] This is a real and present danger and it is crucial that this boundary be set and enforced.

> Even if a staff member does not have ill intent when establishing personal or private business relationships with the families you serve, it sets a precedent which child molesters can exploit.

NO TUTORING

Just like babysitting, staff members should not be permitted to tutor for the families of children in your care. This is not just for the child who is in your program but for any other siblings in the family as well. This includes paid tutoring or offers to tutor the kids at no cost.

If your organization is a school or other educational program, you may offer tutoring as part of your regular program. This boundary is not referring to that scenario. We are addressing individual staff members offering to tutor outside of your standard program offerings. However, if your regular program tutoring services are offered before school, after school, or at lunch, they should "occur in a public and supervised location" as noted by Shakeshaft.[6]

NO VISITS TO PERSONAL RESIDENCES[8, 9, 10, 11, 12]

Study after study has shown that a vast majority of child sexual abuse occurs in a residence. Almost 70 percent of all juvenile sexual assault occurred in a residence and the statistic goes up

> Nearly five of every six sexual assaults of young juveniles occurred in a residence as well as almost 70 percent against older juveniles[7]

to almost 87 percent for children 5 and under.[13] Based on these facts alone, you can significantly lower the risk of children in your care being abused by setting a clear boundary around staff members and children being in a residence together, this includes rectories or other personal residences of church personnel.

So at no time should a staff member visit the house of a child in your organization's care. It's easy for a child molester to use an opportunity such as a child leaving their backpack at school, to reach out to the parent and offer to drop it by their house, thus creating a more personal relationship where additional access can be pursued.

This boundary applies in the opposite direction as well—no staff member should ever have a child in your care at their house either. It's possible your staff members live in the same neighborhood as some of the children in your program, and without this boundary clearly communicated, it's easy for child molesters to try and stand behind their role in your organization to gain private access to kids in their own neighborhood.

Many years ago, there was an incident where a nanny had shown several signs of becoming unusually intertwined with a family in a very short period of time. Early on, the nanny told the children about a new puppy she bought, and soon, she took the kids to her personal residence to show them the puppy. The parents found out and were able to stop those visits and replace the nanny right away. Although this was an independent nanny versus an organization staff member, you can see how crossing this boundary made it possible for this nanny to bring the children to her home where there was increased isolation, in an uncontrolled environment, which put the children at higher risk.

NO SLEEPOVERS[14, 15]

At no time should a staff member personally host a sleepover or overnight visit for children in your organization's care. Overnight visits present increased risk because even if there are multiple kids and/or adults, kids are more vulnerable to molestation when everyone else in the house is sleeping.

Although I didn't realize it was a problem at the time (over thirteen years ago), my daughter's fifth grade teacher (a female) hosted a girl's sleepover at her house right after the end of the school year. I don't believe she had ill intent, but by allowing any staff member to have sleepovers, you set a precedent which increases the risk of abuse and attracts child molesters to your organization.

Looking back, there were other signs of bad boundaries and lack of judgment, including the teacher allowing the girls to slide down her stairs on their sleeping bags and allowing the girls to play outside late at night which resulted in the neighbor calling the police out for disturbing the peace.

There's simply no reason to put kids at risk of being abused and no reason to increase the organization's risk if abuse does occur and the organization had no policy in place to prevent this type of access.

If your organization elects to host a sleepover either on their site or an off-site trip, very strict plans should be approved by the board of directors ahead of time to ensure proper supervision of all kids, by multiple adults, *throughout* the night. This type of event should not be something that happens spontaneously but rather with a conscious thorough risk assessment process.

Staff members should also not be permitted to spend the night at the home of children in your care (or any other location where children in your care are staying). Several years ago, I was talking to the trainer for a local youth mentoring organization about their child sexual abuse prevention policies and she proudly told me that they do not allow their volunteers to have their paired youth spend the night until they have been together for six months. I was shocked at the thought of what a perfect scenario that is for a child molester. They have six months to thoroughly groom that youth—building trust, desensitizing them to touch, testing their ability to keep secrets, gaining complicity in small indiscretions—all the while knowing that at the six-month mark, they will be able to cross the line into fully sexual behavior in an isolated overnight situation. Knowing how child molesters think, I realized that the anticipation would probably make it the most arousing six months of their relationship.

As I talked with her further about her organization's willingness to allow sleepovers, she said it was because they wanted the youth to see how other people live—to be in their environment. I just cannot buy into that rationale. If you really want to show youth how other people live, show them how concerned and caring adults set strong boundaries that protect youth and that does not include spending the night in a one adult–one child situation with a volunteer from a youth program.

Due to allegations of sexual abuse, in 2012, Big Brothers Big Sisters of Puget Sound "sent a letter to all 1,500 adult-child pairings on January 31 that announced an immediate policy change: 'Overnight visits between Bigs and Littles are strictly prohibited except in the event that it is an agency sponsored event.'" It seems the national standards for Big Brother Big Sisters authorizes each of the 370 affiliates to allow overnight visits with Bigs and Littles or ban them if they wish. The sad part about this announcement was the reaction of some of the Bigs. One Big actually resigned because of the loss of overnight access to his Little and the fact that there was not a grandfather clause that allowed existing pairings to continue their overnight stays.[16]

I just cannot stress how important his boundary is, even in the context of mentoring programs. Remember, almost 70 percent of all juvenile sexual assault occurred in a residence.[17] I am grateful that the Puget Sound Affiliate had the courage to make this bold policy change that significantly lowers the risk of abuse for the children in their care.

NO BIRTHDAY PARTIES

Although children may want their favorite teachers, youth leaders, or day care providers to come to their birthday parties, it provides yet another entree for child molesters to gain access to the family and pursue further off-hours access to the kids. The side benefit of this policy is that staff members have a built in excuse to not attend all the kids' birthday parties or risk hurting their feelings.

NO FAMILY GATHERINGS

Staff members should not become family friends with the kids in your care. Again, we must caution allowing this type of extended relationship to develop between your staff and the families of kids in your care. This is exactly the type of access child molesters are looking for and will surely exploit.

> I've talked with some staff members of an after-school program who shared that they have been working at their location for ten-plus years and have had multiple siblings from one family come through the program. Because of that, they have become friends with the families of the kids in their care and frequently attend their family gatherings. This is just the type of opportunity a child molester seeks and a precedent they will try to exploit.

NO DATING

Staff members are not allowed to date youth in their care. This may sound obvious, but this boundary can become a bit blurred when you have programs for teenagers and the staff or volunteers who work for you are in their late teens or early twenties. Outside of a youth-serving organization environment, it would not be that unusual for an eighteen-year-old to date a sixteen- or seventeen-year-old, but when the younger person is part of your program, it's important to remember that *all* on-site and off-site boundaries apply.

Boundaries can become blurred when your organization serves teenagers and has young adults on staff.

Next Steps:

• Review, document, and distribute new Off-Hours Boundaries to staff, parents, and children.

BEST PRACTICE #3

ELECTRONIC COMMUNICATION AND SOCIAL MEDIA BOUNDARIES

Reflection:

Before continuing, complete the questions below regarding electronic communication and social media boundaries

➢ What communication methods do you personally use (cell phone, e-mail, Facebook, Twitter, YouTube, LinkedIn, Instagram, etc.)?

_____

_____

_____

_____

_____

_____

_____

_____

➤ What level of security settings do you use on your social media sites (i.e., what information can be seen by people who are not connected with you?)

_____

_____

_____

_____

_____

_____

_____

_____

➤ Are the kids that your organization serves old enough to have cell phones and/or use e-mail and social media sites? If so, which of these communication methods do you hear about them using?

_____

_____

_____

_____

_____

_____

_____

_____

➤ What formal policies does your organization have in place regarding how staff communicate and interact with the kids you serve via electronic communication? What social media platforms are formally incorporated into your program?

_____

_____

_____

_____

_____

_____

_____

_____

➤ What informal practices do you and/or your organization have in place regarding how staff communicate and interact with the kids you serve via electronic communication?

_____

_____

_____

_____

_____

_____

_____

Are children communicating online? Here is the reality of technology in the hands of children in your care:

- According to a national poll conducted by Common Sense Media,[1]

  - More than half of adolescents log on to a social media site more than once a day.
  - Almost a quarter of teenagers log on to their favorite social media site more than 10 times a day.

- According to a Teens and Technology study by Pew Research Center,[2]

  - 78% of teens now have a cell phone, and almost half of those own smartphones.
  - 74% of teens ages 12–17 say they access the Internet on cell phones, tablets, and other mobile devices at least occasionally.
  - 25% of teens are "cell-mostly" Internet users.

- Another study by the Kaiser Family Foundation in 2010 found,[3]

  - 66% of children ages 8–18 have cell phones.

    - 85% of teens 15–18 years old
    - 69% of tweens 11–14 years old
    - 31% of kids 8–10 years old

  - 93% of all 8- to 18-year-olds live in homes with at least one computer
  - 36% of them have computers in their bedrooms
  - 29% of children ages 8–18 have laptop computers

    - 38% of teens 15–18 years old
    - 27% of tweens 11–14 years old
    - 17% of kids 8–10 years old

So clearly the possibility of staff members being able to access children in your care via electronic communication is a matter of when, not if!

If your organization serves older children and teens, your staff will more than likely receive a Facebook Friend Request or have a child ask them to share their e-mail address, screen name, and/or cell phone number. This opens a whole new arena where inappropriate and risky personal relationships can flourish.

So it's important to establish a clear strict policy around kids' access to your staff members through technology and social media channels in particular. As with Off-Hour Boundaries, your policy should be all inclusive, restricting any technology aided verbal, written or visual (photos and videos) communication between the kids in your organization's care and your staff, regardless of the child's age. The boundaries include but are not limited to the items detailed below.

NO SHARING PHONE NUMBERS[4, 5]

Staff members are not permitted to share their home phone numbers or cell phone numbers with kids in your organization's care and vice versa. It is inappropriate for staff members to be talking on the phone or texting with your teenagers and older children and it should be avoided no matter how innocent it seems.

Using text messaging to send pornographic images is typically referred to as "sexting." Several studies have been done in recent years citing the prevalence of sexting to be between 19–50 percent of the population surveyed. However, there are inconsistencies in these studies including the definition of sexting and the age of the participants (some included young adults). At this time, I have not found a set of results that I am confident reflect the true prevalence of sexting in children.[6]

That said, sending nude pictures of minors via text would be considered child pornography and would likely be subject to child sexual exploitation laws in most states and could land the sender on the sex offender registry for life. Many states have or are in process of drafting laws specific to sexting which further clarify the legal boundaries. Staff members sharing phone numbers with children in your care opens up a world of possibilities that can be exploited by child molesters and create liability exposures for organizations. I highly encourage you to take this boundary seriously.[7]

I have worked with some organizations such as sports training centers that have teenagers in their program who drive themselves to activities. In some cases, a coach may need to reach them at the last minute to reschedule and therefore find it necessary to call or text their athletes. If you have extenuating circumstances such as this that arise as part of your organization's activities, I recommend that you set a clear rule that they use text messaging instead of calling and that they send the message as a group text, including the parents.

Once an electronic line of communication is established between a staff member and a child in your care, it's difficult to stop and almost impossible to manage. A child who is looking for attention that they may not be receiving at home, or who has come to idolize a staff member, may be the one who initiates the contact and this makes them even more vulnerable to a child molester who exploits the given opportunity.

NO SHARING E-MAIL ADDRESSES OR SCREEN NAMES[8, 9]

Staff members are not permitted to share their e-mail addresses or screen names with kids in your organization's care and vice versa. The days of standalone instant messaging applications is all but gone—children primarily use the instant messaging features within the social media applications more and more. Either way, there's really no reason why an instant message needs to be sent to a child in your care, regardless of the platform. If a staff member needs to send information out to the kids in your care, the messages should be sent to the parents via e-mail. Again, if circumstances dictate a teenager needs to be contacted directly, the parent should always be copied.

SET RESTRICTIVE PRIVACY SETTINGS AND USE APPROPRIATE PROFILE PICTURES

Staff should have their privacy controls set to show the least amount of information possible to people who are not "friends" and should always use appropriate profile pictures. This simply limits sharing of personal information—there's no reason for kids to know how staff members spend their personal time. When kids find out personal information about staff members and initiate conversations with them about it, this provides child molesters an opportunity to exploit the child's interest in them and create a more personal and intimate relationship, which is exactly what a child molester is looking to create.

NO BECOMING FRIENDS ON FACEBOOK OR FOLLOWING ON TWITTER[10]

Staff members should not connect with kids in your care via Facebook, Twitter, or any other social networking site. Staff members *should not initiate nor accept* invitations to connect with kids in your care. It's not uncommon for adolescents to want to connect with their caregivers and leaders—it's cool and makes them feel older to be "friends" with adults. However, this creates a situation where inappropriate levels of personal information can be shared intentionally or inadvertently between staff and kids. Depending on privacy settings, it can even provide opportunities for staff member's "friends" to establish direct communication with the kids in your care unbeknownst to your staff member. Child molesters seek these types of opportunities to start private conversations with kids—to gain their trust and build special relationships that build kids up while planting seeds that separate them from other protective adults such as their parents, teachers, and youth leaders. This is a slippery slope which should be avoided.

> Based on a policy set in 2012, "New York City public schoolteachers may not contact students through personal pages on Web sites like Facebook and Twitter, but can communicate via pages set up for classroom use."[11]

If your organization is looking to create "community" among the kids you serve so you can communicate important program information, have a positive influence on their lives and allow them to enjoy a supportive monitored interactive space with friends, Facebook can be an effective tool. We recommend that this be used very thoughtfully and with documented boundaries.

The best way to accomplish this is to set up a Page on Facebook that represents the business—such as a Youth Program at a faith organization. Kids in your care can Like the page which will allow them to see your official posts to the page on their personal Facebook newsfeed. They can also go directly to the page to read other people's comments and responses to official posts. You can use the page to promote upcoming events, share the success of past events, share inspirational thoughts, etc. Posting pictures of past events should be handled with immense caution as to not identify any individual children by name, and of course, since your staff doesn't take photographs, any photos would have been supplied by parents or children. Any photos used should of course be reviewed and approved for appropriateness before posting.

In order to keep kids safe while using this type of Facebook interaction, exchanges should be limited to information that is specific to your program or general messages to all the kids and not a place for personal and private relationships to form. Parents should be invited to join the page as well and staff members should not extend the online relationship to any type of individual connection to children in your care, by "friending" them on Facebook or "following" them in the case of Twitter.

Though connecting personally with others who engage on your organization page is a normal progression, remember staff members and children in your care are not permitted to be "friends" on social media. Keep it strictly business!

I understand social media relationships are difficult to manage which is why they are best avoided altogether. I also understand that simply setting a boundary will not in and of itself stop your staff from connecting with the kids in your care. However, it is the published boundary that clearly states your expectations for creating safety for kids in your care and any staff member who chooses to disregard the boundary is either blatantly trying to gain private access to children or at minimum being insubordinate and not making the welfare of your children a priority. Either way, the established boundary is what substantiates you taking action when it is broken.

It is similar to a restraining order which is simply a piece of paper stating a boundary: "John Johnson cannot come within 100 yards of Jane Johnson." While the piece of paper cannot stop John Johnson from being in contact with Jane Johnson, when notified, the police have the authority to enforce the boundary and impose the pre-established consequences.

NO CONNECTIONS ON MULTIMEDIA SHARING SITES

There are a variety of social networking sites that are primarily geared toward the sharing of multimedia such as photographs and videos including Tumblr, Pinterest, Instagram, Snapchat, and Vine. Staff members should not use these sites to share pictures or videos with the children in your care or to view multimedia that the children may want to share with them. Each application has its own paradigm for how to connect with people (adding, friending, following) and each has a way to break that connection (deleting, unfriending, blocking). If your staff members use these programs for personal use, it is their responsibility to understand how the applications work and ensure that the kids in your care are not able to connect with them. While all of these technologies should be avoided, Snapchat is of particular concern when it comes to child sexual abuse because anything you send through this application is automatically deleted within ten seconds. This provides a great platform for child molesters to groom their victims without parents coming across the information.

NO CONNECTIONS ON VIDEO CHAT APPLICATIONS

There is yet another channel of social media interaction that is focused on live chat between computers, tablets, and even phones. These applications include Skype, Google+, and Facetime to name a few. These applications use the camera on each person's device to capture a live video stream and share it to the other device so it is as if you're talking face-to-face. As you can imagine, this is just another huge opportunity for sexually abusing and exploiting children without leaving behind the evidence of pictures and videos that can be used as evidence against them. Therefore, it is crucial that you forbid the use of these applications between your staff and the children in your care. I would even extend the restriction to forbid use of these applications on your premises at any time.

Technology is changing every day so the recommendations above are reflective of what is available and popular as of the writing of this book. Use these recommendations to gain an understanding of the risk associated with social media tools, especially for children who are already vulnerable because of dysfunction in their family including lack of supervision, neglect, single-parent families, substance abuse as well as emotional and physical abuse that leave children longing to connect with anyone who will show them attention. Use your newfound understanding to keep your policies updated in the future.

Next Steps:

- Review, document, and distribute new Electronic Communication and Social Media Boundaries to staff, parents, and children.

CHILD-TO-CHILD BOUNDARIES

Reflection:

Before continuing, complete the questions below regarding child-to-child boundaries.

➤ What formal policy and/or boundaries does your organization have in place to protect children from inappropriate sexual behavior with another child?

_____

_____

_____

_____

_____

_____

_____

_____

_____

➢ What informal practices do you and/or your organization have in place to protect children from inappropriate sexual behavior with another child?

_____

_____

_____

_____

_____

_____

_____

_____

➢ Are there times and/or locations when children are not fully visible to staff members? Describe.

_____

_____

_____

_____

_____

_____

_____

_____

_____

➢ What is your formal policy regarding monitoring bathroom visits?

_____

_____

_____

_____

_____

_____

_____

_____

➢ What are your informal practices with regards to monitoring bathroom visits?

_____

_____

_____

_____

_____

_____

_____

> ➤ Are your programs separated by age group or do you have activities when a broad range of children are together? What formal policy or informal practices do you have to ensure the safety of younger children during these activities?

_____

_____

_____

_____

_____

_____

_____

_____

_____

This section is primarily focused on boundaries that will minimize children's exposure to abuse at the hands of other children who are predatory in nature as well as those who may simply be reenacting abuse they have endured without understanding their actions.

> 30–40 percent of child sexual abuse happens at the hands of other juveniles.[1, 2, 3]

However, there is a third type of child-on-child abuse which involves others orchestrating or forcing children to abuse each other which was apparent in a research project of sexual abuse in day care centers. This project found that 21 percent of the cases studied fell into this type of abuse and were particularly prevalent in multiple perpetrator situations.[4] I have not included any boundaries in this section specific to this class of abuse because it is inherently covered by the other boundaries that target adult grooming behaviors and legal boundaries as defined by your state, but I would have been remiss to not mention it here.

Let's move on to look at the reasons children may independently be sexually inappropriate with their peers and how you should respond. It's not uncommon for children to explore their sexuality with other children. In fact, according to a study of 339 US child welfare and mental health professionals, 73 percent engaged in sexual behaviors with other children.[5] Sometimes, this is part of natural and healthy sexual behavior, and sometimes, children are simply repeating what they've been exposed to in their home through bad boundaries (such as watching their parents having sex). In these cases, resetting appropriate boundaries is usually all that's required to stop the children from repeating this behavior.

However, in some cases, inappropriate sexual behavior between kids can be a sign that a child has or still is experiencing sexual abuse or in the case of teenagers, it's also possible they could be struggling with a sexual behavior problem that requires treatment. In these cases, additional intervention is typically required to ensure the other kids in your care are protected and that the child displaying the concerning behavior gets the help they need.

It's not your place to determine the cause of sexually inappropriate behavior between children. That should be left to professionals. Instead your role is to:

- Set boundaries that reduce the risk of it happening in the first place;
- Immediately correct inappropriate behavior when encountered;
- Effectively monitor future interactions between these specific children;
- Communicate concerning behavior to others in your organization as appropriate. Notify the parents of all children involved; and

- Report to the authorities if the inappropriate behaviors cause you to suspect a child in your care is being abused or being abusive.

In this Best Practice, we will focus on specific boundaries that can reduce the risk of children being sexually inappropriate with each other while in your care.

While it is not your place to determine the cause of inappropriate sexual behavior between children, it is your responsibility to understand what is inappropriate and whether the behavior is an indication of a sexual behavior problem that requires professional help. I recommend all staff members read the following two pamphlets:

- *Understanding Children's Sexual Behavior: What's Natural and Healthy* by Toni Cavanagh Johnson, PhD. http://www.tcavjohn.com/
- *Helping Children with Sexual Behavior Problems: A Guidebook for Professionals and Caregivers* by Toni Cavanagh Johnson, PhD. http://www.tcavjohn.com/

FULL VISIBILITY AND CLOSE MONITORING DURING NAP TIME

As mentioned earlier, in day care centers "Almost a third of all abuse occurred during nap time." Finkelhor noted that this was the most common time for abuse to happen in the centers he studied.[6] All children should be fully visible and closely monitored during nap time. Napping can be a vulnerable time for children since the room is dark and it's natural to think children don't need as much supervision since they're sleeping. However, the reality is that they're not always

> All children should be fully visible and closely monitored during nap time.

sleeping, and therefore, it presents an opportunity for children to be inappropriate with each other. In addition, facilities are often set up so there are little nooks and crannies where children rest during nap time, making it difficult to see interactions between kids. This makes children even more vulnerable.

> One four-year-old boy, "John," was sent to the bathroom unmonitored with another young boy in his preschool. The boy asked John if he could touch his penis. John said no and told the teacher and his mother that night. Several weeks later, even after John had told the teacher about the first incident, John was again sent to the bathroom with the same boy. This time, the boy got mad at John and smacked his penis. Again, John told his teacher and his mother. His mother escalated the situation to the director of the school and specifically requested that every effort be made to keep John away from this other boy. Yet a few weeks later, John came home and told his mother that during nap time, the same boy told John that he better let him kiss his butt or he wouldn't be his friend any more. It seems that even though they were supposed to be kept away from each other, the two boys were put in a small cubby area during nap time where the two of them were alone and the teachers could not see or hear them. The mother made a decision to remove her son from the school because they simply were not willing to take the necessary precautions to protect her son.

NO UNMONITORED BATHROOM VISITS

As mentioned in the On-Site Boundaries section, bathroom visits can be a very vulnerable time for children because of the inherent exposure of the genitals. Although I already covered these bullets in the On-Site Boundaries section, I have repeated them here with a specific emphasis on minimizing the risk of child-to-child abuse.

- For *older* children, stalls in bathrooms should have doors and the kids should be instructed to close them. If they're old enough to be sent to the bathroom alone, they are old enough to have the full privacy of a closed door.
- For *young* children, bathrooms should be designed with low partitions and open entrances for increased supervision.
- When sending kids to the bathroom, there should be a staff member present to monitor. The staff member should be located where they can see the interaction between the kids, preferably at the door where the staff member is observable by others versus being inside the bathroom with the kids.
- Although I do not recommend sending kids to the bathroom using the buddy system without a staff monitor, if you must, the bathroom visits should be with kids of similar age and developmental level.
- Also if you must use the buddy system, send three kids rather than two. Just the presence of a third child can help to minimize the potential of children touching children, even in an innocent manner.

SEPARATE AGE GROUPS

Children should be separated into groups with kids of similar age and developmental levels for all program activities. 30–40 percent of child sexual abuse happens at the hands of older juveniles, so it is critically important that you pay careful attention to the physical and social power differences between kids and avoid situations that would increase risk.[7, 8, 9] It's natural to think that if there's an older child in the room, the younger kids would need less supervision, but this statistic shows us that quite the opposite is true. If your specific circumstances require you to have older children in the same vicinity with younger children, you will need to provide *increased* supervision to ensure the safety of the younger children.

AVOID DIRECT AND INADVERTENT CREATION OF AUTHORITY

Do not formally delegate responsibility to older kids that would put them in a power position over younger children. As an example, don't step outside the room and ask an older child to keep an eye on the younger kids. Even teens that are part of your volunteer staff should always be supervised by a fully screened adult staff member.

Also be careful not to inadvertently give older kids authority over younger ones by saying things such as "Tom is the leader, now do what he says." This subtle establishment of authority can be used by older kids in the future to get younger children to engage in inappropriate sexual behavior within your program or even after hours outside the program.

PROVIDE CLOSE SUPERVISION

It's simply important to realize that some abusers are children. Until you allow this into your consciousness, you're not likely to provide the right level of supervision needed to protect the children in your care and you may not be able to see abuse that's happening right in front of you.

> Subtle establishment of authority can be used by older kids to get younger children to engage in inappropriate sexual behavior.

Next Steps:

- Review, document, and distribute new Child-to-Child Boundaries to staff, parents, and children.

BEST PRACTICE #3

GIFT BOUNDARIES

Reflection:

Before continuing, complete the questions below regarding gift boundaries.

➤ What formal boundaries does your organization have in place regarding giving gifts to children in your care? How about gifts to the parents?

_____

_____

_____

_____

_____

_____

_____

_____

_____

> What informal boundaries does your organization have in place regarding giving gifts to children in your care? How about gifts to the parents?

_____

_____

_____

_____

_____

_____

_____

_____

_____

_____

NO GIFTS TO CHILDREN[1, 2, 3, 4]

Giving kids gifts is a classic grooming behavior of child molesters and should therefore be avoided. No child should receive a gift that is not a standard benefit of your program which is available to all children who participate. As an example, if your program is serving children living below the poverty level and you provide back-to-school backpacks to all children in your care, that would be acceptable. It would not however be acceptable for one of the children to also receive an iPod or tickets to a sporting event.

Gifts come in all forms—they may include tangible gifts as mentioned above or special outings or privileges not given to other children. Child molesters often use gifts to gain the attention and friendship of a child, but over time, the child molester is expecting something in return for the gifts, eventually leading to inappropriate sexual behavior. Gift giving and special outings can also create a relationship that seems so good, a child doesn't want to give it up, even after a child molester has started to sexually abuse them. Even parents may welcome gifts and outings for their kids, especially if they are not in a financial position to provide them themselves.

> The Jerry Sandusky case is the most extravagant example of gift giving. He gave young disadvantaged boys a chance of a lifetime by inviting them to professional and college sporting events, such as Philadelphia Eagles games, or pre-season practices at Penn State. He gave his victims "a number of gifts, including golf clubs, a computer, gym clothes, dress clothes, and cash." Sandusky also took his victims "to restaurants, swimming at a hotel near Sandusky's home, and to church."[5]

Imagine how difficult it was for these young boys to give up all the "good times" they were having with their offender. The grooming process is specifically designed to confuse children—creating great memories of being loved and honored that so far outweigh the destructive actions of the sexual abuse that the children find it difficult to walk away even after they want to.

Just remember that no child should be set apart as more important or special than any other child and that all children should receive the same benefits through your program and no additional benefits outside your program.

NO GIFTS TO PARENTS OR CARETAKERS[6]

Child molesters are masters of deception and spend an inordinate amount of time focused on image management. As part of that process, it's not unusual for a child molester to make efforts to groom parents and other family members as well.[7] This process is often used to create a special bond between a child molester and the parent which can be exploited for future access and a bond they can draw upon for support if they are ever accused of abuse. Therefore, staff members should not be permitted to give gifts to parents (or any other family member) of the children in your care. Both tangible and intangible gifts can create a conscious or subconscious feeling of indebtedness on behalf of a parent, making it more difficult for them to deflect future overtures that feel uncomfortable.[8]

Implementation of these boundaries will take strong leadership, especially where you have a culture that currently accepts some of these activities such as pulling children out of their regularly scheduled activities or staff members babysitting for your families. Like the case we mentioned at Big Brothers Big Sisters of Puget Sound where one of the Bigs quit because the organization terminated overnight privileges for all Littles, you will be faced with people who don't agree with the new boundaries. They may not believe you will enforce them, but if you have the courage to establish them and the fortitude to enforce them, the children in your care will be significantly less vulnerable to abuse. Believe me, it will likely only take one termination for breaking boundaries before your whole staff will believe that you are serious about the protection of the children in your care and you will not tolerate anyone who is not willing to join you.

Next Steps:

- Review, document, and distribute new Gift Boundaries to staff, parents, and children.

BEST PRACTICE #4

REGULARLY AND ACTIVELY ASSESS BEHAVIORS

Reflection:

Before continuing, complete the questions below regarding assessing behaviors.

> What policies or practices are currently in place that promote conscious proactive assessment of child sexual abuse concerns by your staff?

_____

_____

_____

_____

_____

_____

_____

_____

_____

➤ How do you engage parents in the assessment process? How about children?

_____

_____

_____

_____

_____

_____

_____

_____

➤ Do you have an established process for your *staff members* to communicate concerns about child sexual abuse? If yes, please explain.

_____

_____

_____

_____

_____

_____

_____

_____

➤ Do you have an established process for your *parents* to communicate concerns about child sexual abuse? If yes, please explain.

_____

_____

_____

_____

_____

_____

_____

_____

➤ Do you have an established process for the *children* in your care to communicate concerns about inappropriate behavior? If yes, please explain. Does the process provide an opportunity for them to give feedback on concerns outside of your program (i.e., at home or in other programs)?

_____

_____

_____

_____

_____

_____

_____

_____

➢ How do you keep the process of assessment and communication top of mind for your staff, parents, and children?

_____

_____

_____

_____

_____

_____

_____

_____

➢ How do you ensure the identity of the person submitting feedback on concerning behavior is kept confidential? Do you provide a mechanism for anonymous feedback?

_____

_____

_____

_____

_____

_____

_____

_____

➤ Do you have a single person/position that is responsible for child protection? Is it their primary role?

_____

_____

_____

_____

_____

_____

_____

_____

➤ How does your process for monitoring feedback allow patterns of concern or trends to be spotted?

_____

_____

_____

_____

_____

_____

_____

_____

_____

➢ How and when are concerns communicated to the board of directors or other responsible parties?

_____

_____

_____

_____

_____

_____

_____

_____

_____

➢ Is there a regularly scheduled time for the board of directors or other responsible parties to discuss the protection of children from sexual abuse while in your care?

_____

_____

_____

_____

_____

_____

_____

_____

_____

CREATE STANDARD OPERATING PROCEDURES FOR ASSESSING AND COMMUNICATING CONCERNS

The point of the assessment and communication process is to create a habit of paying attention, of learning to listen with your eyes. In Best Practice #1, I had you look at your enablers and barriers which will be addressed throughout the book and implementation process. In Best Practice #2, you learned the two key objectives in managing access to children and the detailed steps of how to achieve those objectives. In Best Practice #3, you learned over sixty-five specific boundaries that will allow you to better protect children.

It may seem logical to jump directly to the details of what to do if an individual breaks those boundaries, but honestly, one of the biggest challenges in protecting children is that people are not in the habit of paying attention to the details of their surroundings and child molesters work tirelessly to make everything look good on the surface. Believe me, it will not do you any good to know the actions to take when a problem arises if you never notice there's a problem. So let's take some time to focus on creating an environment where staff, parents, and children alike are proactively asked to pay attention.

First, there are four types of issues you are looking for during the assessment process:

- Legal boundaries that have been broken and need to be reported to authorities
- Organizational boundaries that have been broken and need to be reported internally
- Concerning behaviors that are not covered by existing boundaries but need to be addressed with the individual and potentially added to your published boundaries
- Questionable behavior and blurred boundaries that may reflect a potentially dangerous pattern

The first two issues are pretty clear cut because I have identified an extensive list of boundaries in Best Practice #3 that you can use as a guide. The assessment process will slow you down and ask you to reflect in a way that will help to make sure you notice these boundary violations. When you're all paying attention, your staff and families may see additional concerning behaviors that need to be addressed. If you see a particular boundary issue arise repeatedly, you may want to add it as a published boundary. This covers the third issue.

The fourth issue really brings us to an incredibly important concept in the assessment process. Because our communities and specifically our youth-serving organizations typically do not have a means of communicating questionable behavior, many incidents of grooming go unrecognized as seemingly isolated incidents that a child molester can explain away or somehow justify. It is only by bringing these isolated incidents into a single view that the overall picture is likely to be seen and may reveal a potentially dangerous pattern of behavior.

You will be light-years ahead of other organizations simply by implementing the boundaries in Best Practice #3 because until now, behaviors that break those boundaries would have all been thrown into this bucket of questionable behavior that you would need to review for patterns. By formally calling out the known grooming behaviors and setting boundaries that intercede, they are no longer questionable behaviors but instead absolute boundary violations, with associated consequences, which significantly minimize the other questionable behaviors that will remain.

According to van Dam, "To stop these socially skilled child molesters, adults need to ensure that the clues seen in isolation by various community members become known rather than remaining invisible or compartmentalized."[1] She goes on to say that "The known instances of misconduct and the subtle cues that should sound the alarm—all need to be carefully tracked and monitored because of the significance of the overall pattern."[2] Van Dam says, "Communities need to learn to be vigilant without becoming vigilantes"[3] and I couldn't agree more.

While we don't yet have a centralized tracking system for questionable behaviors (clues) within our communities, you can create one within your organization. Although not for the specific reason of identifying patterns, decades ago, the Boy Scouts of America began a process of centralized documentation of volunteers they deemed unfit to be with kids which included reports of suspected sexual abuse and sexual misconduct both within the program and outside of it.

In October of 2012, the Oregon Supreme Court ordered the release of the Boy Scouts of America's ineligible volunteer files to the public. These files included 20,000 confidential documents detailing 1,247 individuals who had been deemed ineligible to volunteer for the Scouts from 1965 to 1985.[4] The Boy Scouts of America had the right idea when they created this centralized process and information repository of volunteers they deemed to be a risk to children, and they successfully protected the kids in *their* care by keeping individuals with inappropriate behavior from having access. This process was instated over 80 years ago, long before mandated reporting laws were in existence. While many are under the impression these were secret files, the "police were involved in nearly two-thirds (63%) of the files and a majority of these files (58%) included information known to the public."[5] Nonetheless, on many occasions the Boy Scouts failed to report suspected abusers to authorities which left those individuals free to prey on other children in the community.

The Boy Scouts have been and continue to be leaders in the protection of children[6] while many organizations have yet to make a commitment or even a concerted effort to protect the children in their care from sexual abuse. I encourage all youth-serving organizations to take the Boy Scouts' lead and establish a centralized repository of information regarding sexually inappropriate behavior but it is crucial that you learn from their and other youth-serving organizations' mistakes and ensure you report concerns to authorities in a timely manner. So let's look at the specific steps you can take to create that centralized file of not only suspected abuse and organizational boundary violations but also other concerning behavior which may reveal potentially dangerous patterns. The steps in the process are as follows:

- Ask for Feedback
- Provide an Assessment and Communication Form
- Establish a Set Time When Assessment and Communication Forms are Submitted
- Establish a Child Sexual Abuse Prevention Communication Team
- Regularly Review Feedback

ASK FOR FEEDBACK

It's far too easy to let our busy lives keep us from slowing down long enough to notice what's happening right in front of us and sometimes what's happening is of concern and we simply miss it. After initial disclosure of abuse, we quite often hear bystanders start listing inappropriate behaviors of the accused or that the person always made them feel uncomfortable, but they never said anything. The process of asking for feedback creates an interruption in your busy schedules and allows you time to engage in a conscious proactive thought process about your surroundings.

Feedback should be requested of staff members, parents, and children. You might also consider extending this if you have any partners, donors, etc,. who are in a position to observe the interactions within your programs.

This process supports the recommendation of researcher Park Dietz who discussed the importance of recognizing and reporting the early warning signs—the red flags—the grooming behaviors and not just obvious sexual acts.[7] Shakeshaft and other experts agree that rumors are an important source of information on educator sexual misconduct.[8, 9] It's important to remember that this assessment and communication process is about bringing what you all see and hear individually into a single centralized view so that the full picture is visible. Grooming signs and even rumors are part of that picture.

> It's far too easy to let your busy lives keep you from slowing down long enough to notice what is happening right in front of you.

PROVIDE AN ASSESSMENT AND COMMUNICATION FORM

Creating a standardized form to be used for assessment and communication provides an effective way to jog the memory of those completing it. The form should be designed to elicit both positive and negative feedback about the protection of children. The standardized form should include the following key areas of feedback:

- Strong, clear boundaries are exhibited
- Good relationships with kids, parents, and/or colleagues
- Legal boundary violations
- Organizational boundaries violations
- Concerning behaviors that are not covered by existing boundaries
- Visual feedback option for children
- Signs of abuse in children

Strong Boundaries and Good Relationships
You will want to elicit positive feedback about staff members both from a perspective of them exhibiting strong and clear boundaries as well as establishing healthy and balanced relationships with

children, parents, and their colleagues. You should look for opportunities to thank them and acknowledge their commitment to the protection of children. However, if you remember, child molesters go out of their way to groom adults into thinking they are honest, helpful, respectable, and trustworthy. So you also want to be prepared to recognize unusual patterns that look like a staff member is going out of their way to make others like them and trust them, this is a red flag.

Legal Boundary Violations

You will want to specifically ask staff, parents, and children if any legal boundaries have been broken. The process of asking makes all of them stop and think about what they have seen, heard, and experienced in the recent period. It allows staff and parents to actively determine if there is any reason to suspect abuse and it gives children permission to tell, even if their offender has threatened to harm them if they do. There are no words to effectively explain the confusion that sexual abuse can create in the hearts and minds of children. The process of asking a direct question may bring the clarity a child needs to recognize sexual abuse for what it is.

You will have shared the legal boundaries with children in an age-appropriate manner during training so they should have a clear understanding of the boundaries (see Best Practice #6). Your form instructions should clearly state that if a legal boundary has been broken, the person completing the form should file a report with the authorities immediately. Staff members should refer to the mandated reporting procedures discussed in Best Practice #7. Parents should immediately contact law enforcement as well as your local child protective services agency (include the phone numbers on your form.)

Organizational Boundary Violations

Remember in Best Practice #3, the first category of boundaries was Legal Boundaries; the other six categories are considered organizational boundaries which intercede with grooming behaviors. Violating organizational boundaries is not illegal but it is unacceptable. Your form should provide a place for your parents and staff to select which type of boundary was violated (i.e., On-Site, Off-Site, Off-Hours, etc.).

Other Concerning Behavior

Although I've made an effort to address the most prominent types of grooming behaviors in my boundaries, there may be additional situations that arise that simply don't seem safe or appropriate and should be addressed with the individual. It's also valuable to document unusual behavior—you may not be able to say it is inappropriate, but it stands out as unusual compared to other people in similar positions. In van Dam's book, *The Socially Skilled Child Molester*, she writes about how the proof is often in the patterns.[10] Please don't let the "little things" seem unimportant— they may not tell a story on their own, but when combined with feedback from a variety of staff members, parents and children over a period of months, the "little things" could present a very clear picture of a child molester.

> Several years ago, a parent brought a Craigslist ad to my attention because of the concerning behavior it included. It was an advertisement for a day care center who touted fun: "When was the last time your child climbed a tree or made mud pies?" The ad pulled on the heartstrings of those parents who were probably too busy to spend quality time with their children. I could see how parents would be drawn in to providing their children with these experiences. However, as I continued to read the advertisement, there was an offer for free day care on Friday nights for single moms only. The ad suggested the kids bring their pillows and sleeping bags so they would be comfortable during movie time. I went to the Web site for this day care center and from the profile I could tell it was owned by a single man who looked to be in his late forties.

I have never had an interaction with the man who runs this day care center and I am not suggesting that he is a child molester. However, I can unequivocally say that the behavior suggested in this advertisement is unusual. I am not in contact with any other forty-year-old men who spend their Friday nights taking care of other people's kids—for free. When you analyze the situation further, there are additional red flags—the ad is specifically directed at vulnerable children coming from broken families; it is specifically directed at women who are likely stressed and overwhelmed, reiterating multiple times in bold font that the offer is for single moms only; the children snuggling up under the cover of sleeping bags; and although the ad didn't say anything about it, I can imagine the lights are turned down during the movie. This scenario sounds not only unusual but dangerous even though there is no evidence of laws being broken or even my recommended organizational boundaries being broken, assuming there are multiple adults present.

I hope that this example provides you a glimpse into what I mean when I say unusual behavior. When looking at the behavior, is it in line with the behavior you see other people exhibiting that are of similar age, gender, and position? If you cannot say yes, then it should be documented on your Assessment and Communication Form as "other concerning behavior."

Visual Feedback for Children

I recommend you incorporate a stop light assessment tool which uses the simple concept of a green, yellow, or red light to reflect a child's feelings. It is easy for even young children to understand. Explain that Green means "Go" and all is well. Yellow means "Proceed with Caution" and that something feels yucky or creepy. Red means "Stop" and that something feels dangerous or scary. Although the children's training discussed later in the book is designed to provide kids with "the language of abuse," the stop light assessment is an easy way to provide feedback even when children don't have the words to describe the way a specific person or interaction makes them feel. You can simply include an image of a stop light on the form and allow children to color in red, yellow, or green for each person they are assessing. Stop Light Assessment Refrigerator Magnets are also available at www.taalk.org/store.

> The stop light assessment is an easy way for children to provide feedback even when they do not have the words to describe the way a specific person or interaction makes them feel.

Signs of Abuse in Children

Although we have been focused on protecting children when they are in your care by looking at the behaviors of child molesters, we would be remiss if we didn't include the opportunity for staff and parents to provide feedback on signs of abuse in a child. These physical, emotional/behavioral, and sexual signs may indicate that abuse has already occurred, either within your organization or elsewhere. The detailed list of these signs was provided in the introduction and can be used to prompt staff and parents to know what to look for.

When you use the assessment form to communicate signs of abuse in children, you are simply assessing the child's behavior instead of a staff member's behavior. Some signs in children are *direct indicators* of sexual abuse such as evidence of physical trauma like blood, swelling, or tears in the skin around the vagina, penis, or anus; complaints of pain during urination or bowel movements; or exhibiting symptoms of genital or urinary tract infections or STDs. In these cases, the person completing the form should report to the authorities immediately as a forensic interview is needed to capture any evidence still available.

Other signs which by themselves may or may not indicate abuse can be documented on the assessment form, but if multiple signs, chronic signs, or major changes in behavior become apparent through this centralized assessment process, it would be grounds to suspect abuse. When you are looking at signs of abuse in children, you may not have any indication who the offender is but that is not required to suspect abuse which is the basis for reporting to authorities. Reporting is simply asking the authorities to look further to see if a problem exists.

Understand that legal boundary violations, organizational boundary violations and concerning behaviors should be communicated for all staff members including contract workers. In addition, a form should be completed for any adult or child who is violating these boundaries or showing concerning behavior while on your premises or during off-site program activities. This might include strangers, relatives of staff members, or relatives of children in your program. It may also include children in your program—remember 30–40 percent of abuse happens at the hands of older or larger children.[11, 12]

Completing the Form

There are a few things your staff and parents can do to make the assessment process most effective:

- Before you start, create a list of all of the kids in your care as well as staff members so that you can systematically focus your attention on each one of them. For parents, this would be mostly staff but could also include the other children in the program.
- Gather the following information: your form, the signs of abuse in children, the grooming behaviors, and the list of legal and organizational boundaries.
- Grab yourself a cup of coffee or a soda and take some time to think.
- It helps to focus on two different visions of your environment—the big picture or aerial view and the details or ground level view.
- Using a military example, first think of yourself as a watchman in a tower who is responsible for surveillance. Look out over the premises and the organization as a whole. Are there areas where your perimeter could be easily infiltrated and needs to be fortified? Are there internal processes and protection systems that are weak and need to be bolstered?
- Then change roles and think of yourself as a ground level soldier who is responsible for being acutely aware of his surroundings, the coming and going of the people around him and any signs of danger. Now think about each child on your list—asking yourself if you see any signs of abuse. Then think about each staff member asking yourself if you see any grooming signs or boundaries that have

been broken. You will also want to specifically take time to think about the interactions between the children in your care and see if any signs of concern come to mind. Lastly, focus on relationships—pay attention to the level of intimacy that exists between staff members and the children around them. The relationships should be professional and not overly personal.

• Remember the intent is to be vigilant without being a vigilante. You are not trying to create something out of nothing. I am just asking you to create a habit of slowing down long enough to notice what's happening around you and recognize any signs of concern.

ESTABLISH A SET TIME WHEN ASSESSMENT AND COMMUNICATION FORMS ARE SUBMITTED

Now that we've asked for feedback and provided a standardized form to jog everyone's memory, how do we actually get people to fill out the form and turn it in? The process needs to be incorporated in some aspect of your existing procedures in order to be readily adopted.

It's not uncommon for businesses to invest time researching and documenting new policies or procedures just to find that they never really take root in the organization. Yes, the policy is officially in place, but they often fail to achieve cultural adoption of the policy where it becomes a natural part of the staff's day-to-day thought process and actions.

Child sexual abuse is a difficult subject for most adults to talk about. So cultural adoption is not likely to happen unless the organiza-

> Child sexual abuse is a difficult topic for most adults to talk about. Formal processes for assessing and communicating concerns can make it easier and more effective.

tion also puts standard operating procedures in place to provide every possible opportunity for the staff, parents, and children to embrace the new policy.

Which standard operating procedure you select depends greatly on how often you want to collect the forms, which in turn depends on how often children participate in your programs. As an example, if your organization provides after-school care five days a week, you may want to request feedback weekly or every other week. If, however, you run a mentoring program where the child only participates two or three times a month, you would likely want to request feedback on a monthly basis instead.

Here are some suggestions for how to incorporate the feedback process into your standard operating procedures but every organization is different—just be sure to tie it to a procedure that is already in place so it's easy to remember and incorporate:

- For staff members, you may require them to turn in their form along with their time sheet, when they pick up their paycheck or when they attend a staff meeting. It doesn't really matter *when* they're asked to turn it in, as long as it is part of some other process that already exists and the expectation is set that everyone turns in the form. We don't want the intervals to be too far apart or people will forget the "little things" that could be key danger signs.

- For parents whose children participate in daily programs, you may want to hand out blank forms on Fridays to be completed over the weekend and have a staff member requesting they drop them in the box as the children are signed in or out on Monday. If their kids only participate a couple of times a month, you may want to e-mail them the form monthly and request that it be returned on the child's next day in the program or by mail. I recommend you add a field to the sign-in sheet that indicates if their form has been turned in for that period, providing a reminder for the parents and staff.

- Children's feedback regarding staff members and other kids should be gathered by the parents and included on the parent's form. This is a great way to encourage open communication between parents and children about their experience in your program and about the child's surroundings in general. Parents can also use this same process to ask kids to provide a Stop Light Assessment of other adults and kids in their lives outside of your program.
- You may want to incorporate a periodic opportunity for children to do a Stop Light Assessment while they're with you. This provides them a safe place to tell even if they're uncomfortable telling their parents. The directions should be expanded to include abuse happening anywhere in the kid's lives, even at home.

> Disclaimer: You may have procedures and/or laws that require parents' permission or at least notification to ask a child to complete such an assessment when they are in your care. So check your specific requirements and gain appropriate professional and/or legal advice before proceeding.

I understand that for large organizations such as schools, a full schedule of assessments would be overwhelming from a sheer volume perspective but that doesn't mean you should forego this practice. Instead, find a way to address the intent and make it work. As an example, you could request feedback from one-third of the families and teachers each month instead of from everyone every week.

While my heart naturally comes from a place of protection for children, it is also important to acknowledge the value of this process for your organization. If one of your staff members was able to get around all of the protection practices you put in place and abuse a child in your care and your organization was sued for negligence, you will be able to provide an extensive amount of evidence regarding your efforts to protect children.

Imagine sitting at the table during a deposition and explaining that you not only followed your child protection focused screening processes and established 65+ boundaries that address known grooming behaviors but that you also requested weekly feedback on inappropriate behaviors and signs of abuse from every family you serve and every staff member. You would be able to show the Assessment and Communication Forms specific to the staff member in question to show that if and when any signs of concern were raised, appropriate and timely action was taken. This is a powerful position to be in and you may have just saved your organization millions of dollars by proving that you were not only not negligent, but indeed diligent in your efforts to protect the children in your care.

> Provide a means for anonymous feedback to protect staff and parent's identity.

Some people may not be comfortable providing honest feedback of a concerning nature, if it's likely everyone will know it was them. So I recommend you create a locked box where staff and families can submit their forms. Since the forms are designed to elicit both positive and negative feedback, set the expectation that every staff member and family submit a form, even if it just indicates that everything's going well and there are no concerns. This helps to protect the privacy and identity of individuals submitting concerns. You can also provide an option for anonymous feedback allowing anyone to mail their form in with no name. You never want to forego the opportunity to gather crucial information just because a particular person doesn't want to be identified. However, it's important for everyone to understand that it can be difficult to take action on anonymous feedback if further information cannot be gathered.

As I mentioned earlier, your silence enables child molesters and this process of open communication creates an environment where child molesters will find it hard to succeed without being detected and therefore they won't want to work or volunteer for your organization.

Your silence enables child molesters.

ESTABLISH A CHILD
SEXUAL ABUSE PREVENTION COMMUNICATION TEAM

When it comes to child molesters, it's difficult to differentiate the guilty from the innocent without looking at patterns over a period of time and across a broad range of children. Van Dam has dedicated a whole book to this topic entitled *The Socially Skilled Child Molester: Differentiating the Guilty from the Falsely Accused.*[13] You have the opportunity to create a process to do just that capture these patterns within your organization and across the children you serve by establishing a Child Sexual Abuse Prevention Communication Team.[14]

First, I recommend that you designate a single position that is responsible for the day-to-day implementation of your child sexual abuse prevention program. For our purposes, I will call this position the Risk Manager. It is important that your prevention program is his primary role, so that the associated duties do not get pushed aside to focus on other assignments. As a matter of fact, according to the 2010 GAO report, schools that receive federal financial assistance are subject to the regulations under Title IX of the Education Amendments of 1972 which "require schools to have procedures in place to protect students from sexual abuse by school personnel"[15] and Shakeshaft's 2004 report says schools must also designate at least one employee to coordinate their Title IX obligations.[16]

I recommend the team consist of at least one board member or high level executive so that it is clear this is not just an administrative task—this is a risk management process that should be taken seriously and have the full attention of the organization's executive team. I addition, the team should include your Risk Manager and one other staff member as well as two parents. Having parents participate on the team is important to create accountability and also as a statement that you are all responsible for the protection of children, not just the organization.

The team's role is to disseminate information about your child sexual abuse prevention program as well as review the Assessment and Communication Forms on a regular basis, in line with the submission frequency. As an example, there's no need to meet weekly if the forms are only submitted twice a month. It's best if the staff members chosen do not have direct involvement with kids as it's less likely (although not unheard of) that a concern will arise about them and create a conflict of interest.

In addition, you should have the team members names published to staff and parents and encourage submissions directly to team members, instead of putting the form in the box, if a concern about one of the team members should arise. A direct submission should be submitted to *at least two* team members to ensure accountability. The form should include a place to indicate the two team members who received the submission.

> Publish a process for providing verbal feedback when time is of the essence.

In situations that are time sensitive, verbal notification should be initiated directly to two team members immediately—thereby avoiding any time delays inherent in the standard process. Forms should be submitted as a follow-up to verbal notification. This immediate submission process should be used in cases where a boundary violation is impending and could be avoided. As an example, you overhear that a staff member is planning to drive one of the kids home at the end of the day.

REGULARLY REVIEW FEEDBACK

The Assessment and Communication Form submission box should be opened during the regularly scheduled Communication Team meeting and all forms reviewed. In reviewing the forms, the team should use the following guidelines during the assessment:

- **Legal Boundary Violations and Suspected Abuse**: Your form instructions should indicate that legal boundary violations should be immediately reported to authorities, but some may still end up in your box. So it is important that the team determines right away if any of the forms indicate a legal boundary has been violated. If so, the team should follow the mandated reporting procedures (see Best Practice #7) and report the alleged abuse to the authorities immediately. There may be other information on a form that makes you suspect abuse, such as multiple or recurring signs of abuse in a child. These cases should also be handled by reporting to authorities as detailed in the mandated reporting procedures. Any previous forms for the violating staff member should be copied and submitted as part of the formal process as well.
- **Organizational Boundary Violations**: Determine if the information on any of the forms meets the criteria for an organizational boundary violation. If so, the team should follow the Standards for Responding to Organizational Boundary Violations as discussed in Best Practice #7. Any previous forms for the violating staff member should be copied and submitted as part of the formal process as well.
- **Arising Patterns**: Compare the remaining forms (that do not meet the criteria for legal boundary violations, suspected abuse, or organizational boundary violations) with forms received for that staff member, parent, or

child in the past to assess if there is a pattern developing that raises concern. If a significant pattern does arise that would cause anyone on the team to suspect abuse, the team should follow the mandated reporting procedures (see Best Practice #7) and report the alleged abuse to the authorities immediately. Remember that some patterns may actually appear in the positive feedback categories if a staff member is working unusually hard to build trusting relationships with parents and children.

Be sure you have clearly designated who on the team will follow through to report legal boundary violations, suspected abuse, or organizational boundary violations. You want to be sure that nothing falls through the cracks.

Disclaimer: All forms submitted and the information contained within them should be considered confidential and kept in a secure location. The information should be shared on a need-to-know basis only with staff that have been established as Assessment and Communication Team members or predetermined escalation points for centralized control of child sexual abuse cases, as discussed in Best Practice #7.

It's possible that state laws, union contracts, or other agreements could prohibit the collection and storing of this information. Seek professional/legal advice to determine how the intent of this Best Practice can be achieved within any specific limitations that apply to your organization.

If your organization is bound by laws or contracts that preclude collection of or extended retention of feedback regarding inappropriate staff behavior that would limit the ability to spot concerning trends, I recommend you make every effort to have these laws modified or have the contracts renegotiated.

ESTABLISH STANDARDIZED BOARD REPORTING

To ensure cultural adoption of the organization's child sexual abuse prevention program, it needs to have consistent high level visibility, even when things are running smoothly and there are no reports of legal or organizational boundary violations.

Therefore, the Risk Manager should be responsible for providing a summary of key program activities to be included in reports prepared for each regularly scheduled board meeting. The activities in the report should include but are not limited to:

- Staff members trained (new and annual)
- Number of new children (families) enrolled
- Parents trained (new and annual)
- Children trained (new and annual)
- Summary of legal boundary violations identified and addressed (completed and pending)
- Summary of organizational boundary violations identified and addressed (complete and pending)
- Summary of other concerning behavior and signs of abuse in children communicated through Assessment and Communication Forms.
- Any recently requested or approved policy changes

The process of providing formal reports on your child sexual abuse prevention program, not only serves to support cultural adoption, it also provides a record of due diligence on the part of the organization to protect the children in your care. It's not likely you'll be able to stop every instance of abuse within and through your programs, but in the unfortunate event that a

> Formal board reporting not only serves to support cultural adoption of your program but also provides a record of due diligence on the part of your organization.

child is sexually abused, this documentation would help to mitigate the risk of losing a civil suit for demonstrable negligence.

Next Steps:

- Review, document, and implement new standard operating procedures for assessing and communicating concerns.
- Establish standardized board reporting procedures for your child sexual abuse prevention program.

BEST PRACTICE #5

CREATE AN ACCOUNTABILITY TEAM

Reflection:

Before continuing, complete the questions below regarding how your organization trains and empowers staff and parents to hold each other accountable.

➤ What training do you currently provide to your *staff* regarding the topic of child sexual abuse?

_____

_____

_____

_____

_____

_____

_____

_____

_____

_____

➢ What formal policies and/or informal practices do you have in place to motivate your staff to hold other staff members accountable for their behavior?

_____

_____

_____

_____

_____

_____

_____

_____

➢ What training do you currently provide to the *parents* of the children in your care regarding the topic of child sexual abuse?

_____

_____

_____

_____

_____

_____

_____

_____

_____

> ➤ What formal policies and/or informal practices do you have in place to engage parents in holding your staff accountable for their behavior?

_____

_____

_____

_____

_____

_____

_____

_____

_____

_____

DELIVER MANDATORY STAFF TRAINING[1, 2]

Mandatory child sexual abuse prevention training for staff is a crucial component of your child sexual abuse prevention program because it provides the basis for everyone in the organization to learn to talk about the pandemic and specifically educates them to recognize grooming behaviors in child molesters as well as signs of abuse in children. It also establishes clear boundaries, both legal and organizational, which intercede with child molesters' behaviors and are therefore crucial to the protection of children. Most importantly, it sets the stage for proactive protection of children in your care which serves as a deterrent to potential offenders who are looking for easy access that would allow them to exploit children.

Training Content

The training program consists of two modules as follows:

Module #1: Child Sexual Abuse Prevention Basics

This training module is a key part of your child sexual abuse prevention program. Participation should be mandatory for every staff member and it should be repeated annually.

The objectives of this module are as follows:

1. To raise your level of awareness of the child sexual abuse pandemic and its consequences
2. To empower you to visualize and transform *your* world into a safer place for kids
3. To equip you to recognize risky behaviors and signs of abuse
4. To teach you about barriers that keep people from talking about abuse and taking appropriate action
5. To help you understand your responsibility to protect kids and respond to abuse

Module #2: Child Sexual Abuse Prevention Boundaries For Youth-Serving Organizations

As I mentioned earlier, written boundaries are at the heart of protecting children. Without them, every day is filled with a myriad of subjective choices that are far too often hindered by our emotions, opinions, relationships, and quest for personal gain (promotion, raise, etc.). When boundaries are established and documented in writing, they provide a mechanism for objective decision making that applies to everyone who comes in contact with children in your care. No exceptions!

This training module covers the boundaries discussed in Best Practice #3 which now need to be communicated to your staff. Training participation should be mandatory for every staff member and the training should be repeated annually.

The objective of this module is to discuss in-depth the boundaries included in the following seven categories:

1. Legal Boundaries
2. On-Site Boundaries
3. Off-Site Boundaries
4. Off-Hours Boundaries
5. Electronic Communication and Social Media Boundaries
6. Child-to-Child Boundaries
7. Gift Boundaries

Training Delivery

The training is available online, which permits each staff member to complete the training as their schedules allow. This can minimize the need for overtime and/or temporary program coverage required to complete the training as a group. The online format is also beneficial for organizations that have remote staff who cannot easily travel to a centralized location for training. The online training is available at www.taalk.org/training.

If your organization would prefer to deliver the training in a group setting that promotes open discussion and collaboration, you may do so by displaying the online training to the group using a laptop and LCD projector. You may also elect to provide your staff the choice of group training *or* online training based on their geographic location, availability, and comfort level.

The training platform provides an option for you to copy the URL link so that you can easily distribute it to your staff via e-mail. There is also an option to copy the "embed code" so that you can easily integrate the training into your own Web site for easier access. Both of these options are accessible by hovering your cursor over the top of the slide, and clicking Embed. Note that this feature does not work in full screen mode, so you will have to exit full screen before accessing.

Training Costs

The cost of training is one of the greatest obstacles youth-serving organizations face in implementing an effective child sexual abuse prevention program, especially for large organizations. Because I believe child sexual abuse is predictable and preventable when we surround children with *knowledgeable* adults, I have decided to offer this training at no charge. This in no way diminishes the value of the training, but instead makes it accessible to every individual and every organization who wants it. Money should not be the deciding factor in learning to protect your children!

Track Training Completion

The online training platform provides a certificate of completion which you should require your staff to submit each year.

Create Opportunities for Interaction

Since one of the most important aspects of child sexual abuse prevention is to break the silence, it is important to create opportunities for your staff to talk about what they've learned in the training and specifically how the boundaries apply to your organization. This is especially important at the beginning because your staff may currently be participating in activities that have now become boundary violations, such as babysitting.

I recommend you arrange a series of face-to-face meetings and/or conference calls to allow your staff to ask questions and discuss the program. I also recommend you create a FAQ sheet from the ensuing discussion, so you can provide the same clarifying information to all current staff members as well as future employees.

Training Handouts

Training handouts are incorporated into the online training and are accessible by hovering your cursor over the top of the slide and clicking Attachments. Note that this feature does not work in full screen mode, so you will have to exit full screen before accessing. You should communicate this to your staff when you send out the announcement for the training.

If you elect to do training as a group, you should download the handouts ahead of time and make copies for all participants.

Acknowledge and Accept Your Policy

After your staff members have provided completion certificates for both online training modules, you should require them to read and accept your child sexual abuse prevention policy.

I recommend you provide a package in writing, with a cover letter for them to sign. The sign-off should ask them to acknowledge that:

- They have received and read the policy including legal and organizational boundaries
- They agree to abide by them
- They agree to hold other staff members accountable to abide by them
- They fully understand the pre-established consequences for accusations of legal boundary violations suspected abuse and organizational boundary violations
- They understand how and when to communicate suspected abuse and boundary violations internally
- They understand that they are mandated reporters either by law or by your policy
- As mandated reporters, they understand their obligation to report as well as the penalties for failure to report

After the initial rollout, the training should be completed as part of your annual in-service training along with a requirement to reconfirm acknowledgement of your policy. For staff members who come on board during the year, training and acknowledgement of the policy should be included as part of the new hire process.

> Disclaimer: I understand that in some situations where employment or union contracts exist, this process may need to be negotiated and approved by interested parties including legal counsel, prior to deployment.

ENGAGE PARENTS IN ENFORCING BOUNDARIES

Although training your staff is essential, it's simply not enough. We need to *surround* children with adults who are knowledgeable about how abuse happens and are specifically aware of the boundaries your organization has put in place to reduce the risk of sexual abuse. This is a crucial component needed to stop child molesters in their tracks.

As an example, if a staff member were to offer to tutor a child after school because the child is struggling with math and the parents were unaware of the established organizational boundaries, the parents would likely welcome the offer. This boundary violation would go undetected, potentially putting the child at risk. On the other hand, if the parents *were* aware of the established organizational boundaries, they could immediately remind the staff member that it's not allowed under the existing policy. In this second scenario, the opportunity for private access to that child is avoided and any risk mitigated. In addition, the parents should report this organizational boundary violation on their next Assessment and Communication Form and the appropriate pre-established consequences would be carried out.

Remember you have already trained your staff on the boundaries. Each staff member has acknowledged in writing that they agree to abide by these boundaries and that they fully understand the pre-established consequences for breaking them. So if a staff member does break one of the boundaries, you must assume they have made a conscious choice to do so. That choice reflects a blatant attempt to gain private access, to establish an inappropriate relationship, or at minimum, a general disregard for the safety of the children in your care. In any case, their actions

> If a staff member breaks a boundary, it reflects either a blatant attempt to gain private access, to establish an inappropriate relationship, or at a minimum, a general disregard for the safety of the children in your care.

pose an increased risk of kids being sexually abused and an increased risk of your organization being held responsible for not protecting them.

This level of accountability is essential to the success of the your program and is only achievable by training parents on the child sexual abuse pandemic, the established boundaries, and engaging them in the enforcement process. Your organization can simply extend access to both online training modules referenced earlier in this section, to the parents and caregivers of children in your care.

Training Content

You may extend the staff training to all parents and other caretakers of the children you serve. See the training content details in the previous section regarding staff training.

Training Delivery

As explained before, the training is available online, which permits parents to complete the training as their schedules allow. This can minimize the need to coordinate training as a group. The online format is also beneficial for organizations that have remote locations where parents cannot easily travel to a centralized location for training. Since some parents may not have access to a computer or the Internet, you should offer the training at your location periodically as well.

Training Costs

As with the online training for your staff, I am offering the training at no charge to parents and caregivers, so that money is not an obstacle in engaging them in the process of protecting their children!

Track Training Completion

The online training platform provides a certificate of completion which you can request the parents copy and turn in. This will allow you to track the percentage of families who have completed the training and even publicize how many knowledgeable adults are now surrounding the children in your care.

Have some fun with this by creating a visual of a large thermometer that tracks how many are trained. Offer an incentive for parents to take the training and turn in their completion certificates. It would be great if you made it a competition between classes or teams and had an ice cream party for the first three groups to get all of their parents to turn in their certificates. I encourage you to find a way to make this difficult subject fun!

Some parents will choose not to participate in the training for a variety of reasons that you may never understand. You should continue to market the training in an effort to gain the highest level of participation possible. The more knowledgeable adults a child has surrounding them, the lower their vulnerability to abuse.

Training Content

See training content for staff members above.

Create Opportunities for Interaction

Since one of the most important aspects of child sexual abuse prevention is to break the silence, it is important to create opportunities for parents to talk about what they've learned in the training and specifically how the boundaries apply to their kids, especially if they are already engaged in activities with staff members that are now considered boundary violations. I recommend you arrange a series of face-to-face meetings to allow your parents to ask questions and discuss the program.

I recommend you create a FAQ sheet from the ensuing discussion so you can provide the same clarifying information to all parents of currently enrolled children as well as future families.

Training Handouts

See training handouts for staff members above.

Acknowledge and Accept Your Policy

Although it is your staff who we are trying to hold accountable to the new boundaries, your parents are an integral part of the process, they are part of the accountability team. So you should require them to read and accept your child sexual abuse prevention policy. Though your policy may be more extensive, at minimum, I recommend you provide a package that includes the boundaries and the assessment and communication process, along with a cover letter for them to sign. The sign-off should ask them to acknowledge that:

- They have received and read the policy including legal and organizational boundaries
- They agree to abide by the boundaries that apply to parents
- They understand the importance of their role in holding staff members accountable to honor the boundaries

- They understand they should call law enforcement to report legal boundary violations and suspected abuse
- They understand they should communicate any organizational boundary violations via the Assessment and Communication Form

Since not all parents will participate in the training, I recommend you send out the package to *all* parents about four weeks after making the training available. You will need to track to make sure you receive confirmations back from all parents.

After the initial rollout, the training should be offered to parents annually along with a requirement to reconfirm acknowledgement of your policy. Make the competition for parents to take the training an annual event as well—and remember to make it fun! For families joining your programs during the year, training and acknowledgement of the policy should be included as part of the standard registration process.

Next Steps:

- Either schedule mandatory group training for your staff or distribute login information for mandatory online training and follow up for completion.
- Create and distribute an acknowledgement of your policy and track receipt of a signed copy from every staff member.
- Either schedule group training for parents of the kids in your program or distribute login information for the online training.
- Develop a fun incentive-based competition to get families to complete the training and celebrate your success.
- Create and distribute an acknowledgement of your policy and track receipt of a signed copy from every family.

BEST PRACTICE #6

EDUCATE AND EMPOWER CHILDREN

Reflection:

Before continuing, complete the questions below regarding how your organization educates and empowers children.

➤ Do you have any laws, rules, or cultural taboos that keep you from talking with kids about sexual protection and empowerment? How can those barriers be overcome?

_____

_____

_____

_____

_____

_____

_____

_____

➤ Do you have any laws that require you to educate the children in your care regarding sex and/or sexual abuse? If so, what do those laws dictate? Where are you in the process of implementing the requirements?

_____

_____

_____

_____

_____

_____

_____

_____

➤ Would it be possible and reasonable to incorporate discussions about sexual protection and empowerment in your program? Be creative—it doesn't have to be part of the formal program. As an example, a softball league might host a special event inviting parents and kids to come and learn.

_____

_____

_____

_____

_____

_____

_____

_____

_____

➤ Do you currently create opportunities to talk with kids about respect for healthy boundaries? If so, how and when do you communicate about this topic?

_____

_____

_____

_____

_____

_____

_____

_____

➤ Can you think of any opportunities when you *could* talk with kids about respect for healthy boundaries that you're not leveraging today? If so, describe those opportunities.

_____

_____

_____

_____

_____

_____

_____

_____

➤ Do you currently create opportunities to talk with kids about sex and sexual abuse? If so, how and when do you communicate about this topic?

_____

_____

_____

_____

_____

_____

_____

_____

_____

➤ Can you think of any opportunities when you *could* talk with kids about sex and sexual abuse that you're not leveraging today? If so, describe those opportunities.

_____

_____

_____

_____

_____

_____

_____

_____

_____

➤ Do you currently create opportunities to talk with kids about having a heart for others? If so, how and when do you communicate about this topic?

_____

_____

_____

_____

_____

_____

_____

_____

_____

➤ Can you think of any opportunities when you *could* talk with kids about having a heart for others that you're not leveraging today? If so, describe those opportunities.

_____

_____

_____

_____

_____

_____

_____

_____

_____

➤ Do you currently create opportunities to talk with kids about recognizing healthy and unhealthy peer relationships? If so, how and when do you communicate about this topic?

_____

_____

_____

_____

_____

_____

_____

_____

➤ Can you think of any opportunities when you *could* talk with kids about recognizing healthy and unhealthy peer relationships that you're not leveraging today? If so, describe those opportunities.

_____

_____

_____

_____

_____

_____

_____

_____

_____

➤ Do you currently create opportunities to talk with kids about establishing healthy relationships with younger kids? If so, how and when do you communicate about this topic?

_____

_____

_____

_____

_____

_____

_____

_____

➤ Can you think of any opportunities when you *could* talk with kids about establishing healthy relationships with younger kids that you're not leveraging today? If so, describe those opportunities.

_____

_____

_____

_____

_____

_____

_____

_____

_____

Now that you've provided mandatory training for your staff and invited your parents to join your accountability team, it's time to empower the children in your care.[1, 2] Similar to adults, kids find it difficult to talk about sexual abuse. Educating and empowering children to experience a life free from sexual abuse is a multi-step process that unfolds as they mature and includes the five key components listed below. Depending on the type of programs your organization offers, you may or may not have the opportunity to engage children in all five components, but at a minimum, every organization should be empowering children with legal boundaries and the organizational boundaries you have established.

1. **Respect Healthy Boundaries:** Tell kids the legal boundaries and the organizational boundaries that stop grooming behavior. Empower them to expect the boundaries to be honored.
2. **Talk about Sex and Sexual Abuse:** Help kids embrace healthy sexuality and teach them the language of abuse, giving them permission to tell.
3. **Have a Heart for Others:** Develop in kids a compassionate heart for others who are hurting.
4. **Recognize Healthy Peer Relationships:** Equip them to create healthy relationships with peers.
5. **Establish Healthy Relationships with Younger Children:** Prepare them to manage their own behavior and boundaries with younger children and to recognize concerning behavior in others.

In the following pages, we will explore each of these components by age group.

RESPECT HEALTHY BOUNDARIES

The vast majority of the boundaries set forth in this program are designed to be managed by staff and parents collectively, especially during the preschool years. However, there are a number of boundaries that could be broken without an adult's knowledge. Therefore, kids need to be empowered by knowing what those boundaries are and instilling in them the expectation that they will be honored.

Boundaries that protect kids from sexual abuse in youth-serving organizations are no different than boundaries or safety rules in other areas of their lives. When a child says they're going to go outside and ride their bike, we naturally respond by saying, "Make sure you wear your helmet and stay out of the street." We don't go into gory detail about mangled bodies that would traumatize them, but we do make sure they know how to put their helmet on and where the sidewalk ends and the street begins (the boundary). In the same way, we don't have to provide kids details about sexually inappropriate acts when we're talking with them about boundaries.

It's a good idea to use the term "boundary" rather than "rules," even if it's a new term for kids. Help them create a visual picture in their mind by drawing a line in the sand or putting a rope down that represents a specific boundary. That line should never be crossed by anyone. This "picture" is more likely to stay with them and help them understand that these are black and white boundaries, which is important because child molesters are masters of deceit and try to get kids to see everything in shades of gray, constantly pushing the child's limits.

Empowering kids to hold others accountable for honoring these boundaries is as easy as 1–2–3!

1. Tell kids the boundaries
2. Tell kids to remind anyone who forgets a boundary
3. Tell kids to tell their parents *and* another staff member when someone forgets

Let the kids know they have two options for telling: they can verbally tell someone right away or they can communicate it on the Assessment and Communication Form by checking the type of boundary that was broken or coloring in the red light on the Stop Light Assessment.

BOUNDARIES COMMON TO ALL AGE GROUPS

Below are five common boundaries that kids of all ages need to be told upon joining your program. They should be shared with the kids and with the parents either as part of a pre-registration process or on their first day.

1. You should never be *left* alone with an adult or older child.

   Note: By adding the word "left" to the sentence, we shift responsibility from the child to the organization's leaders.

2. We don't keep secrets here.
3. No one is allowed to take photographs of you without your parents there.
4. We don't have program activities where we wear masks or blindfolds or use anything to tie someone up.
5. We keep our hands to ourselves and where they can be seen—no hitting, tickle games, sitting on laps, hugs, kisses, or touching private parts (yours or anyone else's).

PRESCHOOL-AGE CHILDREN (THREE TO FIVE YEARS)

There are a limited number of additional boundaries that preschool-age children need to know. Provide a copy of the boundaries to the parents upon registering and ask that they review them with their child before the next time they come back. Ask the parents to sign-off that they have done so. Parents and staff members can then reinforce these and the five common boundaries as opportunities arise.

- Observable Bathroom Monitoring
- No Pulling Children Out of their Regularly Scheduled Program
- No Babysitting
- No Tutoring
- No Visits to Personal Residences
- No Birthday Parties
- No Family Gatherings
- Separate Age Groups
- No Gifts to Children
- No Entering Children's Rooms at Night
- Limit Medical Exams/Treatment by Staff Members

SCHOOL-AGE CHILDREN (SIX TO TWELVE YEARS)

As children get older and become more independent, there are a few additional boundaries that they need to know in order to hold staff accountable. Note that these are in addition to the five common boundaries and the boundaries for preschool-age children.

- No Unauthorized People on the Premises
- No "Chatting" with People on the Computer or Accessing Unauthorized Sites
- No Before or After Program Help
- Approved and Off-Limits Locations

- No Family Members Working Together
- Multiple Adults during Movies and Lights-Out Activities
- Limit Physical Touching: No assisted instruction that includes body-to-body touching (batting, musical instruments, etc.)
- No Lies, Threats, Coercion, or Violence
- No Showering With or Changing Clothes in Front of Staff (or them in front of you)
- Written Authorization for Off-Site Locations
- Control Transportation to Off-Site Locations
- Additional Boundaries for Out-of-Town Travel
- No Sleepovers
- Avoid Inadvertent Creation of Authority

As children approach their teen years, their interest in developing relationships independent of their parents will increase. Electronic communication methods allow these relationships to flourish, making it much more difficult for parents to monitor, thus increasing the risk of inappropriate relationships forming.

These additional electronic communication boundaries should be introduced to children as soon as they are provided access to these technologies but no later than the age of eleven. By age eleven, even if they don't have their own accounts, they will be exposed to these technologies through friends.

- No Sharing Phone Numbers
- No Sharing of E-mail Addresses or Screen Names
- No Becoming Friends on Facebook or Following on Twitter
- No Connections on Multimedia Sharing Sites
- No Connections on Video Chat Applications

TEENAGERS (THIRTEEN TO EIGHTEEN YEARS)

We might think by age thirteen, our kids are old enough, strong enough, and smart enough to not fall prey to a child molester, but it can actually be one of the most vulnerable time periods. According to a US Department of Justice study, a female's year of greatest risk is age fourteen.[3] According to Lanning and Dietz, there are three factors that make older children vulnerable. They say, "Post-pubescent adolescent children are obviously potential targets of a much larger and more diverse population of offenders than are younger, prepubescent children. First, many more adults are aroused by attractive adolescents with secondary sex characteristics than by pre-pubescent children. Second, adolescents more often communicate their sexuality through clothes, makeup, actions, and words than do pre-pubescent children. Third, adolescents spend more time away from their parents and have greater freedom than younger children."[4]

As children's bodies start to change and they become young adults, they change the way they look at themselves and others. They begin to incorporate their relationships with others as a key component of their self-image and self-worth. They're striving to be grown-up and to be respected as mature independent young adults. They're looking for validation, and since it's also a time when they naturally begin pulling away from their parents, they may not look for or want that validation from home. According to Lanning and Dietz, this is when child molesters are more likely to use "ease of sexual arousal, rebelliousness, and curiosity to manipulate the children into sex."[5]

This dynamic provides a very real opportunity for child molesters to step in and be the person who engages teens in adult conversation, who respects their opinions, who treats them as peers, who uses deception to pit them against their parents. Child molesters use these techniques to lure teens into a trusting, intimate emotional relationship—often the most intimate relationship these children currently have in their lives. Then the child molester exploits that relationship to bring them into a new level of intimacy: sexual intimacy.

Since this new sexual relationship is based on the seemingly peer-to-peer adult relationship that was previously established, it's not difficult for the child molester to convince the teen that it's a consensual relationship, especially if the perpetrator is the opposite sex. We frequently see this when school teachers or other authority figures seduce middle school or high school students, often professing a never-ending love for them. It's so important that you don't let your guard down yet and that you continue to talk with teenagers about the real possibility of this type of seduction.

It's the perfect time to introduce the remaining boundaries:

- Legal boundaries prohibiting vaginal or anal intercourse, oral copulation, vaginal penetration with an object, sodomy, masturbation in the presence of a child, voyeurism, exhibitionism, and sexual exploitation for financial gain.
- No unprofessional behavior
- No sexual discussion, no pornography, sexually explicit material, or sexting
- No sharing alcohol, prescription drugs, or street drugs
- No dating

TALK ABOUT SEX AND SEXUAL ABUSE

There are three main objectives in talking with kids about sex and sexual abuse:

- Let kids know it's an acceptable topic of conversation and nothing to be ashamed of
- Teach kids the language of abuse and show them how to talk about it
- Give kids permission to tell

It's not unusual for adults to be uncomfortable talking with children about sex and even more so about sexual abuse. Unfortunately, that discomfort and resulting avoidance of the topic is exactly what child molesters count on and exploit. The longer you wait to start these conversations with kids, the more uncomfortable it becomes and the higher the risk of abuse. In addition, children can sense your discomfort and in the unfortunate event that their sexual boundaries are crossed, they're not likely to see you as a safe adult they can tell.

Since most adults feel uncomfortable talking to kids about sex and sexual abuse, it's not unusual for a child molester to be the only one who *is* talking to them about it and you can bet they're teaching them or more likely threatening them to keep it a secret!

Your organization has the opportunity to lay the foundation for healthy sexual relationships while contrasting inappropriate behaviors.

> Sometimes, child molesters are the only ones talking with kids about sex and sexual abuse.

In the process, you'll teach parents how to be comfortable doing the same. Depending on your program, you may (1) only have brief opportunities to share information or respond to a situation or a child's question, (2) have the opportunity to incorporate this crucial information into your program as is the case with schools and faith organizations, or (3) fall in between and be able to create specific opportunities to disseminate information and encourage communication. In any case, it's important for designated staff members (nurses, counselors, etc.) to increase their knowledge and level of comfort so children know they can come to you. As an organization, your increased knowledge will also allow you to have a variety of tools and resources available for your students and families if a problem should arise.

Some states have passed a law that requires child sexual abuse prevention training for students and teachers. Most have done this by adopting Erin's Law which states, "With respect to the renewal of a Standard Teaching Certificate, provides that continuing professional development activities may include participating in or presenting at in-service training programs on sexual abuse and assault awareness and prevention. It also provides that the Comprehensive Health Education Program requires age-appropriate sexual abuse and assault awareness and prevention education in grades pre-kindergarten through 12 along with training school staff on the prevention of sexual abuse. Effective immediately." Eighteen states have passed the law as of June 2014, nineteen more states are introducing Erin's Law 2014–2015. You can find an updated list of states that have passed Erin's Law along with the wording of the individual state codes at www.erinslaw.org/results. It is important for school districts to know if your state law requires you to provide education to teachers and students.

We live in the technology age and sexual predators have easy access to children through the internet. As a matter of fact, approximately 1 in 7 youth receive unwanted sexual solicitations on the internet.[6] Therefore, it is essential for staff, parents, and children to understand internet safety guidelines as well.

There are so many great resources available that I will not attempt to recreate the wheel, but instead, use this section as an opportunity to provide a list of resources and tools that will allow you to be successful in meeting your organization's goals for effectively empowering children and their families.

PRESCHOOL-AGE CHILDREN (THREE TO FIVE YEARS)

Children's Books and Videos

You should add children's books regarding sexual abuse to your library. We encourage you to not only have them available for group reading time but also to schedule a fun event where parents can come with their children and enjoy a book reading and refreshments. This is a great way to open the lines of communication between parents, kids, and staff members. In a child-friendly way, these books discuss topics such as (1) anatomically correct names for body parts, (2) body safety, (3) inappropriate touch and that it's not okay, (4) kids' right to say no, (5) secrets, and (6) the importance of telling until someone helps you. Here are some resources I recommend you add to your library:

Books

- *Those Are My Private Parts* by Diane Hansen (also available in Spanish)
- *My Body Belongs to Me* by Jill Starishevsky
- *The Birthday Suit* by Kristina Muldoon (also available in Spanish)
- *The Right Touch: A Read-Aloud Story to Help Prevent Child Sexual Abuse* by Sandy Kleven
- *No Trespassing This Is MY Body* by Pattie Fitzgerald
- *I Said NO!* by Kimberly King
- *The Swimsuit Lesson* by Jon Holsten
- *Some Parts Are Not for Sharing* by Julie Federico (also available in Spanish)
- *My Body Is Private* by Linda Walvoord Girard
- *Fred the Fox Shouts NO* by Tatiana Y. Kisil Matthews
- *Sara Sue Learns to Yell and Tell* by Debi Pearl
- *No Secrets Between Us* by Rose Morrisroe
- *My Body Is Special and Belongs to Me* by Sally Berenzweig

Videos

- *My Body Belongs to Me* by Jill Starishevsky
- https://www.youtube.com/watch?v=a-5mdt9YN6I
- *My Body Belongs to Me* by Jill Starishevsky (Spanish version)
- https://www.youtube.com/watch?v=KZ4cpmyoXbU

Adult's Books

Adults should expand their own knowledge on normal sexual development and age-appropriate behavior as well as on discerning inappropriate or concerning behavior in children and adults. Books for adults should include reference books on sex and on sexual abuse and are great for staff members as well as parents to expand their knowledge. Here are some that I would recommend you read: the first one I consider required reading for every adult:

- *The Socially Skilled Child Molester: Differentiating the Guilty from the Falsely Accused* by Carla van Dam, PhD
- *Understanding Children's Sexual Behavior: What's Natural and Healthy* by Toni Cavanagh Johnson, PhD
- *Identifying Child Molesters: Preventing Child Sexual Abuse by Recognizing the Patterns of Offenders* by Carla van Dam, PhD
- *It's Perfectly Normal* by Robie H. Harris
- *It's So Amazing!* by Robie H. Harris
- *How and When to Tell Your Kids About Sex* by Stan and Brenna Jones (Christian Based)
- *Off Limits: A Parent's Guide to Keeping Kids Safe from Sexual Abuse* by Sandy K. Wurtele, PhD and Feather Berkhower, MSW
- *A Risk Reduction Workbook for Parents and Service Providers* by Nora Baladerian
- *Predators and Child Molesters* by Robin Sax

- *It Happens Every Day* by Robin Sax
- *Protecting the Gift: Keeping Children and Teenagers Safe (and Parents Sane)* by Gavin de Becker
- *Safe Kids, Smart Parents* by Rebecca Bailey

Comprehensive Educational Programs

Comprehensive programs regarding child sexual abuse are available and can be fully incorporated into your existing programs. Here are a couple of programs to consider for preschool-age children:

- Talking About Touching: Personal Safety for Pre/K-Grade 3 by Committee for Children
  http://www.cfchildren.org/talking-about-touching.aspx
- Child Lures Prevention (Grades PreK-2)
  http://www.childluresprevention.com/
- Be Safe At Last (Grades K-6)
  https://www.besafeatlast.com/

Broader Empowerment Programs

In addition to programs that are solely designed to address sexual development and/or sexual abuse, there are programs that offer a wider focus on empowering children to be safe and on opening lines of communication on a variety of difficult social topics. Here is one program to consider for preschool-age children:

- New Jersey Child Assault Prevention (Early Childhood edition)
  http://njcap.org/preschool/

SCHOOL-AGE CHILDREN (SIX TO TWELVE YEARS)

As children get older and they can comprehend a broader and deeper level of information, I encourage you to continue providing age appropriate resources.

Children's Books

The books about sex that I recommended earlier can continue to be used, expanding the discussion to an age-appropriate level. There are a limited number of books about child sexual abuse, written specifically for older school-age children, currently on the market. So I encourage you to continue to use the ones in the preschool-age section as long as you can because kids who are being sexually abused can still relate to them. One of the creative ways to continue to reach older children with these books without resistance is to create opportunities where older children read the books to younger children—with adult supervision, of course! That said, there is one book for older children that I highly recommend:

- *Some Secrets Should Never Be Kept* by Jayneen Sanders

Adult's Books

The adult books I mentioned in the preschool-age section will continue to provide great value for working with school-age children. There are a couple of additional resources that I recommend you consider as well:

- Dallas Children's Advocacy Center—Parent/Child Curriculum Package (Ages 8–14) http://trainingcenter.net/product/parent-child-curriculum-package
- The Sex Ed Store provides a variety of books and programs to support sex education discussions with school-age children. http://www.sexedstore.com/purchase-resources

Comprehensive Educational Programs

The comprehensive programs that we mentioned in the preschool-age section will continue to work for younger school-age children, but we recommend that you transition over to the following programs in the later years:

- *Speak Up Be Safe* by Childhelp (Grades 1–6) http://www.childhelp.org/programs/entry/speak-up-be-safe/
- Advocates for Youth Website – Provides Parents and Professionals with Growth and Development as well as Sex Education Materials applicable to kids K-12 and beyond http://advocatesforyouth.org/topics-issues/growth-and-development?task=view
- Child Lures Prevention (Grades 3–4 and 5–6) http://www.childluresprevention.com/
- Be Safe At Last (Grades 7–12) https://www.besafeatlast.com/

Broader Empowerment Programs

If you elected to use the general empowerment program that I recommended for preschool-age children, it should be transitioned over to their program for older children and here are a couple of additional programs to consider:

- New Jersey Child Assault Prevention (Elementary Level edition) http://njcap.org/elementary/
- radKids http://www.radkids.org/
- Kids on the Block http://www.kotb.com/

Internet Safety Programs

- Netsmartz – Internet education for parents, educators, teens, tweens and kids
http://www.netsmartz.org/Parents
- Netsmartz – Scouting
http://www.netsmartz.org/scouting
- Stay Safe Online
http://www.staysafeonline.org/
- PBS Kids Internet Academy
http://pbskids.org/webonauts/about/
- Get Net Wise
http://kids.getnetwise.org/
- Common Sense Media
https://www.commonsensemedia.org/blog/social-networking-tips
- FBI – Parents Guide to Internet Safety
http://www.fbi.gov/stats-services/publications/parent-guide/parent-guide
- Enough is Enough – Internet Safety 101
http://www.internetsafety101.org/

TEENAGERS (THIRTEEN TO SEVENTEEN YEARS)

As the children in your care reach their mid-teens and are spending more and more time away from their parents, we need to continue to remind them of the danger of abuse by adults in their inner circle, but now we also need to expand their skills in protecting themselves from sexual assault by strangers.

Teenager's Books/Resources

- *The Gift of Freedom: A Stronger Safer You* by Stuart Haskins
- *Gift of Fear: Survival Signals That Protect us from Violence* by Gavin de Becker

- *A Risk Reduction Workbook for People with Developmental Disabilities* by Nora Baladerian
- Just Tell Street Teams
  http://www.justtell.org/

Adult's Books/Programs

- Teens, Sex and Health: A Comprehensive Approach to Sexual Education (DVD)
  http://www.amazon.com/TEENS-SEX-HEALTH-Comprehensive-Education/dp/B00155X58S
- The Sex Ed Store provides a variety of books and programs to support sex education discussions with teens.
  http://www.sexedstore.com/purchase-resources

In addition to the new resources listed above, many of the adult books we mentioned in the preschool-age section will continue to provide great value for adults working with teenagers. In addition, adults should read the books listed for teenagers above so they can discuss and reinforce key concepts.

Comprehensive Educational Programs

Some of these program names may sound familiar, but they offer distinct programs for different grade levels so I recommend that you transition over to the age-appropriate resources in the later years:

- The Sex Ed Store provides a variety of books and programs to support sex education discussions with school-age children as well as teens.
  http://www.sexedstore.com/purchase-resources
- Advocates for Youth Web site – Provides Parent and Professionals with Growth and Development and Sex Education Materials applicable to kids K-12 and beyond

http://advocatesforyouth.org/topics-issues/growth-and-development?task=view
- Child Lures Prevention (Grades 7–12)
http://www.childluresprevention.com/
- Be Safe At Last (Grades 7–12)
https://www.besafeatlast.com/

Broader Empowerment Programs

If you are using the materials from New Jersey Child Assault Prevention, you will need to transition over to their teen program in these later years:

- New Jersey Child Assault Prevention – (Teen edition)
http://njcap.org/teen/

Internet Safety Programs

The programs identified in the previous age group have resources that continue to apply to teenagers.

Survivor Stories/Panels

One of the most powerful ways to reach teenagers regarding this topic is to have one or more sexual abuse survivors come and tell their stories in an interactive format, allowing the teens to ask questions. I recommend that you separate the girls and boys and preferably have a survivor of the same sex speak to them. The survivors should use their stories to bring specific points to life while being flexible and letting the discussion flow naturally. Sexual abuse is an uncomfortable discussion but ask the teens to try and stay engaged so they hear all the information in case they or a friend needs it.

You can contact TAALK (www.taalk.org), RAINN (https://www.rainn.org/get-involved/speakers-bureau), or other local child sexual abuse advocacy groups to see if there is a local speaker available to come and talk with your teens or there may be survivors in your organization who are comfortable sharing their story. In any case, there are key points that are important to bring up during the discussion:

- Sexual abuse is any sexual act between an adult and a minor *or* between two minors when one exerts power over the other. Power can include forcing, threatening, bribing, coercing, or persuading. It's a crime.
- Sexual abuse can be contact sexual abuse, visual sexual abuse, and verbal sexual abuse. Give examples of each.
- Sexual abuse happens to 1 in 4 girls and 1 in 6 boys before they turn 18.[7, 8]

Let's see what that might look like in a group this size. Count off and have every fourth girl and every sixth boy stand up. The right people might not be the ones standing, but you can see if you have been abused, you're certainly not alone. As a matter of fact, it's likely some of your closest friends have also been abused.

- o 35–45 percent of abuse happens at the hands of a family member[9, 10]
- o 55–60 percent of abuse is perpetrated by acquaintances that the child knows well such as teachers, coaches, and faith leaders.[11, 12]
- o Juvenile offenders perpetrate 30–40 percent of abuse against minors.[13, 14]
- o Male offenders are responsible for about 90 percent of all abuse against children.[15, 16]
- o But in the case of male victims, females are the perpetrators around 40 percent of the time.[17, 18]
- o Biological mothers are the perpetrators in 8 percent of all substantiated sexual abuse cases.[19]

- Kids who are abused often feel scared, angry, depressed, and ashamed. If they've been abused by someone that was supposed to protect them like a parent or authority figure, they may feel betrayed and abandoned too. This is normal but *help is available and healing is possible.*
- More often than not, survivors feel it was somehow their fault, but *it's never the child's fault.*
- Sexual abuse can have a big impact:

    o   30 percent had post-traumatic stress disorder[20]
    o   Suicide attempts are more than twice as likely[21]
    o   More than one-third of boys experienced substance abuse at some time in their lives[22]
    o   Almost one-third of girls experienced lifetime substance abuse or dependence[23]
    o   Young girls are more likely to develop eating disorders[24, 25]
    o   Boys and girls often act out sexually with 60 percent of teen pregnancies preceded by sexual abuse[26, 27, 28, 29]
    o   47 percent of boys engaged in delinquent acts joined by almost 20 percent of girls[30]
    o   Nearly 60 percent of incarcerated female adolescents were sexually abused[31]
    o   Sexual abuse also has a direct impact on adult health including stress related disorders, heart disease, liver disease, and shorter life expectancies[32, 33]
    o   40 percent increased risk of marrying an alcoholic[34]
    o   40-50 percent increased risk of marital problems[35]

These consequences can be avoided or at least greatly minimized if you get help early. If you've been abused, *it's so important for you to tell someone now and get help.*

- Now think of all the people who were standing up at the beginning—there are survivors of sexual abuse all around you: peers, adults, and younger children. People aren't born depressed, angry, or addicted to drugs, alcohol, or sex and they certainly aren't born to self-mutilate. Something happened. If you know people who are acting out in these ways, tell them you can see they're hurting and ask if they want to talk about it. If a friend tells you they've been abused, it won't help them if you keep their secret, *help them get help.*

- *The risk isn't over yet.* Teenagers are particularly vulnerable to authority figures that are in a position to emotionally or spiritually manipulate you (teachers, faith leaders, coaches, etc.). At this age, it's also not unusual for an abuser to lure you into a "relationship" with them, treating you like an adult and telling you they love you. It's still a crime for an adult to have any sexual relations with a minor, even if they get you to believe it's consensual.
- Risky behaviors to look for:

  o Makes you or others feel uncomfortable by lack of respect for boundaries
  o Engages in excessive physical contact
  o Spends more time with kids than adults his/her own age
  o Spends excessive time e-mailing and texting kids
  o Is unusually aware of kid's trends, terminology, computer games, and music
  o Uses drugs or alcohol excessively or exhibits signs of depression or violent behavior
  o Exploits actual/implied authority or idolatry
  o Overly interested in the sexuality or developing body of pre-teens and teens
  o Arranges to spend uninterrupted time with kids
  o Showers kids with gifts, treats, special outings
  o Let's kids break the rules or get away with inappropriate behavior

- o   Creates a "special" relationship that only you share
- o   Pits you against other trusted adults (parents, teachers, youth leaders)
- o   Offers kids drugs or alcohol
- o   Offers to "teach" kids about sex—what they're not learning at home
- o   Asks kids to keep secrets
- o   Insists on bathing with or washing children who are old enough to do it themselves
- o   Walks in on children when they are dressing
- o   Creates an intimate emotional relationship with kids
- o   Significantly favors one child over another or one age range over another
- o   Watches pornography or has sex in front of kids
- o   Insists on private behind closed doors time with kids
- o   Administers regular enemas or medical checks
- o   Goes into kid's bedroom at night or insists on kids sleeping in their bed

Hearing someone talk comfortably about their story of childhood sexual abuse can put teens at ease. If there are survivors in the group, it may help them connect the dots for the first time and realize that what happened to them was abuse. It also helps them realize they are not alone and models for them how to talk about it, increasing the odds that they will tell. For the rest of the group, hearing the story along with these key points will significantly increase their sensitivity to abuse survivors and in turn their ability to help a friend.

Ask them to take a minute of silence and identify five trusted adults in their lives that they could talk to if they really needed help.

Depending on how much time you have, you can have one survivor tell their story or create a panel by using two or three survivors. Typically, we start by telling our stories and then open it up to questions. Then we walk through the handout which covers the points above, stopping regularly to see if the information raises any questions or concerns they want to discuss. I have found that delivering this information in a relaxed, interactive discussion format makes teenagers feel much more comfortable than using a presentation format.

It's important that you provide this information to the kids as a handout because many survivors who need it most may have completely dissociated and checked out during the discussion. It's also important that you tell kids where they can get help whether through your organization or calling a child abuse hotline. If you're going to present a specific opportunity to talk with someone through your organization, it should be an opportunity that is ongoing or at least over a period of days or weeks to ensure confidentiality. As an example, you wouldn't want to tell them to come to the office during lunch that day, the kids will all be looking to see who's missing at lunch.

Offering Survivor Stories for teens is a powerful way to draw out survivors. We have seen as much as 10 percent disclosure rate after these sessions. Showing teens what it looks like to talk about it and giving them permission to do so will allow them to get help at an early age and could potentially change the course of their lives.

HAVE A HEART FOR OTHERS

One of the key components to resolving the child sexual abuse pandemic is bringing help and healing to survivors as soon as possible before patterns of emotional isolation, addictions, and self-sabotage set in. Since kids spend so much time with other kids, their peers can play an important role in noticing and responding to their pain and helping them get help sooner.

You can teach children to see their peers through the lens of compassion, slow down long enough to notice their pain, create a safe place for them to tell, and know what steps to take if someone does disclose sexual abuse. You can begin to build the foundation for this type of peer-to-peer support from a very early age.

PRESCHOOL-AGE CHILDREN (THREE TO FIVE YEARS)

As soon as children begin to play with siblings and peers, you can start to instill these three very simple concepts as follows:

- When kids are misbehaving, it's usually because they've been hurt (physically or emotionally) or they're not getting what they need to make them feel safe and comfortable.
- When kids are misbehaving, we should try to understand what they're feeling and why they're feeling that way.
- When kids are misbehaving, we should ask if they want to talk about it and what we can do to help them feel better.

These concepts will most likely play out without a lot of depth in the preschool years. However, they lay the foundation for children to experience others' negative behaviors without taking it personally. Further, these concepts teach children how to respond compassionately to others' negative behaviors which will help to diffuse the intensity of those emotions rather than responding with similarly intense emotions which are likely to fuel the fire.

SCHOOL-AGE CHILDREN (SIX TO TWELVE YEARS)

As children get older, you can help them understand that when kids are being hurt by other people, they:

- Are often afraid that it will happen again
- Don't know how to make it stop
- Are sad and sometimes feel very alone
- Take their anger and frustration out on other people

Remind them of the three simple concepts you taught them in the preschool-age years and add this additional concept:

- When kids are misbehaving, it may be their way of calling out for help. If you are concerned about them, talk to a trusted adult and ask them to help.

As kids mature, the resulting conversations with other kids will likely have more depth. Be sure kids know who they can talk to if they're concerned about a friend, discuss the options with them (teacher, parent, faith leader, etc.) Once again, you're laying the foundation for compassionate relationships throughout these kid's lives—in school, in business, in marriage, and as parents.

TEENAGERS (THIRTEEN TO SEVENTEEN YEARS)

By the time survivors reach their teens, their negative behavior usually begins to turn inward. They may still lash out at others, but they also begin to show self-harming behaviors—sometimes because they think they deserve it and sometimes in an effort to mask the pain or become invisible. These behaviors can include:

- Excessive use of drugs and alcohol
- Eating disorders: anorexia, bulimia, binge eating, or overeating
- Sexual promiscuity
- High-risk behavior such as unprotected sex, speeding, driving under the influence, dangerous stunts, etc.
- Self-mutilation such as cutting, pinching, or burning
- Suicide attempts

As teens become more aware, they will likely begin to see these behaviors not only in peers but also in adults around them. Remind them of the four simple concepts you taught them in the school-age years and add this additional concept:

- People are not born addicts, angry, or depressed. What happened to make them act this way?

If we can teach kids to embrace this idea and hold it close to their hearts, they can be instrumental in leading other kids, teens, and even adults to get help

> People are not born addicts, angry, or depressed. What happened to make them act this way?

and free themselves from the pain of their past. Maybe we could even get adults to embrace this idea!

RECOGNIZE HEALTHY PEER RELATIONSHIPS

We are all sexual beings, and it is important that we teach kids to embrace their sexuality and not be ashamed of it. However, it is also important for us to teach kids healthy sexual boundaries. Sexual boundaries are a crucial factor in establishing respect for other people's choices relating to sex as well as for minimizing sexual behavior in public that could make children a target for child molesters on the prowl.

It's not unusual for children who are being sexually abused at home to act out sexually with their peers. It's what they have grown up to understand as normal. As an example, if a young boy has grown up being forced to have oral sex on his father in order to get a meal, it would not be unusual for that same boy to insist that his friend have oral sex on him if he wants him to share his cookies at lunchtime. This example highlights the need for organizations to understand, instill, and enforce healthy sexual boundaries. By doing so, your organization can create a safe environment for all kids in your care and help kids who are being sexually abused recognize if their boundaries are being violated elsewhere.

PRESCHOOL-AGE CHILDREN (THREE TO FIVE YEARS)

We provided an extensive list of resources about sexual development in the "Talking about Sex and Sexual Abuse" section above but the most valuable resource for understanding natural and healthy sexual behaviors in kids is:

- *Understanding Children's Sexual Behavior: What's Natural and Healthy* by Toni Cavanagh Johnson, PhD. http://www.tcavjohn.com/

This pamphlet includes a simple chart that lists a variety of sexual behaviors indicating when that behavior would be considered natural and healthy, when it would be of concern and when it would be advisable to seek professional help. Since natural and healthy sexual behaviors change as children grow, the author has included two separate charts—one for preschool-age children and one for K-Grade 4.

If you come across a situation where a child is clearly exhibiting sexual behavior problems, there are a couple of more resources by the same author that would be valuable to recommend to the parents and/or professionals working with that child as follows:

- *Helping Children with Sexual Behavior Problems: A Guidebook for Professionals and Caregivers* by Toni Cavanagh Johnson, PhD. http://www.tcavjohn.com/
- *Space Invaders: A Game About Boundaries* by Toni Cavanagh Johnson, PhD. http://www.tcavjohn.com/

SCHOOL-AGE CHILDREN (SIX TO TWELVE YEARS)

The information provided in the section above for preschool-age children will provide a solid foundation for school-age children as well.

TEENAGERS (THIRTEEN TO EIGHTEEN YEARS)

As children move into their teens and on to become young adults, the topic of sexual boundaries between peers changes dramatically. Since teens spend so much time without adult supervision, at least in the later years, there is a much higher risk of forcible sexual relations and rape. These violations can happen within an existing relationship, at the hands of a stranger, or with someone they thought was a friend.

The process of educating teens to protect their sexual boundaries with peers is multifaceted and should include instilling trust in their intuition, understanding safe and risky environments, deciding ahead of time what their boundaries are, preparing to be fearless and take swift action, and having the courage to make conscious choices about who they consider to be safe people.

In addition to teens learning to protect themselves within their newfound independence, the teenage years are also a time to learn the risks associated with sexual choices. There are commonly discussed risks such as pregnancy and sexually transmitted diseases which are covered to some extent in health education classes and we have also listed a variety of resources for additional information on these topics throughout this section. It is important that teens understand that there are now multiple sexually transmitted diseases that have no known cure (not just AIDS).

Some sexual behavior may also have significant legal repercussions which are less commonly discussed. As a matter of fact, depending on your state's laws and the specific circumstances, if a teenager innocently texts a naked picture of themselves to their boyfriend or girlfriend (sexting), they could end up

> The stakes are high and we cannot afford to be vague about our expectations of teens.

being charged with distribution of pornography and be listed as a registered sex offender for life.

The stakes are high and we cannot afford to be vague about our expectations of teens. According to Robert Longo, it is important that we communicate the following key points to teenagers:[36]

- Understand the health risks
- Know the law
- Rely on credible sources for information
- Be cautious

Understand the Health Risks: Sexual activity has health risks including pregnancy and sexually transmitted diseases and these risks need to be clearly communicated to teens. I will not go into detail here as this information is typically well covered in our public school system as part of the health curriculum. However, there is a recommendation for a comprehensive sex education program below in the Adult Books/DVD section, if you need it.

Know the Law: Being sexual is risky business whether it's sexualized behavior with a younger child (covered in the next section), as a prank with peers or even as part of a caring intimate relationship. It's crucial that teens understand the laws in their state and how those laws are applied.

Here are a few examples of how Age of Consent laws might apply to sexual relationships between a boyfriend and girlfriend:

- The age of consent differs by state. If you are over the age of consent and engage in sex with your boyfriend or girlfriend who is under the age of consent, it's a crime. This is so even if it was a consensual interaction—someone under the age of consent cannot legally agree to have sex.
- If both of you are over the age of consent but one of you is still under the age of 18, the minor's parent may report

the incident and ask law enforcement to press charges for statutory rape.

• It is also important to understand the definition of consent. Even if both you and your boyfriend or girlfriend are over 18, if one of you is intoxicated or mentally retarded, you could be charged with a sex crime.

As we look at sexual behaviors among friends, we find that some teens are lured into pranks that may seem fun or funny at the time but, in fact, are against the law. A behavior called teabagging is an example of just such a prank. Teabagging is when a boy dips his testicles in and out of another person's mouth as you would a teabag in a cup of hot water. Even a modified version of this prank where a boy dragged his testicles across another boy's face while he was sleeping ended in criminal charges, according to Longo. Sex is no laughing matter and teens need to approach any type of sexualized behavior with respect and caution—sexual behavior could have irreversible consequences on the rest of their lives!

Because laws differ by state and change regularly, I cannot possibly address specifics here. I understand that you may not be able to incorporate this information into your formal programs for a variety of reasons, but if you have the ability to host an annual event where teenagers and their parents can learn from someone in your community who is well versed in your state laws, it would be a gift for the teenagers in your care. We owe it to our teenagers to provide them with credible sources of information so they can make knowledgeable decisions.

Rely on Credible Sources for Information: Sex is a topic that most adults are uncomfortable talking about which often leaves teens turning to their peers for information. Unfortunately, peers are probably the worst source of information as it is highly likely they're in a similar situation, lacking experience and credible resources. At the same time as our teenagers are starving for information, the media is bombarding them with unrealistic images of sexuality and relationships. This is especially true of pornography and teens don't realize that what is being depicted in pornographic material does not reflect real life. The participants are people who are being paid to have sex and act out fantasies. It is not the behavior that is expected in healthy loving relationships. If we aren't able to have this frank conversation with our teens, then how will they know?

We should let teens know that they need to access credible sources of information before they decide to engage in any type of sexual behavior. It would be helpful if your organization can either provide direct access to this information or at least provide a resource and referral list so our teens aren't left to figure this out on their own.

Be Cautious: As a precaution, Longo recommends that we tell teens:

- Don't be sexual under the age of 16 or the age of consent, whichever is higher.
- Don't be sexual with anyone else who is under the age of 16 or the age of consent, whichever is higher.
- Don't be sexual with anyone who is more than 2 years younger or 2 years older than you until you are both over 18.
- Don't engage in any sexual behavior as a joke.

Below are a few resources that can help to prepare teenagers for what lies ahead:

Teenager's Books

- *May I Kiss You?: A Candid Look at Dating, Communication, Respect, and Sexual Assault Awareness* by Mike Domitrz
- *The Gift of Freedom: A Stronger Safer You* by Stuart Haskins

- *Gift of Fear: Survival Signals That Protect us from Violence* by Gavin De Becker
- *Safe People: How to Find Relationships That Are Good For You and Avoid Those That Aren't* by Dr. Henry Cloud and Dr. John Townsend (Christian Based)
- *The Rules of Sex: For Those Who Have Never Been Told* by Nora Baladerian (for people with disabilities)

Adult Books/DVDs

- *Teens, Sex and Health: A Comprehensive Approach to Sexual Education* (DVD). http://www.amazon.com/TEENS-SEX-HEALTH-Comprehensive-Education/dp/B00155X58S

I highly recommend that in addition to viewing this DVD set, you read the books I listed for teens above. This will allow you to open up discussion about the key concepts in the materials and use the information to reinforce the ideas as opportunities arise.

Comprehensive Programs

There are also a couple of interactive courses that your organization can use in more of a classroom style approach as follows:

- Help! My Teen is Dating: Real Solutions to Tough Conversations http://www.datesafeproject.org/help-my-teen-is-dating/
- Save the Date http://heroesandhealthyfamilies.org/programs.html

ESTABLISH HEALTHY RELATIONSHIPS WITH YOUNGER CHILDREN

30–40 percent of abuse happens at the hands of older or larger children.[37, 38] The information that we've provided thus far in the program regarding the risks and prevention strategies around child-to-child sexual abuse has been from the vantage point of the child who is potentially the victim. On the flip-side of that coin however is a child who is the abuser. I would be remiss if I didn't include information on how to proactively create opportunities to talk with children, especially older children about recognizing and managing their own sexual behaviors and when and where to go for help, if needed.

PRESCHOOL-AGE CHILDREN (THREE TO FIVE YEARS)

You may think that talking with preschool-age children about recognizing and managing their own sexual behavior is absurd because of their young age. However, this is a time when you begin to lay the foundation for future more in-depth conversations with school-age children and teenagers.

At this stage, discussions around children's own behavior can be accomplished in two ways:

First, when you are discussing general boundaries your organization has established, especially boundaries around physical touching, simply expand your conversations to include a statement such as "The boundaries apply to everyone, even other children, as a matter of fact, even you."

Secondarily, on an as needed basis, you can use the information in Cavanagh Johnson's pamphlet below to guide children to understand boundaries for their own sexual behavior (i.e., masturbation in public versus in private, exploration with other children, etc.)

- *Understanding Children's Sexual Behavior: What's Natural and Healthy* by Toni Cavanagh Johnson, PhD. http://www.tcavjohn.com/

SCHOOL-AGE CHILDREN (SIX TO TWELVE YEARS)

As children move into their school-age years, continue to emphasize that they should expect the boundaries established by your organization to be respected, especially those around physical touching. Expand the conversation to let them know that as they get older, other younger children will look up to them as role models. Therefore, it is important for them to respect the boundaries of younger children, especially when it comes to respecting their right to body privacy.

You can refer back to some of the children's books that you elected to share from the Talk about Sex and Sexual Abuse topic discussed earlier in this chapter and use specific examples. As a matter of fact, having older children read the books to the younger children is an excellent way to empower the younger children and establish child-to-child boundary expectations for the older children.

On an as needed basis, you can use the information in Cavanagh Johnson's pamphlet to guide children to understand boundaries for their own sexual behavior, especially as it relates to respecting other children's right to body privacy (i.e., exploration with other children).

- *Understanding Children's Sexual Behavior: What's Natural and Healthy* by Toni Cavanagh Johnson, PhD. http://www.tcavjohn.com/

At this stage, it's also important to let children know that sometimes children have a difficult time respecting other kid's boundaries and that if they find this to be a struggle for them, they should ask someone on your staff or another trusted adult for help. In order to reinforce this option to get help, consider doing a project to have kids write a list of five trusted adults in their lives that they can go to for help.

TEENAGERS (THIRTEEN TO EIGHTEEN YEARS)

As we mature, we are held accountable for our actions more and more each year. When it comes to inappropriate sexual behavior with younger children, teenagers may be held legally accountable and potentially even tried as an adult, depending on the circumstances and your state's laws. It's important for teens to understand what constitutes sexual abuse so they have a clear vision of the expectations they are being held to.

> Disclaimer: Child sexual abuse laws vary by state so I'm unable to effectively represent all variations in this document. However, the list presented below will serve as a foundation for teens to understand the expected boundaries.

Sexual abuse is any type of sexual act between an adult and a minor or between two minors when one uses authority, force, threats, bribery, coercion, or persuasion to gain power over the other.

Depending on your state's laws, child sexual abuse can include:

Contact Sexual Abuse

- Touching a child's private parts
- Making a child touch someone else's private parts
- Oral-genital contact in either direction
- Rape or any penetration with objects or body parts
- Kissing: prolonged or open mouth
- Making children touch each other

Visual Sexual Abuse

- Watching a child undress or go to the bathroom: voyeurism
- Exposing private parts to a child: exhibitionism
- Asking a child to play sexual games and expose themselves
- Showing pornography or making a child watch sexual acts
- Taking sexual pictures

Verbal Sexual Abuse

- Using obscene or sexual language around children with the intent of sexual gratification
- Talking about specific sexual acts

It's crucial for teens to respect boundaries that keep them from engaging in any of these behaviors or even being put in a position of being falsely accused of any of these behaviors. These boundaries apply to teens that are around younger children in your program as well as with their siblings or any other children in their life.

The teenage years are a time when inappropriate sexual thoughts and feelings toward younger children may arise for a variety of reasons. The feelings may even go as far as being sexually aroused by younger children.

> Tell Teens: If someone younger than you arouses you, that's a problem. Don't act on it. Talk to a trusted adult immediately.

However, acting on those thoughts and feelings is a problem, as a matter of fact, depending on the circumstances it could be a crime. One study of offenders by Elliott found that "A third of the men were under the age of 16 when first attracted sexually to children. All of these men committed their first offense as juveniles, 1 to 3 years after becoming sexually attracted to children."[39] and 83 percent of the offenders said they didn't seek help because they either didn't realize they needed it or there was no help available.[40]

As mentioned in the last section, the stakes are high and we cannot afford to be vague about our expectations of teens. It's crucial that you tell teens very directly: If someone younger than you arouses you, that's a problem. Don't act on it. Talk to a trusted adult immediately.

Teens that struggle with sexual behavior problems do not necessarily have a sexual disorder and are not doomed to a life of pedophilia. There is very effective treatment available, but it's important for them to seek help as soon as possible. The following pamphlet will help you better understand children with sexual behavior problems and how to guide them to getting the help they need.

- *Helping Children with Sexual Behavior Problems: A Guidebook for Professionals and Caregivers* by Toni Cavanagh Johnson, PhD. http://www.tcavjohn.com/

Next Steps:

- Review, establish, and implement new boundaries education for the children in your care.
- Review, select, and implement any additional child sexual abuse prevention related education for your staff.
- Review, select, and implement any additional child sexual abuse prevention related education for the children in your care.
- Schedule group or individual training as necessary to support additional education programs selected above.

BEST PRACTICE #7

PRE-ESTABLISH YOUR RESPONSE AND TAKE BOLD ACTION

Reflection:

Before continuing, complete the questions below regarding what you and your organization have done to pre-establish your response to observed, disclosed, or suspected child sexual abuse as well as boundary violations.

➤ What would make you suspect a child is being sexually abused?

_____

_____

_____

_____

_____

_____

_____

_____

➤ Do you know if you are a mandated reporter? If you are, have you received formal mandated reporter training?

_____

_____

_____

_____

_____

_____

_____

_____

➤ If you are a mandated reporter, what is your state's process for reporting abuse?

_____

_____

_____

_____

_____

_____

_____

_____

_____

➢ Does your organization require you to make an internal report for suspected child sexual abuse? If so, what is the process for internal reporting?

_____

_____

_____

_____

_____

_____

_____

_____

_____

➢ What factors should be considered before reporting internally?

_____

_____

_____

_____

_____

_____

_____

_____

➤ If your organization requires you to make an internal report when you suspect child sexual abuse, is the internal report to be made *prior to* or *after* you submit a report to the authorities?

_____

_____

_____

_____

_____

_____

_____

_____

_____

➤ What is your reporting policy for staff members who are *not* mandated reporters (i.e. volunteers, unclassified employees)?

_____

_____

_____

_____

_____

_____

_____

_____

_____

_____

➤ What organizational consequences are currently in place for staff members who are accused of child sexual abuse? Who is responsible for making the decision about whether consequences are invoked? When do those consequences go into effect?

_____

_____

_____

_____

_____

_____

_____

_____

➤ Are there any laws, employment contracts, union agreements, etc., in place that limit the possible consequences after a staff member is accused of child sexual abuse? If so, what are the limits?

_____

_____

_____

_____

_____

_____

_____

➢ How do the limits impact your ability to protect the kids in your care?

_____

_____

_____

_____

_____

_____

_____

_____

_____

➢ If your organization has existing organizational boundaries, what is the notification and escalation process for reporting violations?

_____

_____

_____

_____

_____

_____

_____

_____

_____

➤ If your organization has existing organizational boundaries, what consequences are in place for breaking those boundaries?

_____

_____

_____

_____

_____

_____

_____

_____

➤ Who is responsible for invoking consequences for organizational boundary violations?

_____

_____

_____

_____

_____

_____

_____

_____

_____

➤ How are established consequences for organizational boundary violations currently communicated to staff? Is the method effective?

_____

_____

_____

_____

_____

_____

_____

_____

➤ Are the consequences for organizational boundary violations equally enforced for all staff members? If not, what are the exceptions?

_____

_____

_____

_____

_____

_____

_____

_____

_____

➤ What existing contractual arrangements dictate your response to organizational boundary violations (employment contracts, volunteer policies, union agreements, state law, etc.)? What do those agreements dictate? What are their limitations?

_____

_____

_____

_____

_____

_____

_____

_____

➤ How do the limitations impact your ability to protect the kids in your care?

_____

_____

_____

_____

_____

_____

_____

_____

> ➤ If limitations exist that negatively impact your ability to protect the kids in your care, what is the process for modifying the contracts? Whose approval is required? When can they be modified?

_____

_____

_____

_____

_____

_____

_____

_____

_____

ADOPT STANDARDS FOR RESPONDING TO LEGAL BOUNDARY VIOLATIONS AND SUSPECTED ABUSE

Child sexual abuse is a crime and cases should never be handled "in-house." Unfortunately, through many high profile cases, we've seen the devastating impact of organizations attempting to resolve the issue internally. Examples include individual cases such as Penn State employees covering up observed and suspected abuse by Jerry Sandusky, as well as the widespread cover-ups in the Catholic church. In these cases, child molesters were not held accountable for their actions, and in many cases, they

> Child sexual abuse is a crime and cases should never be handled "in-house."

continued to have access to children resulting in additional victims.

As I've worked with organizations who serve youth, staff members often ask, "What constitutes child sexual abuse or what would make me suspect abuse is happening?" Though I covered the definition and examples of abusive behavior in the introduction, it is important that I bring it front and center again, as I outline your responsibility as it relates to legal boundary violations and suspected abuse.

SEXUAL BEHAVIOR BETWEEN CHILDREN

First, remember that not all sexual abuse is between an adult and a minor—some sexual encounters are between minors. In addition, not all sexual interactions between minors are abusive, some of them are a normal part of childhood exploration. It is important for you to be able to differentiate between what is normal sexual behavior between children and what is abusive so that you can respond appropriately. According to Cavanagh Johnson, it is considered normal and healthy when:

- Sexual behavior is between children of similar ages
- Sexual behavior is spontaneous
- Sexual behavior is *not* intended to be secret or purposefully in private
- Sexual behavior does not cause fear, shame, or guilt
- The behavior stops when repeatedly corrected by an adult[1]

In cases that appear to be normal and healthy, your staff should intercede to stop the inappropriate behavior and clearly communicate the expected boundaries. If a child is unable to stop after being repeatedly corrected by an adult, child protective services should be notified so the child can be properly evaluated and the family can get the help they need.

Now let's address behavior that is abusive in nature. Child sexual abuse is any sexual act between and adult and a minor *or* between two minors when there is a power differential between them. Differences in power include age, size, emotional maturity, advanced sexual knowledge, as well as forcing, threatening, bribing, or coercing. When a staff member observes or hears about sexual interactions between children that do not seem normal and healthy but instead have a significant power differential involved, they should treat the situation as if it were illegal—reporting to authorities and allowing them to investigate for further details.

FORMS OF SEXUAL ABUSE

Child sexual abuse can come in several forms—contact, visual, or verbal as detailed below. Child sexual abuse laws vary by state, but below are examples of inappropriate behaviors that may be considered sexual abuse in your state.

- **Contact Sexual Abuse**

    o Touching a child's private parts
    o Making a child touch someone else's private parts, including adults or other children
    o Oral-genital contact in either direction
    o Vaginal or anal rape or any penetration with objects or body parts
    o Kissing: prolonged or open mouth

- **Visual Sexual Abuse**

    o Watching a child undress or go to the bathroom: voyeurism
    o Exposing private parts to a child: exhibitionism
    o Asking a child to play sexual games and expose themselves
    o Showing pornography or making a child watch sexual acts

- ° Masturbating in front of children
- ° Taking sexual pictures of children
- ° Viewing, creating, buying, and selling child pornography

- **Verbal Sexual Abuse**

  - ° Using obscene or sexual language around children
  - ° Discussing sex acts or sexual gratification

Remember for our purposes, the definition of private parts includes the breasts (for girls *and* boys), butt, anus, penis, vagina, and *mouth*. Also remember that the less invasive behaviors indicated in the verbal abuse category may be a small part of a bigger picture so I recommend that you take all of these behaviors seriously and allow the professionals to investigate and determine the full extent of the abuse. So what action should you take if any of these behaviors come to your attention?

HOW TO RESPOND TO SEXUAL ABUSE

Observed Sexual Abuse

Observed sexual abuse is a crime in progress and should be treated as such. You should be mentally and emotionally prepared to respond as if it were second nature. Consider how you would respond to a hit and run car accident: you would quickly look at the car and make a mental note of the make and color as well as the license plate number; you would imprint a description of the driver in your mind; you would call 911; you would quickly run to the victim and check to see if they are okay, pulling them to safety if needed; you would of course stay with the victim until the authorities arrive; and then you would provide a statement to the police providing as much detail as possible about what you witnessed.

If you observe child sexual abuse, you should be prepared to respond in the same fashion. While you might think this response would be the obvious one, I am still dumbfounded by two distinct incidents in the Jerry Sandusky case where a fellow staff member visually saw him raping a boy in the shower and neither one of them called the police, neither one of them stayed with the victim, neither one of them even identified who the victim was.[2,3] They just left, probably in shock.

You need to acknowledge the possibility of this kind of shock and prepare yourself to respond appropriately. My hope is that if you have a plan already figured out, your mind will recall it and put it into action automatically. Here is what you need to do:

- Take a picture on your cell phone and e-mail it to yourself immediately (hard evidence!)
- Interrupt the crime and attempt to protect the child
- Call the police immediately (911)
- Stay with the child until the authorities arrive
- Make note of the environment/evidence
- Attempt to identify the victim and the suspect, including a detailed description of both
- Document the date, time, location, and what you saw (in detail: all five senses)
- Write down any words exchanged among all parties

Take the time to embrace and engrain this response into your thought process. It would be helpful to say it out loud a few times and visualize yourself walking through these logical steps. This will help you to make it second nature so you can take action basically on autopilot, even if you are shocked by what you have seen.

Disclosed Sexual Abuse

If a child discloses through verbal, written, simulated, or artistic communication being involved in any of the above sexually abusive behaviors, it should be reported to authorities immediately, but first, you will need to respond to the child's disclosure with the following important steps:

- Let the child know that you believe them!
- Let them know that it's safe to talk to you about it.
- Let them know that it's *not* their fault.
- Ask open-ended questions to determine the basics: "What happened next?" or "Tell me more about that." These types of questions allow you to clarify what you have seen or heard, even if it is a picture a child has drawn that is sexual in nature.
- Do not investigate yourself but gather just enough information to file a report. Find out who, what, where, and when, if possible.
- File a report with child protective services *and* law enforcement. You should file with child protective services where the child lives, regardless of where the crime occurred. However, the police have specific geographical jurisdictions so you will need to report to the law enforcement agency where the crime occurred. Refer to the mandated reporting section later in this chapter.
- Protect the child from their perpetrator, if possible and as necessary. As an example, if a child just disclosed that their cousin rapes them every day after school and the cousin is coming to pick the child up in an hour, you should call the authorities immediately and allow them to make the decision whether to allow the child to go home with the alleged perpetrator.

Your requirement to report disclosed abuse to the authorities is certain even if the child discloses to someone else, who then in turn tells you. You should also report regardless of who the identified offender is—someone within your organization such as a staff member, volunteer, contract worker, or another child as well as anyone outside of your program such as a family member, family friend, or another acquaintance.

Suspected Abuse

If you have received any information directly or indirectly that would cause you to *suspect* that any of these sexually abusive behaviors have happened to a child, it should be reported to authorities immediately. Although your good sense may tell you not to believe rumors, according to experts in the field, it is important to realize that rumors are a good source of information[4] and signs of abuse in children are strong indicators as well. While a single sign does not necessarily mean that abuse has occurred, if you see multiple signs, chronic signs, or major changes in behavior, it should be cause for you to suspect abuse has occurred. I have included these signs below as a reminder.

Physical Signs

- Evidence of physical trauma: blood, swelling, or tears in the skin around the vagina, penis, or anus
- Complaints of pain during urination or bowel movements
- Exhibiting symptoms of genital or urinary tract infections or STDs: offensive odor, itching, redness, rashes, blisters, or discharge in the genital area or the mouth and throat
- Stress-related illnesses: chronic stomach aches or recurring migraine headaches
- Self-mutilation: pinching themselves, burning themselves with cigarettes, puncturing themselves with pins, or cutting their bodies with knives or razor blades without intending to commit suicide

Emotional or Behavioral Signs

- Anxiety, panic attacks, phobias, and signs of post-traumatic stress disorder
- Extreme fear
- Aggressive behavior toward friends and family
- Withdrawal from friends, family, or activities they previously enjoyed
- Fear of certain people, places, or activities
- Excessive sadness, depression, or suicide attempts
- Decreased school performance
- Eating disorders, loss of appetite, gagging
- Sleep disturbances, nightmares, and screaming
- Regressive behaviors, bedwetting, separation anxiety
- Numbing their pain with alcohol, drugs, or cutting
- Perfection and signs of obsessive-compulsive disorder
- Loss of memory of certain years or large blocks of time

Sexual signs

- Increased questions about human sexuality
- Excessive masturbation or masturbating in public
- Increased sexual play with friends, pets, or toys
- Talking about or acting out specific sexual acts
- Increased choice of sexually revealing clothing or covering up
- Signs of promiscuity
- Teen pregnancy
- Depicting people in a sexual way in pictures

Let's look further into the word "suspect" so we are all on the same page. The definition of suspect is to "have an idea or impression of the existence, presence, or truth of (something) without certain proof."[5] It is not up to you to prove that abuse has taken place before reporting to authorities. You simply have to have an idea or impression that something has taken place.

Sax, says, "Reporting your suspicion is not the same as making an accusation. You are just asking the authorities to investigate the possibility that there may be a problem."[6] The mandated reporting laws which I will cover in the next section require you to report suspicions of abuse, not just incidents where you have facts or hard evidence. You should not rely on proof to get an investigation but instead on the investigation to get proof.

> You should not rely on proof to get an investigation but instead on the investigation to get proof.

MANDATED REPORTERS

Disclaimer: Since mandated reporting laws vary by state and are subject to change, I cannot reflect requirements specific to your organization in this document. However, it is your responsibility as an organization that serves children to thoroughly understand and abide by the mandated reporting laws that govern your state. The Child Welfare Information Gateway (www.childwelfare.gov) is a good starting point for understanding mandated reporting requirements but ultimately, you should seek the advice of an attorney who is familiar with your state's mandated reporting laws.

Also note that mandated reporting laws extend to other types of abuse including physical abuse, emotional abuse and neglect which are beyond the scope of this book and therefore have not been mentioned in this document.

Who Must Report Sexual Abuse

Youth-serving organizations play a critical role in the identification and reporting of child sexual abuse simply by virtue of how much time children spend in these organizations. States have recognized this crucial role and "Approximately 48 States, the District of Columbia, American Samoa, Guam, the Northern Mariana Islands, Puerto Rico, and the Virgin Islands designate professions whose members are mandated by law to report child maltreatment. Individuals designated as mandatory reporters typically have frequent contact with children," according to the Child Welfare Information Gateway.[7] These professions may include youth organization staff positions such as teachers, principals, and other school personnel; directors, employees, and volunteers at entities that provide organized activities for children, such as camps, day camps, youth centers, and recreation centers; members of the clergy; and faculty, administrators, athletics staff, and other employees and volunteers at institutions of higher learning, including public and private colleges and universities and vocational and technical schools.[8]

Some states require all adults to report. "In approximately 18 states and Puerto Rico, any person who suspects child abuse or neglect is required to report," regardless of profession.[9] It is your responsibility to know the mandated reporting laws in your state and effectively communicate those laws to your staff as part of your overall child sexual abuse prevention policy.

Reporting Procedures

In addition to the designation of who should report, each state typically establishes specific procedures for mandated reporters to notify authorities, which may include child protective services, law enforcement, or both. These procedures are well defined by each state indicating where mandated reporters should call to report abuse, what paperwork should be submitted as a follow up to the call, and the timelines associated with the process (i.e., the form must be submitted within twenty-four hours of the verbal report, etc.).

I have always encouraged anyone reporting abuse to report to both the police and child protective services to be sure they are both aware and they can coordinate who will take the lead. Lanning and Dietz warn that "Many mandated reporting laws were passed at a time when lawmakers were focused on emerging awareness of intrafamilial child abuse, with little recognition of acquaintance molestation, and these statutes have not necessarily been updated." They go on to say that, "Organizations need to understand that in many jurisdictions, suspicions of sexual victimization of a child by an acquaintance (i.e., not a parent or a guardian) will not be accepted or investigated by a local social welfare agency such as Child Protective Services."[10] You would never want a case to go without a thorough investigation because one agency didn't believe it was in their jurisdiction and the other agency wasn't notified. So I encourage you to include in your policy that all suspicions of child sexual abuse be reported to both your local law enforcement agency and child protective services. As noted earlier in this chapter, your report to law enforcement should be made to the agency where the crime occurred. So if the child discloses that an uncle molested him at their beach house in another county or state, the report should be made with the police department that has jurisdiction over the city where the beach house is. Child protective services reports should be made to the county where the child lives.

> I encourage you to include in your policy that all suspicions of child sexual abuse be reported to both your local law enforcement agency and child protective services.

Training for Mandated Reporters

Most states also have a mechanism for training mandated reporters, which you should research and make available to your staff. However, this training typically addresses only the process for reporting and high level definitions of abuse but does not address the detailed signs that indicate when you should suspect that sexual abuse has occurred. The 2014 GAO report states, "An expert from a risk management firm we spoke with told us that training on mandatory reporting requirements, such as who is considered a mandatory reporter and to whom reports should be made, generally does not adequately focus on preventing child sexual abuse in the first place."[11] In an effort to prepare your staff to be an effective mandated reporter, module #1 of the online training should be used to augment any state-provided mandated reporter training.

Mandated reporters are typically required to give their name when reporting but can request confidentiality. In addition, immunity from civil or criminal liability is granted in most states to mandated reporters who report in good faith.

It is your responsibility to put collegial and institutional loyalties aside and report observed, disclosed, or suspected abuse, even if you find it hard to believe. Your kids are counting on you!

Failure to Report

"Approximately 48 States, the District of Columbia, American Samoa, Guam, the Northern Mariana Islands, and the Virgin Islands impose penalties on mandatory reporters who knowingly or willfully fail to make a report when they suspect that a child is being abused or neglected."[12] Depending on the state and the specific circumstances, the charges can be misdemeanor or felony charges and penalties can include "jail terms ranging from 30 days to 5 years, fines ranging from $300 to $10,000, or both."[12] In some states, mandated reporters that fail to report may also be civilly liable. Institutions may also be fined for failure to report or preventing someone from reporting.[12] The GAO survey further differentiated between requirements to report suspected *sexual abuse* versus *sexual misconduct*[13] so it is important to have a clear understanding of what you are required to report.

In addition to the legal consequences of failure to report, I recommend that you establish harsh organizational penalties for failure to report, such as termination. It is important to create an environment of zero tolerance not only for offenders but for mandated reporters who are obligated to report and choose not to. If you have a staff member who fails to report and you terminate them, it would certainly send a message to the rest of your staff that you're serious about the safety of the kids in your care and you expect all staff members to actively participate in their protection.

One of the biggest challenges with failure to report was summed up well by van Dam when she said, "Once the organization fails to properly address the first complaint, they become entrenched in continuing to placate the parents while supporting the employee. With each new complaint they become more locked into pursuing the initial course of action."[14] I cannot emphasize how important it is to step up and report, even if you didn't do so when you first suspected. Not only are the victims counting on you to be their voice but with each new indication of abuse whether by the same staff member or a different staff member, you are digging yourself and your organization into a deeper level of liability. It is best to come clean and admit that you probably should have reported earlier than to continue in denial. The current climate is ripe for both civil lawsuits and criminal charges against those who fail to report. I implore you to do the right thing—for your kids and for your organization!

NON-MANDATED REPORTERS (PASSIVE REPORTERS)

Whether required by law or not, I believe all staff members who work for an organization that serves children (paid or volunteer) should be expected to report observed, disclosed, or suspected abuse to the authorities. As a matter of fact, I hope that all adults would accept this as a moral/ethical responsibility and step up courageously to protect children.

If you have staff members who are *not* considered mandated reporters by law, I recommend that you make reporting mandatory anyway, as part of your organization's policy. Adopt the organizational consequences for failure to report that you put in place for mandated reporters for non-mandated reporters as well. You should provide non-mandated reporters with all the same information you give to your mandated reporters including the mandated reporter laws; the specific reporting procedures and timelines; make the state provided mandatory reporter training available to them; and of course all staff members will be required to take module #1 of my training, as recommended in Best Practice #5. Of course, you will need to document and effectively communicate that they are not legally required to report and thus the state imposed failure to report consequences do not apply but that your organization's consequences for failure to report do apply. Clearly communicate your expectations and pre-established consequences.

Just in case a non-mandated reporter is too uncomfortable to report observed, disclosed, or suspected abuse to the authorities themselves, I recommend you let them know ahead of time that they can report to your Risk Manager who would make the report to authorities with them. This is important because non-mandated staff members are typically volunteers who may be young adults or even teenagers who may not have the clarity and emotional strength to follow through. To ensure reporting is handled properly when escalated, the Risk Manager should be a mandated reporter.

INTERNAL REPORTING PROCESSES

I've spoken with many organizations that have a formal internal reporting process that is to be followed so that all reports to authorities go through a centralized person. Unfortunately, this approach of internal reporting *before* reporting to authorities assumes that everyone involved in the internal process will believe what the reporter believes and respond in a way that is in the best interest of the child, which is *not* always in the best interest of the organization. Unfortunately, we have seen time and time again that this is a faulty assumption. The extensive scandal within the Catholic church and the more recent Penn State scandal prove that we cannot rely on other people in the organization to follow through.

In addition, internal reporting processes can interfere with the investigations of authorities. According to a 2014 Government Accountability Office report, "…three of the six school districts GAO visited have policies requiring suspected sexual abuse or misconduct to be reported to school administrators. Local investigative officials reported that such policies can be confusing, as they imply reports should only be made to school officials. This can result in a failure to report to the proper law enforcement or CPS authorities and interfere with investigations."[15]

Mandated reporting laws are very specific about the procedures for institutions that have internal reporting requirements. According to the Child Welfare Information Gateway:

- "In 10 States, the District of Columbia, and the Virgin Islands, the staff member who suspects abuse notifies the head of the institution first, and then the head or his or her designee is required to make the report.
- In eight States, the individual reporter must make the report to the appropriate authority first and then notify the institution that a report has been made.
- Laws in 14 States make clear that regardless of any policies within the organization, the mandatory reporter is not relieved of his or her responsibility to report.

- In 15 States, an employer is expressly prohibited from taking any action to prevent or discourage an employee from making a report."[16]

The GAO noted similar findings in their 2014 report on Child Welfare.[17] So once again, it is crucial that you understand the laws in your state to ensure any internal reporting procedures you set up are in agreement with them.

Organizations should not have policies in place that could deter someone who suspects abuse from making an immediate independent report to the authorities and doing what they believe is in the best interest of the child. My recommendation is that whenever allowable by law, any internal reporting policies call for the internal report to be completed *after* the report to authorities, but even then, the specific circumstances of any case can be complex.

> The choice to report observed, disclosed, or suspected child sexual abuse to authorities is clear cut—if you suspect, you report. The choice to also report that same abuse internally has many factors to consider.

Considerations for Reporting Internally

While there are very tangible benefits of reporting observed, disclosed, or suspected abuse internally (after having reported to authorities), there are also drawbacks. There are several important factors to consider when determining whether to report internally. My hope is that your organization would acknowledge and communicate the following considerations to your staff and support their resulting choices.

- Is it required by law?

  ◦ Your mandated reporter training process should clearly communicate if there are any legal requirements for mandated reporters to notify someone within their organization, either before or after they report to authorities.

- Is it recommended by law enforcement or the child protective services agency you reported to?

  ◦ During the reporting process, mandated reporters should specifically ask the agency they are reporting to if they should notify someone internally. Since I recommend you report to both child protective services and law enforcement, this question should be posed to both agencies as their opinions could be different. If you get opposing answers, I would notify them both of this fact and ask them to coordinate and come to an agreement before you proceed to report internally.

  ◦ If the alleged offender works for the organization, authorities may recommend the mandated reporter immediately report the allegations internally so the organization can take appropriate action to revoke the alleged offender's access to kids and/or notify the child's parents. If there is no legal requirement for the mandated reporter to report internally and they do not feel comfortable doing so, they may request the authorities to make the internal notification instead.

  ◦ On the other hand, if the situation includes extenuating circumstances such as a broader allegation that other organization members knew about the abuse or that one of the parents is the accused perpetrator, authorities may specifically direct the mandated reporter not to tell anyone within the organization or the child's parents, as it may interfere with their investigation strategy.

- Is it in the child's best interest?

  ○ If there are no legal requirements dictating whether the mandated reporter report internally and the authorities have not given them any specific mandate, they should consider what is in the best interest of the child.

  ○ Some organizations have reporting policies that require their staff to make an internal report before they report to the authorities. However, when you ask a staff member to report internally first, you run the risk of someone within the organization talking them out of reporting. In some cases, other staff members question their evidence causing them to doubt their initial belief or some staff members may directly try to persuade them that it's best handled internally. For this reason, it is critically important for the mandated reporter to make the report to authorities first, even if they intend to tell the organization leadership afterward as it would certainly not be in the child's best interest if a staff member was talked out of reporting suspected abuse.

  ○ If the alleged offender is a staff member and has access to kids, especially the child in question, it's very important to make an internal report, assuming the mandated reporter has confidence that organization leadership will take steps to revoke the alleged offender's access to kids immediately.

  ○ If the mandated reporter suspects the alleged offender will find out about the report and still have access to the child in question after they notify organization leadership, it may result in danger to the child or elevate the seriousness of threats, further traumatizing the child. If the mandated reporter thinks this is possible, it is best not to make the internal report, but instead let the authorities notify them at the right time in the formal investigation.

- Is it in the best interest of the case?

  o As mentioned above, it's not unusual for offenders to threaten their victims and significantly increase the seriousness of threats if they find out the child has disclosed. At this point, the offender's goal is to get the child to recant their story. If this happens, the district attorney has lost their star witness and it's unlikely there will be enough evidence for the district attorney to pursue criminal charges. The case will be closed, the offender will not be held accountable, and the victim and potentially other children will continue to be at risk of abuse by this offender. So if the mandated reporter thinks the offender is likely to be notified and have a chance to sway the testimony of the victim, they should not make an internal report.

  o Because 80 percent of child sexual abuse cases happen in one perpetrator–one child situations,[18,] [19] disclosures often become a he said/she said situation and authorities lack the evidence needed for the district attorney to pursue criminal charges. There is a brief time early in the process before the alleged offender has been notified of the disclosure when authorities can develop and execute a strategy to gather additional evidence beyond the victim's testimony such as use of search warrants to gather hard evidence or covert phone calls to capture inadvertent confessions. The 2014 GAO report noted that law enforcement officials they spoke with prefer to use the element of surprise which is often lost when other investigations begin without them.[20] If the mandated reporter thinks that making an internal report would result in the alleged offender being notified before the authorities can gather all the evidence, it would not be in the best interest of the case to make an internal report.

- Is it in your best interest?

  o Mandated reporters' identity is confidential in most states except where disclosure is required by law and then only to those on a need-to-know basis. Obviously, this is not the case if you personally notify organization leadership. According to the Child Welfare Information Gateway, California is a good example of a state that has made provisions for this. The California law specifies that "internal procedures shall not require any employee required to make reports to disclose his or her identity to the employer."[21] Allowing internal reports to be submitted anonymously is an excellent way for organizations to help staff members avoid this challenge of needing to protect themselves.

  o Although most state's mandatory reporting laws provide both criminal and civil protection for reports made in good faith, how people will react internally is an unknown. Each situation is different and mandated reporters will need to decide for themselves if they think being identified as the reporter will cause difficulties with their superiors, colleagues, parents, the alleged perpetrator, or union. They may feel being identified would put their person, their family, and/ or their job at risk.

- ○ If mandated reporters (1) have no legal requirement to make an internal report; (2) the authorities are not directing them to make an internal report; (3) to the best of their knowledge, it would not have a detrimental impact on a child's safety; and (4) it will not have a negative impact on the case, then they should consider what is in their own best interest.
- ○ Even if a mandated reporter decides not to make an internal report initially, they can choose to do so at any time and share their reason for the delay based on the thought process outlined above.

As we've discussed, making a choice to report observed, disclosed, or suspected child sexual abuse to the authorities is clear cut—if you suspect, you report. However, the choice to *also* report internally has many factors to consider.

CENTRALIZED CONTROL OF LEGAL BOUNDARY VIOLATIONS AND SUSPECTED SEXUAL ABUSE CASES

Whether you elect to implement an internal reporting process or an allegation of sexual abuse is brought to your attention by law enforcement or child protective services based on a direct report to them, you will need centralized control. This centralized approach for child sexual abuse cases is critical so that communication with the authorities, your staff, your board, your families, the general public, and the media can be properly managed.

You should pre-establish a process where a minimum of three escalation points are notified immediately upon becoming aware of an allegation of abuse. Your internal reporting policy should designate these people/positions are to be copied on the report and *anyone* who inquires should be limited to communication with the first two key individuals, at least initially.

- The first escalation point should be the highest level staff member in the organization or within that division/department for larger organizations. This would likely be positions such as the executive director, regional vice president, program director, or senior pastor. For our purposes, we will refer to this position as the Policy Enforcement Director, as this is their role in the process. The Policy Enforcement Director should have the responsibility to work directly with law enforcement and child protective services personnel to support further investigation and coordinate, as necessary. In addition, the Policy Enforcement Director should have the authority to execute or coordinate approval for predetermined consequences to allegations of legal boundary violations when the accused is a staff member (i.e., termination, administrative leave, revoke access to children, etc.). This position should be the first point of contact for all incoming inquires from the authorities, your staff, your board, your families, the general public, and the media regarding any child sexual abuse cases.

- The second escalation point to be notified should be the Risk Manager that we identified in Best Practice #2. This same person should be involved in all cases of alleged legal boundary violations as well as cases where abuse of a child is suspected from someone outside of the organization. These cases may or may not come up through the Assessment and Communication process that the Risk Manager is already involved in. This person should be the alternative contact for both internal and public inquiries.

- The third escalation point should be the board of directors or other governing body that was established as having ultimate responsibility for your child sexual abuse prevention program, as discussed in Best Practice #2.

There may be one or more people to notify based on who is ultimately responsible. These individuals will generally play an oversight position and be involved in making policy decisions versus the day-to-day execution of the approved plan. However, they are ultimately responsible and will be intimately involved in decisions regarding settlements of individual lawsuits that may arise as a result of staff abuse. Because they will not necessarily be up to date on the day-to-day workings of a case, internal and public inquiries should not be escalated to them.

- Your organization should keep the identity of the victims confidential. The identity of the alleged offender should also be kept confidential until such time as your Policy Enforcement Director, in conjunction with the authorities, decides to make it public. Therefore, I encourage you to use caution in what information is included in any communication about the case, especially if information is sent electronically and perhaps to personal e-mail addresses, in the case of board members in smaller organizations.

ORGANIZATIONAL CONSEQUENCES OF LEGAL BOUNDARY VIOLATIONS

Accusations of child sexual abuse should be taken very seriously and it's essential that your organization take every precaution to ensure the accused perpetrator does not come in contact with a child that you suspect has been abused for several reasons as follows:

- You'll want to ensure there are no additional opportunities for abuse to happen.
- You'll want to avoid a potentially traumatizing experience for the child. Since it's common for offenders to threaten their victims to keep them silent, if a child has disclosed

or knows you suspect abuse has taken place, just seeing the offender can trigger in the child an overwhelming sense of fear that the offender will actually follow through with the threats.

- You'll want to ensure the alleged offender does not have an opportunity to talk to the child and potentially increase their threats, causing the child to recant their story.

It's also important to keep the alleged offender from coming in contact with any of the child's family members who might find it difficult to control their anger or even have their allegiance swayed by the offender's excuses, leaving the child feeling betrayed.

Of course, we want to ensure the accused offender has no access to other children either. This is not only to protect the children from the risk of abuse, but it also ensures the alleged offender does not have a chance to increase threats toward other children who may also be victims.

Based on these real and present dangers for additional abuse, coercion, threats, and violence, we recommend that if one of your staff members has been accused of sexual abuse, they be immediately removed from their position and the premises but only *after* agreement from law enforcement has been received. Remember, you want to protect the element of surprise law enforcement needs to obtain additional evidence. The Policy Enforcement Director will need to work closely with law enforcement to communicate with the victim's family during this time, to (1) ensure the child is protected, even if the alleged offender is still on premises and (2) they understand the importance of confidentiality during this initial phase of evidence gathering. Once removed, the accused should not be allowed back on the premises until the legal process has come to a conclusion.

Sometimes, the legal process can take a year or more and depending on your state laws and employment contracts, you may be able to terminate the staff member's employment or you may be required to place them on a paid administrative leave.

It behooves you to fully understand what factors control your potential course of action and attempt to renegotiate contracts and/or begin the legal reform process to create a structure where you can effectively protect children without undue financial burden on your organization.

We saw this dilemma in full view in the Los Angeles Unified School District (LAUSD) as they dealt with the case of convicted child molester, Mark Berndt. The Los Angeles Sheriff's Department requested that LAUSD not conduct their own side by side investigation so that potential victims would not have to be interviewed multiple times which could possibly hurt the criminal case and traumatize the children. LAUSD fired Mark Berndt, but he appealed. Because the district had no evidence of their own to prove the allegations and the Sheriff's Department was not yet in a position to turn needed evidence over to the District, they elected to offer Berndt a $40,000 settlement to retire, instead of going forward to fight the termination decision. However, retirement afforded Berndt additional benefits. According to LA Weekly, "he retains lifetime health coverage and his pension, totaling $3,891.17 monthly in pretax benefits. If he lives to the average age of a man in California, he'll reap about $1 million."[22] While I understand the District may have made what they thought was the least expensive decision available to them at the time, it cost the tax payers potentially a million dollars to remove this alleged sex offender from his position working with children. This scenario is a perfect example of terms that need to be renegotiated with the teacher's union and addressed in state law.

REPORTING TO APPROPRIATE LICENSING AGENCIES

In addition to reporting observed, disclosed, or suspected abuse to law enforcement and child protective services, it is important that you also report allegations of abuse to any licensing agencies where the alleged offender holds credentials.[23] This may apply to teachers, nurses, coaches, physical therapists, etc. This assures that their licenses are suspending and/or revoked as appropriate based on the pending and final outcome of the investigation, state law, and agency provisions. In addition, it provides for centralized documentation of sexual misconduct which can be communicated to future potential employers during their background checks. In some cases, state law allows state licensing agencies to conduct their own investigations as well.[24]

> Disclaimer: While I recommend that accused perpetrators should not be allowed back on the premises until the legal investigation has come to a conclusion, it is your organization's responsibility to seek legal advice to determine the correct course of action based on governing laws and any employment contracts that are in place.

INCIDENT REVIEW AND RISK ASSESSMENT[25, 26]

Every time there are allegations of sexual abuse within your organization, whether they are substantiated or not, the incident should be thoroughly evaluated by your organization to understand how the offender allegedly gained access to the child and was able to perpetrate the abuse. Just because there is not enough evidence to lead to a conviction does not mean that the alleged incident didn't happen. Remember child sexual abuse prevention is a continuous improvement process, not a one-time event. Though it is unfortunate to have incidents of abuse, every one of them should be looked at as a learning tool and an opportunity to continue to close the gaps that leave children in your care vulnerable to abuse.

VICTIM HARASSMENT

We see staff members supporting or protecting the alleged offender, time and time again—through verbal support, rallies, wearing t-shirts that claim the innocence of the offender, and threatened legal retaliation. Child molesters are so good at grooming the community that the parents, staff, and even authorities sometimes find it difficult to believe the allegations. Here are some examples of harassing behavior:

Harassing Parents: In her book, *The Socially Skilled Child Molester*, van Dam shares the following example: "A group of parents who were worried about a teacher's conduct toward their children complained to the school principal. The complaint resulted in a number of attacks against them. The teacher's lawyer threatened to sue them for defamation of character; the teacher's union threatened them with lawsuits. Other teachers accused them of being on a witch hunt. One of the parents said, 'Everywhere we turned we were made to feel like we had done something wrong.'"[27]

Harassing Children: Shakeshaft shares a story in her paper on educator sexual misconduct which is another good example of this kind of extreme loyalty to the alleged offender: "A typical example is the case of a 6th-grade girl whose friend reported the abuse, ultimately leading to a teacher's arrest. Other teachers wore armbands in support of their colleague and collected money from students and parents to support his legal defense, including collecting money in the female victim's classroom, in front of her. Other teachers called her a 'slut' and accused her of 'trying to ruin the career of a good man.' The accused teacher confessed to sexually abusing the student. The female victim left the school because she was harassed daily by adults and students."[28]

I want you to take the time to stop and really think about how this little girl must have felt. We ask children to tell and when they muster up the courage to do so, we call them liars. Research has shown that only 1–2 percent of children's reports of sexual abuse were fictitious.[29, 30] So we have no valid reason not to believe children. The alleged offenders are adults and they can defend themselves.

This kind of harassing behavior can also have a serious negative impact on the case because 70 percent of offenders have between 1 and 9 victims, 23 percent have between 10 and 40 victims, and 7 percent have between 41 and 450 victims.[31] When one child discloses, it could be the first time other victims feel safe enough to come forward but imagine instead how they feel when they see the community rallying around their offender. What do you think the chances are that they will disclose their own abuse if they run the risk of being called a liar?

Harassing behavior is simply inappropriate and should not be tolerated from staff members, parents, or other children. You should set the example and communicate that unless someone observed the abuse themselves, they can't know the facts and should respectfully allow the evidence of the case to unfold throughout the investigation. Shakeshaft calls for school districts to "ensure that students who report abuse are themselves protected from harassment, and the districts also must provide support systems for student victims."[32] This holds true for all youth-serving organizations. If you do not have the internal resources to provide the necessary support, you should work with child protective services to arrange for counselors for the victims and their families.

If you don't stand up for your kids when they disclose, you are sending them a message that this behavior is normal or that they deserved it which will have an immeasurably negative impact on their boundaries and self-worth leaving them more vulnerable to revictimization and even to abuse themselves.

BOARD UPDATES

The Risk Manager should be responsible for submitting regular updates to the board of directors until a case is deemed closed by law enforcement, child protective services, licensing agencies, and your organization. If the case is in an active state, weekly updates will likely be necessary. If the investigation is proceeding quietly without much outward activity, you can adjust the timing of your board updates accordingly. Once an incident that was raised by your Assessment and Communication process is identified as a suspected legal boundary violation or suspected abuse by someone outside the organization, the records should be permanently transferred to this centralized control process. However, the team should be notified periodically of the status of the case in a manner that does not break confidentiality but does ensure accountability.

As addressed in Best Practice #2, the board of directors should have ultimate responsibility for the establishment and execution of the child sexual abuse prevention program within your organization. Since the board is not typically involved in the day-to-day activities, their notification as part of the escalation process is essential and they have the responsibility to intervene if:

- The response process is not being followed
- The response process is not proceeding in a timely manner
- The pre-established consequences are not enforced objectively

ADOPT STANDARDS FOR RESPONDING TO ORGANIZATIONAL BOUNDARY VIOLATIONS

Although organizational boundary violations are taken very seriously and have pre-defined consequences, the violation in and of itself does not indicate a crime has been committed. So cases of organizational boundary violations can be handled "in-house" according to the established and documented policy.

CENTRALIZED CONTROL OF ORGANIZATIONAL BOUNDARY VIOLATION CASES

I recommend the same escalation points for reporting organizational boundary violations as I did for reporting legal boundary violations earlier in this chapter. The same contacts should be designated for all inquiries from your staff and your families as well. However, because no laws have been broken, there is no need to report to or coordinate your efforts with law enforcement or child protective services. You will not likely have any inquiries by the general public or the media either.

INTERNAL INVESTIGATION

The Risk Manager and Policy Enforcement Director should work together on an internal investigation to determine if indeed an organizational boundary was violated. They may need to interview adults and children that were involved, as well as bystanders, to make a final determination.

Sometimes, organizational boundary violations are just the tip of the iceberg and your internal investigation may reveal that legal boundaries have also been violated. It is essential that the Risk Manager and Policy Enforcement Director are both cognizant of this possibility during their investigation and immediately switch to the mandated reporting process at the first sign of suspected abuse.

CONSEQUENCES OF ORGANIZATIONAL BOUNDARY VIOLATIONS

Importance of Establishing Consequences

Organizational boundaries are put in place to protect children. All staff members should have been trained on the established boundaries and signed-off, acknowledging that:

- They have received and read the boundaries
- They agreed to abide by them
- They agree to hold other staff members accountable to abide by them
- They fully understand the pre-established consequences for organizational boundary violations

So if a staff member breaks one of the organizational boundaries, you must assume they have made a conscious choice to do so. That choice reflects a blatant attempt to gain private access, to establish an inappropriate relationship with kids, or at minimum, a general disregard for the safety of the children in your care. In any case, their actions pose an increased risk of your kids being sexually abused as well as an increased risk of your organization being held responsible for not protecting them.

Therefore, it's important that your organization not only establish the organizational boundaries but that they also establish direct consequences for breaking them. There's simply no point in having boundaries if there are no consequences for breaking them. The consequences should be established as part of the planning process, long before emotion comes into play. This approach enables objective

> There is simply no point in having boundaries if there are no consequences for breaking them.

enforcement of boundaries. The policy applies equally to all, without the opportunity to be swayed by any individual based on trust, respect, or power.

Severity of Consequences

Since organizational boundary violations have a direct correlation to the safety of your children, I recommend every organization establish the most stringent consequences allowed by law and other determining factors such as employment contracts, volunteer policies, and union agreements.

If permissible, I recommend that the established consequence of an organizational boundary violation is immediate termination of employment (volunteer status, position on the board, etc., as applicable). This response establishes a very clear no tolerance policy.[33] An immediate termination response would typically be an acceptable consequence if you have an "at will" employment contract, volunteer policy and/or board agreement where the relationship can be legally terminated by the organization, with or without cause at any time. However, if your employment, volunteer, or union contracts have specific stipulations regarding termination, they must be honored, and of course, any termination policy must be within the guidelines of all applicable laws.

> Consequences should communicate a no tolerance policy.

Disclaimer: This recommendation for immediate termination is based on my intent to protect children and is not to be misconstrued as legal advice. Your organization is solely responsible for seeking appropriate professional advice and determining the legality of any policies you choose to adopt.

If you are unable to terminate employment based on existing contractual agreements, I recommend these stipulations be brought up for modification in future contract negotiations.

If for any reason your organization is unable to establish an immediate termination policy as a consequence for organizational boundary violations, I recommend you establish the most stringent policy you can based on your organization's specific circumstances. Other options to consider include, but are not limited to, temporary suspension, reassigning the staff member to a position where there are no children present, or utilizing applicable contractual processes required to legally terminate a staff member for cause (i.e., written warnings, improvement plans, etc.).

Under no circumstances should you reassign a staff member to the same role in a different location where they continue to have access to kids. This would not provide any additional protection for kids and in fact would likely diminish the awareness of and focus on their past violations putting kids at increased risk. Unfortunately, we've seen the detrimental effects of this approach in the Catholic church and other youth-serving organizations.

> Child sexual abuse evidence is often found in the ongoing behavior patterns of child molesters and centralized documentation helps to make those patterns visible.

Regardless of your established consequences, I recommend all organizational boundary violations be formally documented, reviewed with the staff member, and included in their permanent personnel file, if able to do so under state law and existing contracts. Child sexual abuse evidence is often found in the ongoing behavior patterns of child molesters and centralized documentation helps to make those patterns visible.

If the consequence for violations is anything other than termination of service, supervision of the staff member should be increased to minimize the potential of future violations.

COMMUNICATION OF INCIDENT CLOSURE

When the investigation is complete, the Policy Enforcement Director should take the lead to communicate to either an individual family that was affected or all of the families, as appropriate. If a parent was aware of and approved of the organizational boundary violation (i.e., a staff member tutoring their child), they should be reminded of the organization's established boundaries and asked to help you keep the staff accountable to honoring them. The Policy Enforcement Director should follow up by sending a letter to the parents documenting their discussion along with a copy of the organization's current boundaries. The letter should be sent within forty-eight hours of the discussion and a copy kept on file.

BOARD UPDATES

The Risk Manager should be responsible for submitting regular updates to the board of directors until a case of organizational boundary violations is closed by your organization. Internal investigations of alleged organizational boundary violations tend to move more quickly than legal investigations so weekly updates should suffice for this short period of time.

All other aspects of the board update process for legal boundary violations applies to organizational boundary violations as well.

Next Steps:

- Create and implement an updated child sexual abuse prevention policy that incorporates all applicable best practices outlined in this book. Some of these practices may be implemented over time based on your strategic plan so document and implement all that are applicable for the current period and then update as you continue to expand your protection efforts.

BEST PRACTICE #8

PROVIDE SUPPORT
AND RESOURCE REFERRALS

Reflection:

Before continuing, complete the questions below regarding how your organization provides support and referrals for those impacted by child sexual abuse.

➤ Does your organization currently provide any direct support services for families who have been impacted by child sexual abuse? If so, what support services are available? How do your families access these services?

_____

_____

_____

_____

_____

_____

_____

_____

_____

_____

➢ Does your organization currently provide any resource referrals for families who have been impacted by child sexual abuse? If so, what types of referrals are available? How are these resources communicated to families?

_____

_____

_____

_____

_____

_____

_____

_____

_____

Twenty percent of the population in America has been sexually abused.[1,2] That is more people than the Center for Disease Control estimates will get the flu each year.[3]

Twenty percent of the population in America has been sexually abused.[4,5] That is more people than the Center for Disease Control estimates will get the flu each year.[6] So needless to say, as you implement these practices, you will be talking with children, teens, and adults who have personally experienced sexual abuse as well as parents who know or suspect their child has been abused. It's also inevitable that at some point, you will be speaking with someone who is attracted to children who may or may not have crossed the line and offended against a child.

In any case, it's irresponsible to talk about child sexual abuse without providing the resources and referrals your families may need. If your organization has expertise, you may provide direct support services. If not, provide referrals or coordinate with child protective services or local advocacy groups to provide needed services.

I've included an example of a resource card that I use as a handout at all my presentations. I encourage you to create a similar card for distribution at group trainings, in your initial announcement package, and your future registration packages. You should also have them on display at key locations in your facility.

I keep the resource referral card short and simple, including the basic resources that are not likely to change. Because the broader set of resources is ever changing, I direct people to our worldwide child sexual abuse prevention and support resource directory for a more extensive list of resources (https://taalk.org/resources/global-resource-directory.html). You are welcome to direct them to our directory or any databases available for local resources.

Report Abuse – 911 & local Child Protection Agency

Suspect Abuse – 1-800-4AChild

Concerned about Inappropriate Thoughts/Behaviors

1-888-PREVENT or www.stopitnow.org/help

Suicide Hotline – 1-800-SUICIDE

Survivor Support

- taalk.org   - malesurvivor.org

- siawso.org   - 1in6.org

- thelamplighters.org   - psychologytoday.com

Non-Offending Parents of Survivors

- taalk.org   - comfortinthestorm.com/

- mosac.net   - network54.com/forum/6443

www.taalk.org - 1-888-808-6558   Talk About Abuse to Liberate Kids

Next Steps:

- Create and distribute a child sexual abuse resource handout.

CONCLUSION

Now that you have read the whole book, you may be thinking that this all sounds well and good, but what does it have to do with my organization's mission and my personal passion? What does it have to do with reading, writing, and arithmetic? What does it have to do with building a child's personal relationship with God? What does it have to do with conditioning an athlete's body and mind to be an Olympic champion? What does it have to do with preparing children to be all that they can be?

Everything! It has everything to do with the vision and passion that calls you to do what you do for children. Our children are destined for greatness, if they are given a chance, but all that you do to unleash the potential in the children you serve will be undermined if they are secretly living with fear and intimidation; shame and guilt; violation and threats of violence; feelings of worthlessness and hopelessness; and self-destructive behavior. You must protect the children in your care from those whose focus is hurtful, selfish, inappropriate, and illegal or their dreams will be destroyed—your dreams for them will go unrealized.

The children in your care can and will go on to become all that they are destined to be—in themselves, in their families, in your community, and in our nation, if we all do our part. Their future is in your hands. What will you do to protect it?

It starts with you. Be a change agent.

NEXT STEPS

As I mentioned in the introduction, I believe people want to do the right thing if they only knew what that was. If you are one of those people, now you know what to do. You are knowledgeable about the child sexual abuse pandemic and your role in resolving it. I want to say a special thank you from all of the kids in your care now and in the future for choosing to make a difference!

So what's next?

Take the Training: If you have not already done so, go to www.taalk.org/training and complete module #1 and module #2 of the Youth-Serving Organization training.

Get Started: Remember child sexual abuse prevention is a continuous process not a one-time event. Now that you have the knowledge, it's time to go back and work through the implementation process for each best practice, one step at a time. Use the Child Sexual Abuse Prevention Assessment and Strategic Planning Guide to assess your organization's current state, identify where your policies and procedures fall short of informed best practices, and create a strategy and timeline to close the gaps. Return to the Getting Started chapter earlier in the book for details on implementing this as a formal program within your organization.

Visit the TAALK Web site Periodically (www.taalk.org): I will post updates to the Youth-Serving Organization community page as they become available including sample forms, question-naires, upcoming webinars, etc. Register for our Youth-Serving Organization newsletter on that same page to receive notification of new tools and training. I have some exciting things planned for the future such as our online training in Spanish!

Join the Forum: If you are interested in connecting with others who are working to make youth-serving organizations a safer place for kids, join the Child Sexual Abuse Best Practices for Youth-Serving Organizations forum topic at www.taalk.org/forum. This is the great place to ask questions which allows us to continue to learn from real life situations and share our combined learning with others.

Spread the Word: Remember the best practices you learned about apply to every adult in the community as well as youth-serving organizations. I hope that you will share your vision for protecting kids and the information you learned with other individuals and organizations in your community. Remember child sexual abuse is predictable and preventable when we surround children with knowledgeable and outspoken adults and we all play a part in the solution. Please invite them to do their part by taking our free training.

Thank you for your commitment to the safety of the children in your care and for doing *your* part! I look forward to working together and would welcome your feedback at csabestpractices@taalk.org.

According to Lanning and Dietz, to better protect children, organizations should do the most that the law allows instead of the least that the law requires.[1]

Child Sexual Abuse Prevention Assessment and Strategic Planning Guide

* Status Key: NA = Not Applicable, IM - Implemented, NR = Needs Revision, IP = In Process, FP = Future Plans

	Status (NA, IM, NR, IP, FP *)	Priority to Implement (High,Med,Low)	Target Date	Lead Staff Member	Possible Barriers (Legal, Emp.Contract, Insurance, Cultural, Cost, Time)
Best Practices #1 - Determine Your Starting Point					
Compile your formal child sexual abuse prevention policies					
Schedule a staff meeting to discuss responses to the reflection questions					
Document your informal child sexual abuse prevention practices					
Document identified organizational or cultural barriers and enablers					
Best Practices #2 - Manage Access to Children					
Establish responsibility for your child sexual abuse best practices program					
Determine who is responsible					
Document who is responsible					
Communicate who is responsible to parents and staff					
Integrate child protection into the applicant screening process					
Use a standardized application form					
Incorporate personal interviews					
Respect your intuition					
Conduct multiple interviews					
Include character focused interview questions					
Include boundary focused interview questions and 'what if?' scenarios					
Discuss your child sexual abuse best practices program					
Formalize the feedback process from interviewers					
Conduct a thorough reference check process					
Require criminal background checks					
Thoroughly investigate red flags					
Institute a thirty-day probationary period					

"Full-size PDF and electronic versions of the Planning Guide are available on the Youth-Serving Organization Community page at www.taalk.org."

Child Sexual Abuse Prevention Assessment and Strategic Planning Guide

* Status Key: NA = Not Applicable, IM = Implemented, NR = Needs Revision, IP = In Process, FP = Future Plans

Best Practices #3 - Set, Document and Enforce Boundaries	Status (NA, IM, NR, IP, FP *)	Priority to Implement (High, Med, Low)	Target Date	Lead Staff Member	Possible Barriers (Legal, Emp. Contract, Insurance, Cultural, Cost, Time)
Legal boundaries - research, document and communicate					
Vaginal or anal intercourse					
Oral copulation					
Vaginal penetration with an object					
Sodomy					
Touching a child's private parts or having them touch some else's					
Masturbation in the presence of a child					
Exhibitionism					
Voyeurism					
Child pornography and sexual exploitation					
Lewd or lascivious acts					
Annoying a minor					
Molesting a child					
Incest					
Positions of power					
Body parts that are off-limits by law					
Age of consent					
Statute of limitations					
On-site boundaries					
Access					
Secure the facility and limit access to children					
Restrict access and/or monitor registered sex offenders					

"Full-size PDF and electronic versions of the Planning Guide are available on the Youth-Serving Organization Community page at www/taalk.org."

Child Sexual Abuse Prevention Assessment and Strategic Planning Guide

* Status Key: NA = Not Applicable, IM = Implemented, NR = Needs Revision, IP = In Process, FP = Future Plans

Best Practices #3 - (continued)

	Status (NA, IM, NR, IP, FP *)	Priority to Implement (High,Med,Low)	Target Date	Lead Staff Member	Possible Barriers (Legal, Emp.Contract, Insurance, Cultural, Cost, Time)
☐ Restrict and monitor internet access					
☐ Isolation					
☐ No one adult - one child situations					
☐ Approved and off-limits locations					
☐ No pulling children out of their regularly scheduled program					
☐ No before or after program help					
☐ Two adults with infants, toddlers, and nonverbal children					
☐ Video cameras in locations that serve children with disabilities & high risk areas					
☐ No family members working together					
☐ Two adults monitoring nap time					
☐ Multiple adults during movies or other lights-out activities					
☐ Observable diapering and bathroom monitoring					
☐ Designate and schedule rovers					
☐ Provide parental access and supervision					
☐ Behavioral					
☐ No unprofessional behavior					
☐ No intimidation: secrets, lies, threats, coercion, or violence					
☐ No sexual discussion, exposing children to porn or sexually explicit material					
☐ Limit physical touching					
☐ No showering with children or changing clothes in front of each other					
☐ No entering children's rooms at night					
☐ Limit medical exams/treatment by staff members					

"Full-size PDF and electronic versions of the Planning Guide are available on the Youth-Serving Organization Community page at www/taalk.org."

Child Sexual Abuse Prevention Assessment and Strategic Planning Guide

* Status Key: NA = Not Applicable, IM = Implemented, NR = Needs Revision, IP = In Process, FP = Future Plans

Best Practices #3 - (continued)	Status (NA, IM, NR, IP, FP *)	Priority to Implement (High,Med,Low)	Target Date	Lead Staff Member	Possible Barriers (Legal, Emp.Contract, Insurance, Cultural, Cost, Time)
No sharing alcohol or prescription, over the counter, or street drugs					
No photographs of kids					
No hands in other people's pockets					
Keep hands where they can be seen					
No masks, blindfolds, scatting, fetishisms, or rituals					
Off-site boundaries					
When off-site, all on-site boundaries apply					
Written authorization for off-site locations					
Pre-approved activities					
Pre-approved locations					
Pre-approved frequency and duration					
Designated list of individuals authorized to approve					
Increased supervision needs identified and secured					
Internal written request and approval process					
Parent approval process					
Parent chaperones					
Control transportation to off-site locations					
Additional boundaries for out of town travel					
When traveling, all other off-site boundaries apply					
Increased supervision needs identified and secured					
Staff members and children should not enter each other's hotel rooms					
No use of alcohol or street drugs					

"Full-size PDF and electronic versions of the Planning Guide are available on the Youth-Serving Organization Community page at www/taalk.org."

Child Sexual Abuse Prevention Assessment and Strategic Planning Guide

* Status Key: NA = Not Applicable, IM = Implemented, NR = Needs Revision, IP = In Process, FP = Future Plans

Best Practices #3 - (continued)	Status (NA, IM, NR, IP, FP *)	Priority to Implement (High,Med,Low)	Target Date	Lead Staff Member	Possible Barriers (Legal, Emp,Contract, Insurance, Cultural, Cost, Time)
Off-hours boundaries					
When in public, all on-site and off-site boundaries apply					
No babysitting					
No tutoring					
No visits to personal residences					
No sleepovers					
No birthday parties					
No family gatherings					
No dating					
Electronic communication and social media boundaries					
No sharing phone numbers					
No sharing email addresses or screen names					
Set restrictive privacy settings and use appropriate profile pictures					
No becoming friends on Facebook or following on Twitter					
No connections on multimedia sharing sites					
No connection on video chat applications					
Child-to-child boundaries					
Full visibility and close monitoring during naptime					
No unmonitored bathroom visits					
Separate age groups					
Avoid direct or inadvertent creation of authority					
Provide close supervision					

"Full-size PDF and electronic versions of the Planning Guide are available on the Youth-Serving Organization Community page at www/taalk.org."

Child Sexual Abuse Prevention Assessment and Strategic Planning Guide

* Status Key: NA = Not Applicable, IM = Implemented, NR = Needs Revision, IP = In Process, FP = Future Plans

	Status (NA, IM, NR, IP, FP *)	Priority to Implement (High,Med,Low)	Target Date	Lead Staff Member	Possible Barriers (Legal, Emp.Contract, Insurance, Cultural, Cost, Time)
Best Practices #3 - (continued)					
Gift boundaries					
No gifts to children					
No gifts to parents or caretakers					
Review, document and distribute all new boundaries to staff, parents and kids					
Best Practices #4 - Regularly and Actively Assess Behaviors					
Create standard operating procedures for assessing & communicating concerns					
Ask for feedback					
Provide an assessment and communication form					
Establish a set time when assessment and communication forms are submitted					
Establish a child sexual abuse prevention communication team					
Regularly review feedback					
Establish standardized board reporting					
Best Practices #5 - Create an Accountability Team					
Deliver mandatory staff training					
Existing staff					
Provide or direct staff to training handouts					
Complete training module #1					
Complete training module #2					
Track training completion					
Create opportunities for interaction					
Secure acknowledgement and acceptance of your policy					

"Full-size PDF and electronic versions of the Planning Guide are available on the Youth-Serving Organization Community page at www/taalk.org."

Child Sexual Abuse Prevention Assessment and Strategic Planning Guide

* Status Key: NA = Not Applicable, IM - Implemented, NR = Needs Revision, IP = In Process, FP = Future Plans

Best Practices	Status (NA, IM, NR, IP, FP *)	Priority to Implement (High,Med,Low)	Target Date	Lead Staff Member	Possible Barriers (Legal, Emp.Contract, Insurance, Cultural, Cost, Time)
Best Practices #5 - (continued)					
Institute an annual training process					
Incorporate training into the new hire process					
Engage parents in enforcing boundaries					
Existing parents					
Create a fun and motivating participation campaign					
Provide or direct parents to training handouts					
Offer training module #1					
Offer training module #2					
Track training completion					
Create opportunities for interaction					
Secure receipt and agreement to follow your policy					
Institute an annual training process					
Incorporate training into the new family registration process					
Best Practices #6 - Educate and Empower Children					
Deliver training for children					
Determine legal factors regarding training children (can do/can't do/must do)					
Existing children					
Respect healthy boundaries (mandatory)					
Talk about sex and sexual abuse					
Have a heart for others					
Recognize healthy peer relationships					
Establish healthy relationships with younger children					

"Full-size PDF and electronic versions of the Planning Guide are available on the Youth-Serving Organization Community page at www/taalk.org."

Child Sexual Abuse Prevention Assessment and Strategic Planning Guide

* Status Key: NA = Not Applicable, IM = Implemented, NR = Needs Revision, IP = In Process, FP = Future Plans

	Status (NA, IM, NR, IP, FP *)	Priority to Implement (High,Med,Low)	Target Date	Lead Staff Member	Possible Barriers (Legal, Emp,Contract, Insurance, Cultural, Cost, Time)
Best Practices #6 - (continued)					
Institute an annual training process					
Incorporate training into the new family registration process					
Provide suggested resources list to parents					
Best Practices #7 - Pre-Establish Your Response and Take Bold Action					
Adopt standards for responding to legal boundary violations and suspected abuse					
Provide clarirification of observed, disclosed and suspected sexual abuse					
Mandated reporters					
Provide state reporting procedures and legal consequences for failure to report					
Provide state sponsored training					
Non-mandated reporters (passive reporters)					
Establish and communicate that all staff are organizationally mandated reporters, even if they are not legally mandated reporters					
Provide state reporting procedures and organizational consequences for failure to report					
Provide state sponsored training					
Communicate your internal reporting process					
Provide considerations for reporting internally					
Centralize control of legal boundary violations and suspected abuse cases					
Establish and communicate organizational consequences of legal boundary violations					
Establish and communicate reporting requirements to licensing agencies					
Establish a process for incident review and risk assessment					

"Full-size PDF and electronic versions of the Planning Guide are available on the Youth-Serving Organization Community page at www/taalk.org."

Child Sexual Abuse Prevention Assessment and Strategic Planning Guide

* Status Key: NA = Not Applicable, IM - Implemented, NR = Needs Revision, IP = In Process, FP = Future Plans

	Status (NA, IM, NR, IP, FP *)	Priority to Implement (High,Med,Low)	Target Date	Lead Staff Member	Possible Barriers (Legal, Emp.Contract, Insurance, Cultural, Cost, Time)
Best Practices #7 - (continued)					
Establish and communicate a no victim harassment policy					
Establish a process of regular board updates					
Adopt standards for responding to organizational boundary violations					
Centralize control of organizational boundary violation cases					
Standardize your internal investigation process					
Establish and communicate consequences of organizational boundary violations					
Establish a process to communicate incident resolution					
Establish a process of regular board updates					
Create and implement an updated prevention policy that includes all best practices					
Best Practices #8 - Provide Support and Resource Referrals					
Create and distribute a child sexual abuse resource handout					

"Full-size PDF and electronic versions of the Planning Guide are available on the Youth-Serving Organization Community page at www/taalk.org."

NOTES

Introduction

1. *Merriam-Webster,* accessed June 26, 2014, http://www. merriam-webster.com/dictionary/predict.

2. David Finkelhor, Anne Shattuck, Heather A. Turner, and Sherry L. Hamby "The Lifetime Prevalence of Child Sexual Abuse and Sexual Assault Assessed in Late Adolescence," *J Adolesc Health* 55, no. 3 (Sep 2014): 3, doi:10.1016/j. jadohealth.2013.12.026.

3. "State & County QuickFacts," United States Census Bureau, accessed November 1, 2014, http://quickfacts. census.gov/qfd/states/00000.html.

4. This calculation is extremely conservative as it does not include children. It includes only adults who were likely abused when they were children. The calculation was made using the numbers in the most current topical report by David Finkelhor's cited here and the U.S. Census Bureau report, as follows: 2013 U.S. Population Estimate = 316 million, less 23% of the population under 18 years old = 23M, total adult population = 243M, 51% female population = 124M, 49% male population = 119M, 26.6%

of females are abused = 32.9M, 5.1% of males are abused = 6M, total adult population abused = 38.9M.

5. Carla van Dam, *Identifying Child Molesters: Preventing Child Sexual Abuse by Recognizing the Patterns of the Offender* (Binghamton: The Haworth Maltreatment and Trauma Press, 2001), 4.

6. Carla van Dam, *The Socially Skilled Child Molester: Differentiating the Guilty From the Falsely Accused* (Binghamton: The Haworth Press, Inc., 2006), 3.

7. Howard N. Snyder, *Sexual Assault of Young Children as Reported to Law Enforcement: Victim, Incident, and Offender Characteristics*, A NIBRS Statistical Report, National Center for Juvenile Justice (2000): 10, NCJ-182-990.

8. David Finkelhor, Heather Hammer, and Andrea J. Sedlak, *Sexually Assaulted Children: National Estimates and Characteristics*, NISMART, U.S. Department of Justice, Office of Juvenile Justice and Delinquency Prevention (August 2008): 7.

9. Shanta R. Dube et al, "Long-Term Consequences of Childhood Sexual Abuse by Gender of Victim," *Am J Prev Med* 28, no.5 (2005): 430, doi:10.1016/j. amepre.2005.01.015.

10. Cynthia Simpson, Rebecca K. Odor, and Saba Masho, *Childhood Sexual Assault Victimization in Virginia* (2004): 1.

11. "Seasonal Influenza (Flu)," Center for Disease Control and Prevention, accessed August 5, 2014, http://www.cdc. gov/flu/about/qa/disease.htm.

12. Toni Cavanagh Johnson, *Understanding Children's Sexual Behaviors - What's Natural and Healthy* (San Diego: 2013). http://www.tcavjohn.com/products.php#Fundamentals.

13. Kamala London et al, "Disclosure of Child Sexual Abuse: What Does the Research Tell Us About the Ways That Children Tell?" *Psychology, Public Policy and Law* 11, no. 1 (2005): 194–226, doi:10.1037/1076-8971.11.1.194.

14. Joshua J. Broman-Fulks et al, "Sexual Assault Disclosure in Relation to Adolescent Mental Health: Results From the National Survey of Adolescents," *Journal of Clinical Child and Adolescent Psychology* 36, no. 2 (Apr 2007): 260–266, doi:10.1080/15374410701279701.

15. Dean G. Kilpatrick, Benjamin E. Saunders, and Daniel W. Smith, *Youth Victimization: Prevalence and Implication*, U.S. Department of Justice, Office of Justice Programs, National Institute of Justice (2003): ii.

16. John Briere and Diana M. Elliott, "Prevalence and Psychological Sequelae of Self-Reported Childhood Physical and Sexual Abuse in a General Population Sample of Men and Women," *Child Abuse & Neglect* 27 (2003): 1211-1214, 1217, doi:10.1016/j.chiabu.2003.09.008.

17. Dean G. Kilpatrick, Benjamin E. Saunders, and Daniel W. Smith, *Youth Victimization: Prevalence and Implication*, U.S. Department of Justice, Office of Justice Programs, National Institute of Justice (2003): 9, 10.

18. Joshua J. Broman-Fulks et al, "Sexual Assault Disclosure in Relation to Adolescent Mental Health: Results From the National Survey of Adolescents," *Journal of Clinical Child and Adolescent Psychology* 36, no. 2 (Apr 2007): 260–266, doi:10.1080/15374410701279701.

19. Dean G. Kilpatrick et al, "Risk Factors for Adolescent Substance Abuse and Dependence Data from a National Sample," *Journal of Consulting and Clinical Psychology* 68, no. 1 (February 2000): 19–30.

20. Dean G. Kilpatrick et al, "Violence and Risk of PTSD, Major Depression, Substance Abuse/Dependence, and Comorbidity: Results From the National Survey of Adolescents," *Journal of Consulting and Clinical Psychology* 71, no. 4 (2003): 692–700, doi:10.1037/0022-006X.71.4.692.

21. Stephen A. Wonderlich, Richard W. Wilsnack, Sharon C. Wilsnack, and T. Robert Harris "Childhood Sexual Abuse and Bulimic Behavior in a Nationally Representative

Sample" *American Journal of Public Health* 86, no. 8 (August 1996): 1.

22.   Cynthia Simpson, Rebecca K. Odor, and Saba Masho, *Childhood Sexual Assault Victimization in Virginia* (2004): 3.

23.   Shanta R. Dube et al, "Long-Term Consequences of Childhood Sexual Abuse by Gender of Victim," *Am J Prev Med* 28, no.5 (2005): 434, doi:10.1016/j.amepre.2005.01.015.

24.   Vincent J. Felitti, "The Relation Between Adverse Childhood Experiences and Adult Health: Turning Gold into Lead," *The Permanente Journal* 6, no. 1 (Winter 2002): 44–47.

25.   Vincent J. Felitti and Robert F. Anda, "The Relationship of Adverse Childhood Experiences to Adult Medical Disease, Psychiatric Disorders and Sexual Behavior: Implications for Healthcare," in *The Impact of Early Life Trauma on Health and Disease: The Hidden Epidemic*, eds. Ruth A. Lanius, Eric Vermetten, and Clare Pain, (Cambridge University Press, 2010): 77–87.

26.   Martha Irvine and Robert Tanner, "AP: Sexual Misconduct Plagues US Schools," *The Washington Post*, October 21, 2007, accessed July 14, 2014, http://www.washingtonpost.com/wp-dyn/content/article/2007/10/21/AR2007102100144.html.

27.   Charol Shakeshaft, "Know the Warning Signs of Educator Sexual Misconduct," *Kappan Magazine* (February 2013): 9, 13.

28.   Charol Shakeshaft, *Educator Sexual Misconduct: A Synthesis of Existing Literature*, U.S. Department of Education, Office of the Under Secretary (2004).

29.   Michael Martinez and Paul Vercammen, "Attorneys to Release Confidential Boy Scouts Files on Alleged Child Sex Abusers," *CNN Justice*, October 18, 2012, accessed August 14, 2014, http://www.cnn.com/2012/10/17/justice/boys-scouts-sex-abuse/.

30. "The Nature and Scope of Sexual Abuse of Minors by Catholic Priests and Deacons in the United States 1950–2002," prepared by John Jay College of Criminal Justice for the United States Council of Catholic Bishops, (2004): 10-13.

31. David Finkelhor, Linda Meyer Williams, and Nanci Burns, *Nursery Crimes: Sexual Abuse in Day Care* (Newbury Park: Sage Publications, 1988), 18, 21, 28, 38, 50.

32. Megan Chuchmach, "U.S. Olympic Committee Tackling Sexual Abuse in Sport," *ABC News,* September 29, 2010, accessed August 14, 2014, http://abcnews.go.com/Blotter/Swimming/us-olympic-committee-tackling-sexual-abuse-sport-usa/story?id=11756440.

33. "Big Brothers' Leader Gets 10 Years for Sexual Abuse," *The Blade,* January 27, 2005, accessed November 1, 2014, http://news.google.com/newspapers?nid=1350&dat=20050127&id=JmhPAAAAIBAJ&sjid=VgQEAAAAIBAJ&pg=5761,3176659

34. Penn State Scandal Fast Facts, *CNN U.S.,* April 6, 2014, accessed August 14, 2014, http://www.cnn.com/2013/10/28/us/penn-state-scandal-fast-facts/.

35. Kenneth V. Lanning and Park Dietz, "Acquaintance Molestation and Youth-Serving Organizations," *J Interpers Violence* (May 2014): 4, doi:10.1177/0886260514532360.

36. "Private School Universe Survey," National Center for Education Statistics, accessed August 14, 2014, http://nces.ed.gov/surveys/pss/tables/table_2004_06.asp.

37. "America After 3PM: The Most In-Depth Study of How America's Children Spend Their Afternoons," (October 2009): 3, 4, http://www.afterschoolalliance.org/AA3_Full_Report.pdf.

38. "Mandatory Reporters of Child Abuse and Neglect (State Statutes Current Through November 2013)," Child Welfare Information Gateway, U.S. Department of Health

and Human Services (2014): 1, accessed August 14, 2014, https://www.childwelfare.gov/systemwide/laws_policies/statutes/manda.cfm.

39. "Mandatory Reporters of Child Abuse and Neglect (State Statutes Current Through November 2013)," Child Welfare Information Gateway, U.S. Department of Health and Human Services (2014): 2, https://www.childwelfare.gov/systemwide/laws_policies/statutes/manda.cfm.
40. Cynthia Simpson, Rebecca K. Odor, and Saba Masho, *Childhood Sexual Assault Victimization in Virginia* (2004): 1.
41. Howard N. Snyder, *Sexual Assault of Young Children as Reported to Law Enforcement: Victim, Incident, and Offender Characteristics*, A NIBRS Statistical Report, National Center for Juvenile Justice (2000): 15, NCJ-182-990.
42. Cynthia Simpson, Rebecca K. Odor, and Saba Masho, *Childhood Sexual Assault Victimization in Virginia* (2004): 1.
43. Howard N. Snyder, *Sexual Assault of Young Children as Reported to Law Enforcement: Victim, Incident, and Offender Characteristics*, A NIBRS Statistical Report, National Center for Juvenile Justice (2000): 15, NCJ-182-990.
44. Kenneth V. Lanning and Park Dietz, "Acquaintance Molestation and Youth-Serving Organizations," *J Interpers Violence* (May 2014): 2, doi:10.1177/0886260514532360.
45. Cynthia Simpson, Rebecca K. Odor, and Saba Masho, *Childhood Sexual Assault Victimization in Virginia* (2004): 10.
46. Kenneth V. Lanning and Park Dietz, "Acquaintance Molestation and Youth-Serving Organizations," *J Interpers Violence* (May 2014): 1,3, doi:10.1177/0886260514532360.
47. Carla van Dam, *The Socially Skilled Child Molester: Differentiating the Guilty From the Falsely Accused* (Binghamton: The Haworth Press, Inc., 2006), 3.
48. Kenneth V. Lanning and Park Dietz, "Acquaintance Molestation and Youth-Serving Organizations," *J Interpers Violence* (May 2014): 2, doi:10.1177/0886260514532360.

49. Charol Shakeshaft, "Know the Warning Signs of Educator Sexual Misconduct," *Kappan Magazine* (February 2013): 11.

50. Cynthia Simpson, Rebecca K. Odor, and Saba Masho, *Childhood Sexual Assault Victimization in Virginia* (2004): 1.

51. Howard N. Snyder, *Sexual Assault of Young Children as Reported to Law Enforcement: Victim, Incident, and Offender Characteristics*, A NIBRS Statistical Report, National Center for Juvenile Justice (2000): 13, NCJ-182-990.

52. Howard N. Snyder, *Sexual Assault of Young Children as Reported to Law Enforcement: Victim, Incident, and Offender Characteristics*, A NIBRS Statistical Report, National Center for Juvenile Justice (2000): 13, NCJ-182-990.

53. Cynthia Simpson, Rebecca K. Odor, and Saba Masho, *Childhood Sexual Assault Victimization in Virginia* (2004): 1.

54. Shanta R. Dube et al, "Long-Term Consequences of Childhood Sexual Abuse by Gender of Victim," *Am J Prev Med* 28, no.5 (2005): 430, doi:10.1016/j.amepre.2005.01.015.

55. Cynthia Simpson, Rebecca K. Odor, and Saba Masho, *Childhood Sexual Assault Victimization in Virginia* (2004): 11.

56. John Briere and Diana M. Elliott, "Prevalence and Psychological Sequelae of Self-Reported Childhood Physical and Sexual Abuse in a General Population Sample of Men and Women," *Child Abuse & Neglect* 27 (2003): 1210, doi:10.1016/j.chiabu.2003.09.008.

57. John Eldredge, *The Utter Relief of Holiness: How God's Goodness Frees Us From Everything That Plagues Us* (New York: Faith Words, Hachette Book Group, 2013).

58. Charol Shakeshaft, "Know the Warning Signs of Educator Sexual Misconduct," *Kappan Magazine* (February 2013), 9-11.

59. Anna C. Salter, *Treating Child Sex Offenders and Victims* (Newbury Park: Sage Publications, 1988), 48.

60. Carla van Dam, *The Socially Skilled Child Molester: Differentiating the Guilty From the Falsely Accused* (Binghamton: The Haworth Press, Inc., 2006), 43-44.
61. Robert J. Shoop, *Sexual Exploitation in Schools: How to Spot It and Stop It* (Thousand Oaks: Corwin Press, A Sage Publications Company, 2004), 3, 6.
62. Charol Shakeshaft, "Know the Warning Signs of Educator Sexual Misconduct," *Kappan Magazine* (February 2013): 9.
63. Charol Shakeshaft, "Know the Warning Signs of Educator Sexual Misconduct," *Kappan Magazine* (February 2013): 10-11.
64. Kenneth V. Lanning and Park Dietz, "Acquaintance Molestation and Youth-Serving Organizations," *J Interpers Violence* (May 2014): 11, doi:10.1177/0886260514532360.
65. Kenneth V. Lanning and Park Dietz, "Acquaintance Molestation and Youth-Serving Organizations," *J Interpers Violence* (May 2014): 12, doi:10.1177/0886260514532360.
66. Kenneth V. Lanning and Park Dietz, "Acquaintance Molestation and Youth-Serving Organizations," *J Interpers Violence* (May 2014): 6, doi:10.1177/0886260514532360.

Best Practice #1 - Determine Your Starting Point

1. John Briere and Diana M. Elliott, "Prevalence and Psychological Sequelae of Self-Reported Childhood Physical and Sexual Abuse in a General Population Sample of Men and Women," Child Abuse & Neglect 27 (2003): 1205, doi:10.1016/j.chiabu.2003.09.008.
2. Cynthia Simpson, Rebecca K. Odor, and Saba Masho, *Childhood Sexual Assault Victimization in Virginia* (2004): 1.
3. Shanta R. Dube et al, "Long-Term Consequences of Childhood Sexual Abuse by Gender of Victim," *Am J Prev Med* 28, no.5 (2005): 430, doi:10.1016/j.amepre.2005.01.015.

4. Noemi Pereda et al, "The Prevalence of Child Sexual Abuse in Community and Student Samples: A Meta-Analysis," *Clinical Psychology Review* 29 (2009): 7, doi:10.1016/j.cpr.2009.02.007.

5. Marije Stoltenborgh et al, "A Global Perspective on Child Sexual Abuse: Meta-Analysis of Prevalence Around the World," *Child Maltreatment* 16, no. 2 (2011): 80, 84, doi:10.1177/1077559511403920.

6. David Finkelhor, Anne Shattuck, Heather A. Turner, and Sherry L. Hamby "The Lifetime Prevalence of Child Sexual Abuse and Sexual Assault Assessed in Late Adolescence," *J Adolesc Health* 55, no. 3 (Sep 2014): 3, doi:10.1016/j.jadohealth.2013.12.026.

7. J. Barth et al, "The Current Prevalence of Child Sexual Abuse Worldwide: A Systematic Review and Meta-Analysis," *Int J Public Health* 58, no. 3 (2013): 469, doi:10.1007/s00038-012-0426-1.

8. Kenneth V. Lanning and Park Dietz, "Acquaintance Molestation and Youth-Serving Organizations," *J Interpers Violence* (May 2014): 1, 3, doi:10.1177/0886260514532360.

9. Carla van Dam, *The Socially Skilled Child Molester: Differentiating the Guilty From the Falsely Accused* (Binghamton: The Haworth Press, Inc., 2006), 3.

10. Kenneth V. Lanning and Park Dietz, "Acquaintance Molestation and Youth-Serving Organizations," *J Interpers Violence* (May 2014): 5, doi:10.1177/0886260514532360.

11. Charol Shakeshaft, *Educator Sexual Misconduct: A Synthesis of Existing Literature*, U.S. Department of Education, Office of the Under Secretary (2004): 35, 36.

12. Sandy K. Wurtele, "Preventing the Sexual Exploitation of Minors in Youth-serving Organizations," *Children and Youth Services Review* (2012): 2445, doi:10.1016/childyouth.2012.09.009.

13. "K-12 Education: Selected Cases of Public and Private Schools That Hired and Retained Individuals with Histories

of Sexual Misconduct," Report to the Chairman, Committee on Education and Labor, House of Representatives, United States Government Accountability Office, (2010).

14. "Child Welfare: Federal Agencies Can Better Support State Efforts to Prevent and Respond to Sexual Abuse by School Personnel," Report to the Ranking Member, Committee on Education and the Workforce, House of Representatives, United States Government Accountability Office (2014).

15. "2012 National Youth Protection Symposium Executive Summary," accessed August 3, 2014, 5, http://www.national youthprotectionsymposium.org/wp-content/uploads/2013/09/Executive_Summary%E2%80%932013-06-06.pdf

16. Charol Shakeshaft, *Educator Sexual Misconduct: A Synthesis of Existing Literature*, U.S. Department of Education, Office of the Under Secretary (2004): 35, 47.

17. Janet Saul and Natalie C. Audage, "Preventing Child Sexual Abuse Within Youth-serving Organizations: Getting Started on Policies and Procedures," U.S. Department of Health and Human Services, Centers for Disease Control and Prevention (2007): 29-32.

18. Robin Sax, *It Happens Every Day: Inside the World of a Sex Crimes DA* (Amherst: Prometheus Books, 2010), 187.

19. "Child Welfare: Federal Agencies Can Better Support State Efforts to Prevent and Respond to Sexual Abuse by School Personnel," Report to the Ranking Member, Committee on Education and the Workforce, House of Representatives, United States Government Accountability Office (2014): 28.

20. Kenneth V. Lanning and Park Dietz, "Acquaintance Molestation and Youth-Serving Organizations," *J Interpers Violence* (May 2014): 5, doi:10.1177/0886260514532360.

21. Carla van Dam, *The Socially Skilled Child Molester: Differentiating the Guilty From the Falsely Accused* (Binghamton: The Haworth Press, Inc., 2006), 64.

22. "2012 National Youth Protection Symposium Executive Summary," accessed August 3, 2014, 5, http://www.national youthprotectionsymposium.org/wp-content/uploads/2013/09/Executive_Summary%E2%80%932013-06-06.pdf
23. Charol Shakeshaft, "Know the Warning Signs of Educator Sexual Misconduct," *Kappan Magazine* (February 2013): 11.
24. Charol Shakeshaft, "Know the Warning Signs of Educator Sexual Misconduct," *Kappan Magazine* (February 2013): 9.

Best Practice #2 - Manage Access to Children

1. Howard N. Snyder, *Sexual Assault of Young Children as Reported to Law Enforcement: Victim, Incident, and Offender Characteristics*, A NIBRS Statistical Report, National Center for Juvenile Justice (2000): 7, NCJ-182-990.
2. Anna C. Salter, *Predators, Pedophiles, Rapists, & Other Sex Offenders: Who They Are, How They Operate, and How We Can Protect Ourselves and Our Children*, (New York: Basic Books, 2003), 2, 3.
3. Carla van Dam, *The Socially Skilled Child Molester: Differentiating the Guilty From the Falsely Accused* (Binghamton: The Haworth Press, Inc., 2006), 1.
4. Kenneth V. Lanning and Park Dietz, "Acquaintance Molestation and Youth-Serving Organizations," *J Interpers Violence* (May 2014): 1, 3, doi:10.1177/0886260514532360.
5. Carla van Dam, *The Socially Skilled Child Molester: Differentiating the Guilty From the Falsely Accused* (Binghamton: The Haworth Press, Inc., 2006), 3.
6. Janet Saul and Natalie C. Audage, "Preventing Child Sexual Abuse Within Youth-serving Organizations: Getting Started on Policies and Procedures," U.S. Department of Health and Human Services, Centers for Disease Control and Prevention (2007): 4.

7.   Eric Bailey, "Janitor Convicted of Rape and Murder," *Los Angeles Times,* August 31, 2000, accessed August 15, 2014, http://articles.latimes.com/2000/aug/31/news/mn-13289.

8.   Eric Bailey, "Janitor Convicted of Rape and Murder," *Los Angeles Times,* August 31, 2000, accessed August 15, 2014, http://articles.latimes.com/2000/aug/31/news/mn-13289.

9.   Robin Sax, *Predators and Child Molesters: What Every Parent Needs to Know to Keep Kids Safe: A Sex Crimes DA Answers 100 of the Most Asked Questions* (Amherst: Prometheus Books, 2009), 25.

10.   Dean G. Kilpatrick, Benjamin E. Saunders, and Daniel W. Smith, *Youth Victimization: Prevalence and Implication*, U.S. Department of Justice, Office of Justice Programs, National Institute of Justice (2003): ii.

11.   "K-12 Education: Selected Cases of Public and Private Schools That Hired and Retained Individuals with Histories of Sexual Misconduct," Report to the Chairman, Committee on Education and Labor, House of Representatives, United States Government Accountability Office, (2010): Abstract.

12.   Charol Shakeshaft, *Educator Sexual Misconduct: A Synthesis of Existing Literature*, U.S. Department of Education, Office of the Under Secretary (2004): 47.

13.   Janet Saul and Natalie C. Audage, "Preventing Child Sexual Abuse Within Youth-serving Organizations: Getting Started on Policies and Procedures," U.S. Department of Health and Human Services, Centers for Disease Control and Prevention (2007): 4, 5.

14.   Charol Shakeshaft, *Educator Sexual Misconduct: A Synthesis of Existing Literature*, U.S. Department of Education, Office of the Under Secretary (2004): 48.

15.   Robin Sax, *Predators and Child Molesters: What Every Parent Needs to Know to Keep Kids Safe: A Sex Crimes DA Answers*

100 of the Most Asked Questions (Amherst: Prometheus Books, 2009), 70.

16. Robin Sax, *Predators and Child Molesters: What Every Parent Needs to Know to Keep Kids Safe: A Sex Crimes DA Answers 100 of the Most Asked Questions* (Amherst: Prometheus Books, 2009), 70.

17. Sandy K. Wurtele, "Preventing the Sexual Exploitation of Minors in Youth-serving Organizations," *Children and Youth Services Review* (2012): 2446, doi:10.1016/childyouth.2012.09.009.

18. Janet Saul and Natalie C. Audage, "Preventing Child Sexual Abuse Within Youth-serving Organizations: Getting Started on Policies and Procedures," U.S. Department of Health and Human Services, Centers for Disease Control and Prevention (2007): 5

19. Janet Saul and Natalie C. Audage, "Preventing Child Sexual Abuse Within Youth-serving Organizations: Getting Started on Policies and Procedures," U.S. Department of Health and Human Services, Centers for Disease Control and Prevention (2007): 5, 6.

20. "K-12 Education: Selected Cases of Public and Private Schools That Hired and Retained Individuals with Histories of Sexual Misconduct," Report to the Chairman, Committee on Education and Labor, House of Representatives, United States Government Accountability Office, (2010): 7.

21. Goodreads, http://www.goodreads.com/quotes/23182-intuition-is-always-right-in-at-least-two-important-ways.

22. Goodreads, http://www.goodreads.com/quotes/23182-intuition-is-always-right-in-at-least-two-important-ways.

23. "The Six Pillars of Character," Josephson Institute, accessed December 11, 2011, http://josephsoninstitute.org/sixpillars.html.

24. Kenneth V. Lanning and Park Dietz, "Acquaintance Molestation and Youth-Serving Organizations," *J Interpers Violence* (May 2014): 9, doi:10.1177/0886260514532360.

25. Kenneth V. Lanning and Park Dietz, "Acquaintance Molestation and Youth-Serving Organizations," *J Interpers Violence* (May 2014): 9, doi:10.1177/0886260514532360.

26. Carla van Dam, *Identifying Child Molesters: Preventing Child Sexual Abuse by Recognizing the Patterns of the Offender* (Binghamton: The Haworth Maltreatment and Trauma Press, 2001), 168.

27. Sandy K. Wurtele, "Preventing the Sexual Exploitation of Minors in Youth-serving Organizations," *Children and Youth Services Review* (2012): 2446, doi:10.1016/childyouth.2012.09.009.

28. Robert J. Shoop, *Sexual Exploitation in Schools: How to Spot It and Stop It* (Thousand Oaks: Corwin Press, A Sage Publications Company, 2004).

29. Kenneth V. Lanning and Park Dietz, "Acquaintance Molestation and Youth-Serving Organizations," *J Interpers Violence* (May 2014): 15, doi:10.1177/0886260514532360.

30. Janet Saul and Natalie C. Audage, "Preventing Child Sexual Abuse Within Youth-serving Organizations: Getting Started on Policies and Procedures," U.S. Department of Health and Human Services, Centers for Disease Control and Prevention (2007): 4.

31. "Groupthink," L.P. CRM Learng, November 8, 2013, accessed January 23, 2014, https://www.youtube*in*.com/watch?v=SBw0ased8Sw.

32. "Groupthink," Wikipedia, accessed January 23, 2013, http://en.wikipedia.org/wiki/Groupthink.

33. Janet Saul and Natalie C. Audage, "Preventing Child Sexual Abuse Within Youth-serving Organizations: Getting Started on Policies and Procedures," U.S. Department of Health and Human Services, Centers for Disease Control and Prevention (2007): 5.

34. "K-12 Education: Selected Cases of Public and Private Schools That Hired and Retained Individuals with Histories

of Sexual Misconduct," Report to the Chairman, Committee on Education and Labor, House of Representatives, United States Government Accountability Office, (2010): 3, 4, 17.

35.   Janet Saul and Natalie C. Audage, "Preventing Child Sexual Abuse Within Youth-serving Organizations: Getting Started on Policies and Procedures," U.S. Department of Health and Human Services, Centers for Disease Control and Prevention (2007): 7.

36.   Janet Saul and Natalie C. Audage, "Preventing Child Sexual Abuse Within Youth-serving Organizations: Getting Started on Policies and Procedures," U.S. Department of Health and Human Services, Centers for Disease Control and Prevention (2007): 7.

37.   "Child Welfare: Federal Agencies Can Better Support State Efforts to Prevent and Respond to Sexual Abuse by School Personnel," Report to the Ranking Member, Committee on Education and the Workforce, House of Representatives, United States Government Accountability Office (2014): 19.

38.   Charol Shakeshaft, *Educator Sexual Misconduct: A Synthesis of Existing Literature*, U.S. Department of Education, Office of the Under Secretary (2004): 48.

39.   Robin Sax, *Predators and Child Molesters: What Every Parent Needs to Know to Keep Kids Safe: A Sex Crimes DA Answers 100 of the Most Asked Questions* (Amherst: Prometheus Books, 2009), 70.

40.   Charol Shakeshaft, "Know the Warning Signs of Educator Sexual Misconduct," *Kappan Magazine* (February 2013): 11.

41.   Janet Saul and Natalie C. Audage, "Preventing Child Sexual Abuse Within Youth-serving Organizations: Getting Started on Policies and Procedures," U.S. Department of Health and Human Services, Centers for Disease Control and Prevention (2007): 7.

42.   Charol Shakeshaft, *Educator Sexual Misconduct: A Synthesis of Existing Literature*, U.S. Department of Education, Office of the Under Secretary (2004): 48.

43.   Janet Saul and Natalie C. Audage, "Preventing Child Sexual Abuse Within Youth-serving Organizations: Getting Started on Policies and Procedures," U.S. Department of Health and Human Services, Centers for Disease Control and Prevention (2007): 7.

44.   Robin Sax, *Predators and Child Molesters: What Every Parent Needs to Know to Keep Kids Safe: A Sex Crimes DA Answers 100 of the Most Asked Questions* (Amherst: Prometheus Books, 2009), 70.

45.   Charol Shakeshaft, "Know the Warning Signs of Educator Sexual Misconduct," *Kappan Magazine* (February 2013): 11.

46.   John E. B. Myers, *Myers on Evidence in Child, Domestic and Elder Abuse Cases 1 (Aspen Publishers, 2005): 446, http:// books.google.com/books?id=-krZZF9dl-sC&pg=PA446&lpg =PA446&dq=3+percent+chance+of+getting+caught+abel&so urce=bl&ots=EIo6PlhwVy&sig=BEtofv2L4IJZnvKCeFeUU ZuWfZ0&hl=en&sa=X&ei=TbZWVIuXFdTgoASboYGAA Q&ved=0CB4Q6AEwAA#v=onepage&q=3%20percent%20 chance%20of%20getting%20caught%20abel&f=false.*

47.   "Child Welfare: Federal Agencies Can Better Support State Efforts to Prevent and Respond to Sexual Abuse by School Personnel," Report to the Ranking Member, Committee on Education and the Workforce, House of Representatives, United States Government Accountability Office (2014): 16.

48.   "Child Welfare: Federal Agencies Can Better Support State Efforts to Prevent and Respond to Sexual Abuse by School Personnel," Report to the Ranking Member, Committee on Education and the Workforce, House of Representatives, United States Government Accountability Office (2014): 16.

49. "Background Screenings," ChildCare Aware, accessed August 1, 2014, http://childcareaware.org/child-care-providers/management-plan/background-screenings.

50. "K-12 Education: Selected Cases of Public and Private Schools That Hired and Retained Individuals with Histories of Sexual Misconduct," Report to the Chairman, Committee on Education and Labor, House of Representatives, United States Government Accountability Office, (2010): 25.

51. Charol Shakeshaft, *Educator Sexual Misconduct: A Synthesis of Existing Literature*, U.S. Department of Education, Office of the Under Secretary (2004): 46.

52. Charol Shakeshaft, *Educator Sexual Misconduct: A Synthesis of Existing Literature*, U.S. Department of Education, Office of the Under Secretary (2004): 37-41.

53. "Child Welfare: Federal Agencies Can Better Support State Efforts to Prevent and Respond to Sexual Abuse by School Personnel," Report to the Ranking Member, Committee on Education and the Workforce, House of Representatives, United States Government Accountability Office (2014): 17.

54. "K-12 Education: Selected Cases of Public and Private Schools That Hired and Retained Individuals with Histories of Sexual Misconduct," Report to the Chairman, Committee on Education and Labor, House of Representatives, United States Government Accountability Office, (2010): 5, 8, 9, 25.

55. "K-12 Education: Selected Cases of Public and Private Schools That Hired and Retained Individuals with Histories of Sexual Misconduct," Report to the Chairman, Committee on Education and Labor, House of Representatives, United States Government Accountability Office, (2010): 6.

56. "K-12 Education: Selected Cases of Public and Private Schools That Hired and Retained Individuals with Histories of Sexual Misconduct," Report to the Chairman, Committee

on Education and Labor, House of Representatives, United States Government Accountability Office, (2010): 6, 25.

57. Kenneth V. Lanning and Park Dietz, "Acquaintance Molestation and Youth-Serving Organizations," *J Interpers Violence* (May 2014): 14, doi:10.1177/0886260514532360.

58. Sandy K. Wurtele, "Preventing the Sexual Exploitation of Minors in Youth-serving Organizations," *Children and Youth Services Review* (2012): 2446, doi:10.1016/childyouth.2012.09.009.

59. Janet Saul and Natalie C. Audage, "Preventing Child Sexual Abuse Within Youth-serving Organizations: Getting Started on Policies and Procedures," U.S. Department of Health and Human Services, Centers for Disease Control and Prevention (2007): 7.

60. "K-12 Education: Selected Cases of Public and Private Schools That Hired and Retained Individuals with Histories of Sexual Misconduct," Report to the Chairman, Committee on Education and Labor, House of Representatives, United States Government Accountability Office, (2010): 10.

61. Robin Sax, *Predators and Child Molesters: What Every Parent Needs to Know to Keep Kids Safe: A Sex Crimes DA Answers 100 of the Most Asked Questions* (Amherst: Prometheus Books, 2009), 69.

62. "Child Welfare: Federal Agencies Can Better Support State Efforts to Prevent and Respond to Sexual Abuse by School Personnel," Report to the Ranking Member, Committee on Education and the Workforce, House of Representatives, United States Government Accountability Office (2014): 19.

63. "K-12 Education: Selected Cases of Public and Private Schools That Hired and Retained Individuals with Histories of Sexual Misconduct," Report to the Chairman, Committee on Education and Labor, House of Representatives, United States Government Accountability Office, (2010): 4.

64.   Sandy K. Wurtele, "Preventing the Sexual Exploitation of Minors in Youth-serving Organizations," *Children and Youth Services Review* (2012): 2446, doi:10.1016/childyouth.2012.09.009.

65.   "Child Welfare: Federal Agencies Can Better Support State Efforts to Prevent and Respond to Sexual Abuse by School Personnel," Report to the Ranking Member, Committee on Education and the Workforce, House of Representatives, United States Government Accountability Office (2014): 17.

66.   "K-12 Education: Selected Cases of Public and Private Schools That Hired and Retained Individuals with Histories of Sexual Misconduct," Report to the Chairman, Committee on Education and Labor, House of Representatives, United States Government Accountability Office, (2010): 10.

67.   Charol Shakeshaft, *Educator Sexual Misconduct: A Synthesis of Existing Literature*, U.S. Department of Education, Office of the Under Secretary (2004): 40.

68.   Janet Saul and Natalie C. Audage, "Preventing Child Sexual Abuse Within Youth-serving Organizations: Getting Started on Policies and Procedures," U.S. Department of Health and Human Services, Centers for Disease Control and Prevention (2007): 8.

69.   Janet Saul and Natalie C. Audage, "Preventing Child Sexual Abuse Within Youth-serving Organizations: Getting Started on Policies and Procedures," U.S. Department of Health and Human Services, Centers for Disease Control and Prevention (2007): 8.

70.   Sandy K. Wurtele, "Preventing the Sexual Exploitation of Minors in Youth-serving Organizations," *Children and Youth Services Review* (2012): 2446, doi:10.1016/childyouth.2012.09.009.

71.   Kenneth V. Lanning and Park Dietz, "Acquaintance Molestation and Youth-Serving Organizations," *J Interpers Violence* (May 2014): 14, doi:10.1177/0886260514532360.

72.   "K-12 Education: Selected Cases of Public and Private Schools That Hired and Retained Individuals with Histories of Sexual Misconduct," Report to the Chairman, Committee on Education and Labor, House of Representatives, United States Government Accountability Office, (2010): 6.

73.   Robin Sax, *Predators and Child Molesters: What Every Parent Needs to Know to Keep Kids Safe: A Sex Crimes DA Answers 100 of the Most Asked Questions* (Amherst: Prometheus Books, 2009), 69.

74.   Janet Saul and Natalie C. Audage, "Preventing Child Sexual Abuse Within Youth-serving Organizations: Getting Started on Policies and Procedures," U.S. Department of Health and Human Services, Centers for Disease Control and Prevention (2007): 7.

75.   "K-12 Education: Selected Cases of Public and Private Schools That Hired and Retained Individuals with Histories of Sexual Misconduct," Report to the Chairman, Committee on Education and Labor, House of Representatives, United States Government Accountability Office, (2010): 8, 25.

76.   "K-12 Education: Selected Cases of Public and Private Schools That Hired and Retained Individuals with Histories of Sexual Misconduct," Report to the Chairman, Committee on Education and Labor, House of Representatives, United States Government Accountability Office, (2010): 5.

77.   Janet Saul and Natalie C. Audage, "Preventing Child Sexual Abuse Within Youth-serving Organizations: Getting Started on Policies and Procedures," U.S. Department of Health and Human Services, Centers for Disease Control and Prevention (2007): 7.

78.   Janet Saul and Natalie C. Audage, "Preventing Child Sexual Abuse Within Youth-serving Organizations: Getting

Started on Policies and Procedures," U.S. Department of Health and Human Services, Centers for Disease Control and Prevention (2007): 7, 8.

79. Sandy K. Wurtele, "Preventing the Sexual Exploitation of Minors in Youth-serving Organizations," *Children and Youth Services Review* (2012): 2446, doi:10.1016/childyouth.2012.09.009.

80. Kenneth V. Lanning and Park Dietz, "Acquaintance Molestation and Youth-Serving Organizations," *J Interpers Violence* (May 2014): 15, doi:10.1177/0886260514532360.

81. Kenneth V. Lanning and Park Dietz, "Acquaintance Molestation and Youth-Serving Organizations," *J Interpers Violence* (May 2014): 14, doi:10.1177/0886260514532360.

82. Charol Shakeshaft, *Educator Sexual Misconduct: A Synthesis of Existing Literature*, U.S. Department of Education, Office of the Under Secretary (2004): 48.

83. Robin Sax, *Predators and Child Molesters: What Every Parent Needs to Know to Keep Kids Safe: A Sex Crimes DA Answers 100 of the Most Asked Questions* (Amherst: Prometheus Books, 2009), 70.

Best Practice #3 - Set, Document, and Enforce Boundaries

1. Carla van Dam, *Identifying Child Molesters: Preventing Child Sexual Abuse by Recognizing the Patterns of the Offender* (Binghamton: The Haworth Maltreatment and Trauma Press, 2001), 52, 186.

2. Charol Shakeshaft, *Educator Sexual Misconduct: A Synthesis of Existing Literature*, U.S. Department of Education, Office of the Under Secretary (2004): 47.

3. Carla van Dam, *The Socially Skilled Child Molester: Differentiating the Guilty From the Falsely Accused* (Binghamton: The Haworth Press, Inc., 2006), 3.

4. Charol Shakeshaft, "Know the Warning Signs of Educator Sexual Misconduct," *Kappan Magazine* (February 2013): 12.

5.   Kenneth V. Lanning and Park Dietz, "Acquaintance Molestation and Youth-Serving Organizations," *J Interpers Violence* (May 2014): 10, 11, doi:10.1177/ 0886260514532360.

Best Practice #3 - Legal Boundaries

1.   Charol Shakeshaft, *Educator Sexual Misconduct: A Synthesis of Existing Literature*, U.S. Department of Education, Office of the Under Secretary (2004): 40.
2.   "Age of Consent," accessed August 12, 2014, http://www. ageofconsent.us/.
3.   Charol Shakeshaft, *Educator Sexual Misconduct: A Synthesis of Existing Literature*, U.S. Department of Education, Office of the Under Secretary (2004): 47.
4.   "Child Welfare: Federal Agencies Can Better Support State Efforts to Prevent and Respond to Sexual Abuse by School Personnel," Report to the Ranking Member, Committee on Education and the Workforce, House of Representatives, United States Government Accountability Office (2014): 59.
5.   Michael L. Bourke and Andres E. Hernandez, "The 'Butner Study' Redux: A Report of the Incidence of Hands-on Child Victimization by Child Pornography Offenders," *Journal of Family Violence* 24 (2009): 183–191, doi:10.1007/ s10896-008-9219-y.
6.   "California Penal Code," Official California Legislative Information, accessed August 12, 2014, http://www. leginfo.ca.gov/cgi-bin/calawquery?codesection=pen&code body=&hits=20.
7.   Robin Sax, *Predators and Child Molesters: What Every Parent Needs to Know to Keep Kids Safe: A Sex Crimes DA Answers 100 of the Most Asked Questions* (Amherst: Prometheus Books, 2009), 41.

8. Michele Elliott, Kevin Browne, and Jennifer Kilcoyne, "Child Sexual Abuse Prevention: What Offenders Tell Us," *Child Abuse & Neglect* 19, no. 5 (1995): 584-6, doi:10.1016/0145-2134(95)00017-3.

Best Practice #3 - On-Site Boundaries: Access

1. Kenneth V. Lanning and Park Dietz, "Acquaintance Molestation and Youth-Serving Organizations," *J Interpers Violence* (May 2014): 4, doi:10.1177/0886260514532360.
2. Janet Saul and Natalie C. Audage, "Preventing Child Sexual Abuse Within Youth-serving Organizations: Getting Started on Policies and Procedures," U.S. Department of Health and Human Services, Centers for Disease Control and Prevention (2007): 12.
3. Charol Shakeshaft, "Know the Warning Signs of Educator Sexual Misconduct," *Kappan Magazine* (February 2013): 12.
4. Andrew Knittle, "McLoud Parents Sue School District in Wake of Sexual Abuse Allegations," *NewsOK*, March 27, 2012, accessed August 12, 2014, http://newsok.com/mcloud-parents-sue-school-district-in-wake-of-sexual-abuse-allegations/article/3661042.
5. Laura Hibbard, "Kimberly Crain, Oklahoma Teacher, Resigns After Allegations Of Filming Students In Lingerie," *The Huffington Post*, November 30, 2011, accessed August 12, 2014, http://www.huffingtonpost.com/2011/11/30/kimberly-cain-oklahoma-te_n_1121558.html.
6. Tim Talley, "Kimberly Ann Crain, Former Teacher, Charged With Child Porn For Photos Of Students," *The Huffington Post, May 21, 2012, accessed August 12, 2014, http://www.huffingtonpost.com/2012/05/21/kimberly-ann-crain-teacher-child-porn-oklahoma_n_1534672.html.*

Best Practice #3 - On-Site Boundaries: Isolation

1. Gavin de Becker, Foreword to *Predators, Pedophiles, Rapists, & Other Sex Offenders: Who They Are, How They Operate, and How We Can Protect Ourselves and Our Children,* by Anna C. Salter, (New York: Basic Books, 2003), xi.

2. Robin Sax, *Predators and Child Molesters: What Every Parent Needs to Know to Keep Kids Safe: A Sex Crimes DA Answers 100 of the Most Asked Questions* (Amherst: Prometheus Books, 2009), 86.

3. Howard N. Snyder, *Sexual Assault of Young Children as Reported to Law Enforcement: Victim, Incident, and Offender Characteristics,* A NIBRS Statistical Report, National Center for Juvenile Justice (2000): 10, NCJ-182-990.

4. David Finkelhor, Heather Hammer, and Andrea J. Sedlak, *Sexually Assaulted Children: National Estimates and Characteristics,* NISMART, U.S. Department of Justice, Office of Juvenile Justice and Delinquency Prevention (August 2008): 7.

5. Sandy K. Wurtele, "Preventing the Sexual Exploitation of Minors in Youth-serving Organizations," *Children and Youth Services Review* (2012): 2447, doi:10.1016/childyouth.2012.09.009.

6. Janet Saul and Natalie C. Audage, "Preventing Child Sexual Abuse Within Youth-serving Organizations: Getting Started on Policies and Procedures," U.S. Department of Health and Human Services, Centers for Disease Control and Prevention (2007): 11.

7. Howard N. Snyder, *Sexual Assault of Young Children as Reported to Law Enforcement: Victim, Incident, and Offender Characteristics,* A NIBRS Statistical Report, National Center for Juvenile Justice (2000): 10, NCJ-182-990.

8. "Youth Protection and Adult Leadership," Boy Scouts of America, accessed August 11, 2014, http://www.scouting.org/scoutsource/HealthandSafety/GSS/gss01.aspx.

9. "Sandusky Grand Jury Presentment," *ABC News,* accessed November 10, 2011, 5, 6, http://abcnews.go.com/US/page/ gerald-sandusky-grand-jury-presentment-14924522.
10. David Finkelhor, Linda Meyer Williams, and Nanci Burns, *Nursery Crimes: Sexual Abuse in Day Care* (Newbury Park: Sage Publications, 1988), 87.
11. Charol Shakeshaft, *Educator Sexual Misconduct: A Synthesis of Existing Literature,* U.S. Department of Education, Office of the Under Secretary (2004): 33.
12. David Finkelhor, Linda Meyer Williams, and Nanci Burns, *Nursery Crimes: Sexual Abuse in Day Care* (Newbury Park: Sage Publications, 1988), 85.
13. Kenneth V. Lanning and Park Dietz, "Acquaintance Molestation and Youth-Serving Organizations," *J Interpers Violence* (May 2014): 15, doi:10.1177/0886260514532360.
14. Michele Elliott, Kevin Browne, and Jennifer Kilcoyne, "Child Sexual Abuse Prevention: What Offenders Tell Us," *Child Abuse & Neglect* 19, no. 5 (1995): 588, doi:10.1016/0145-2134(95)00017-3.
15. Charol Shakeshaft, "Know the Warning Signs of Educator Sexual Misconduct," *Kappan Magazine* (February 2013): 12.
16. Sandy K. Wurtele, "Preventing the Sexual Exploitation of Minors in Youth-serving Organizations," *Children and Youth Services Review* (2012): 2447, doi:10.1016/ childyouth.2012.09.009.
17. Greg Garrison, "Sex Abuse Victim Files Lawsuit Against Children's Pastor, Baptist Church," *AL.com,* July 23, 2014, accessed July 24, 2014, http://www.al.com/news/ birmingham/index.ssf/2014/07/sex_abuse_victim_files_ lawsuit.html.
18. David Finkelhor, Linda Meyer Williams, and Nanci Burns, *Nursery Crimes: Sexual Abuse in Day Care* (Newbury Park: Sage Publications, 1988), 87.

19. Robin Sax, *Predators and Child Molesters: What Every Parent Needs to Know to Keep Kids Safe: A Sex Crimes DA Answers 100 of the Most Asked Questions* (Amherst: Prometheus Books, 2009), 86.

20. "Sandusky Grand Jury Presentment," *ABC News,* accessed November 10, 2011, 3, http://abcnews.go.com/US/page/gerald-sandusky-grand-jury-presentment-14924522.

21. Carla van Dam, *Identifying Child Molesters: Preventing Child Sexual Abuse by Recognizing the Patterns of the Offender* (Binghamton: The Haworth Maltreatment and Trauma Press, 2001), 17, 105.

22. Howard N. Snyder, *Sexual Assault of Young Children as Reported to Law Enforcement: Victim, Incident, and Offender Characteristics,* A NIBRS Statistical Report, National Center for Juvenile Justice (2000): 10, NCJ-182-990.

23. David Finkelhor, Heather Hammer, and Andrea J. Sedlak, *Sexually Assaulted Children: National Estimates and Characteristics,* NISMART, U.S. Department of Justice, Office of Juvenile Justice and Delinquency Prevention (August 2008): 7.

24. Sandy K. Wurtele, "Preventing the Sexual Exploitation of Minors in Youth-serving Organizations," *Children and Youth Services Review* (2012): 2447, doi:10.1016/childyouth.2012.09.009.

25. Michael Winter, "Ex-bus Driver Gets 160 Years for Abusing Disabled Kids," *USA Today,* February 22, 2013, accessed August 12, 2014, http://www.usatoday.com/story/news/nation/2013/02/22/new-hampshire-bus-driver-prison-sex-abuse/1940359/.

26. "California Penal Code," Official California Legislative Information, accessed August 12, 2014, http://www.leginfo.ca.gov/cgi-bin/calawquery?codesection=pen&code body=&hits=20.

27. "Spousal Privilege," Wikipedia, accessed August 12, 2014, http://en.wikipedia.org/wiki/Spousal_privilege.
28. David Finkelhor, Linda Meyer Williams, and Nanci Burns, *Nursery Crimes: Sexual Abuse in Day Care* (Newbury Park: Sage Publications, 1988), 39.
29. David Finkelhor, Linda Meyer Williams, and Nanci Burns, *Nursery Crimes: Sexual Abuse in Day Care* (Newbury Park: Sage Publications, 1988), 87.
30. Charol Shakeshaft, *Educator Sexual Misconduct: A Synthesis of Existing Literature*, U.S. Department of Education, Office of the Under Secretary (2004): 33.
31. David Finkelhor, Linda Meyer Williams, and Nanci Burns, *Nursery Crimes: Sexual Abuse in Day Care* (Newbury Park: Sage Publications, 1988), 97.
32. Cynthia Simpson, Rebecca K. Odor, and Saba Masho, *Childhood Sexual Assault Victimization in Virginia* (2004): 1.
33. David Finkelhor, Heather Hammer, and Andrea J. Sedlak, *Sexually Assaulted Children: National Estimates and Characteristics*, NISMART, U.S. Department of Justice, Office of Juvenile Justice and Delinquency Prevention (August 2008): 2.
34. David Finkelhor and Jennifer Dziuba-Leatherman, "Children as Victims of Violence: A National Survey," *Pediatrics* 94, no. 4 (October 1994): 414.
35. David Finkelhor, Linda Meyer Williams, and Nanci Burns, *Nursery Crimes: Sexual Abuse in Day Care* (Newbury Park: Sage Publications, 1988), 86.
36. David Finkelhor, Linda Meyer Williams, and Nanci Burns, *Nursery Crimes: Sexual Abuse in Day Care* (Newbury Park: Sage Publications, 1988), 149.

Best Practice #3 - On-Site Boundaries: Behavioral

1. Robin Sax, *Predators and Child Molesters: What Every Parent Needs to Know to Keep Kids Safe: A Sex Crimes DA Answers*

100 of the Most Asked Questions (Amherst: Prometheus Books, 2009), 86.

2.   Carol Shakeshaft, "Know the Warning Signs of Educator Sexual Misconduct," *Kappan Magazine* (February 2013): 9, 10.

3.   Sandy K. Wurtele, "Preventing the Sexual Exploitation of Minors in Youth-serving Organizations," *Children and Youth Services Review* (2012): 2449, doi:10.1016/childyouth.2012.09.009.

4.   Joe Kemp, "Daughter-in-Law of Nike Co-Founder Busted for Sex Abuse: Authorities, *Daily News,* July 23, 2014, accessed July 26, 2014, http://www.nydailynews.com/news/crime/daughter-in-law-nike-co-founder-busted-sex-abuse-authorities-article-1.1876827.

5.   Kenneth V. Lanning and Park Dietz, "Acquaintance Molestation and Youth-Serving Organizations," *J Interpers Violence* (May 2014): 8, doi:10.1177/0886260514532360.

6.   David Finkelhor, Linda Meyer Williams, and Nanci Burns, *Nursery Crimes: Sexual Abuse in Day Care* (Newbury Park: Sage Publications, 1988), 92-96.

7.   Robin Sax, *It Happens Every Day: Inside the World of a Sex Crimes DA* (Amherst: Prometheus Books, 2010), 135.

8.   Michele Elliott, Kevin Browne, and Jennifer Kilcoyne, "Child Sexual Abuse Prevention: What Offenders Tell Us," *Child Abuse & Neglect* 19, no. 5 (1995): 579, 582, 586, doi:10.1016/0145-2134(95)00017-3.

9.   Carla van Dam, *Identifying Child Molesters: Preventing Child Sexual Abuse by Recognizing the Patterns of the Offender* (Binghamton: The Haworth Maltreatment and Trauma Press, 2001), 30-35.

10.   Robin Sax, *Predators and Child Molesters: What Every Parent Needs to Know to Keep Kids Safe: A Sex Crimes DA Answers 100 of the Most Asked Questions* (Amherst: Prometheus Books, 2009), 86.

11. Michele Elliott, Kevin Browne, and Jennifer Kilcoyne, "Child Sexual Abuse Prevention: What Offenders Tell Us," *Child Abuse & Neglect* 19, no. 5 (1995): 579, 585, 586, doi:10.1016/0145-2134(95)00017-3.

12. Carla van Dam, *The Socially Skilled Child Molester: Differentiating the Guilty From the Falsely Accused* (Binghamton: The Haworth Press, Inc., 2006), 53.

13. Kenneth V. Lanning and Park Dietz, "Acquaintance Molestation and Youth-Serving Organizations," *J Interpers Violence* (May 2014): 6, doi:10.1177/0886260514532360.

14. Sandy K. Wurtele, "Preventing the Sexual Exploitation of Minors in Youth-serving Organizations," *Children and Youth Services Review* (2012): 2451, doi:10.1016/childyouth.2012.09.009.

15. Carla van Dam, *Identifying Child Molesters: Preventing Child Sexual Abuse by Recognizing the Patterns of the Offender* (Binghamton: The Haworth Maltreatment and Trauma Press, 2001), 12, 21-22, 43, 46, 155, 156, 182.

16. Carla van Dam, *Identifying Child Molesters: Preventing Child Sexual Abuse by Recognizing the Patterns of the Offender* (Binghamton: The Haworth Maltreatment and Trauma Press, 2001), 30-35.

17. "Youth Protection and Adult Leadership," Boy Scouts of America, accessed August 11, 2014, http://www.scouting.org/scoutsource/HealthandSafety/GSS/gss01.aspx.

18. Sandy K. Wurtele, "Preventing the Sexual Exploitation of Minors in Youth-serving Organizations," *Children and Youth Services Review* (2012): 2447, doi:10.1016/childyouth.2012.09.009.

19. Kenneth V. Lanning and Park Dietz, "Acquaintance Molestation and Youth-Serving Organizations," *J Interpers Violence* (May 2014): 15, doi:10.1177/0886260514532360.

20. Michele Elliott, Kevin Browne, and Jennifer Kilcoyne, "Child Sexual Abuse Prevention: What Offenders

Tell Us," *Child Abuse & Neglect* 19, no. 5 (1995): 585, doi:10.1016/0145-2134(95)00017-3.

21. "Sandusky Grand Jury Presentment," *ABC News,* accessed November 10, 2011, 18, 19, http://abcnews.go.com/US/page/gerald-sandusky-grand-jury-presentment-14924522.

22. Janet Saul and Natalie C. Audage, "Preventing Child Sexual Abuse Within Youth-serving Organizations: Getting Started on Policies and Procedures," U.S. Department of Health and Human Services, Centers for Disease Control and Prevention (2007): 11.

23. Carla van Dam, *Identifying Child Molesters: Preventing Child Sexual Abuse by Recognizing the Patterns of the Offender* (Binghamton: The Haworth Maltreatment and Trauma Press, 2001), 30-35.

24. Robin Sax, *Predators and Child Molesters: What Every Parent Needs to Know to Keep Kids Safe: A Sex Crimes DA Answers 100 of the Most Asked Questions* (Amherst: Prometheus Books, 2009), 86.

25. David Finkelhor, Linda Meyer Williams, and Nanci Burns, *Nursery Crimes: Sexual Abuse in Day Care* (Newbury Park: Sage Publications, 1988), 95.

26. Kenneth V. Lanning and Park Dietz, "Acquaintance Molestation and Youth-Serving Organizations," *J Interpers Violence* (May 2014): 16, doi:10.1177/0886260514532360.

27. Marc Benjamin and Paula Lloyd, "Feds Say Clovis Teacher Lured Girl for Oral Sex, *Clovis Independent,* January 30, 2012, accessed August 12, 2014, http://www.fresnobee.com/2012/01/30/2702997/clovis-unified-teacher-recorded.html.

28. Colleen Curry, "Los Angeles Teacher Had 200 More Student Bondage Photos: Cops," *ABC News,* February 8, 2012, accessed August 12, 2014, http://abcnews.go.com/US/los-angeles-school-fourth-teacher-accused-misconduct/story?id=15540602.

29. Laura Hibbard, "Kimberly Crain, Oklahoma Teacher, Resigns After Allegations Of Filming Students In Lingerie," *The Huffington Post*, November 30, 2011, accessed August 12, 2014, http://www.huffingtonpost.com/2011/11/30/kimberly-cain-oklahoma-te_n_1121558.html.

30. Carla van Dam, *Identifying Child Molesters: Preventing Child Sexual Abuse by Recognizing the Patterns of the Offender* (Binghamton: The Haworth Maltreatment and Trauma Press, 2001), 13, 111.

31. Carla van Dam, *The Socially Skilled Child Molester: Differentiating the Guilty From the Falsely Accused* (Binghamton: The Haworth Press, Inc., 2006), 89.

32. David Finkelhor, Linda Meyer Williams, and Nanci Burns, *Nursery Crimes: Sexual Abuse in Day Care* (Newbury Park: Sage Publications, 1988), 87.

33. Kenneth V. Lanning and Park Dietz, "Acquaintance Molestation and Youth-Serving Organizations," *J Interpers Violence* (May 2014): 8, doi:10.1177/0886260514532360.

34. Janet Saul and Natalie C. Audage, "Preventing Child Sexual Abuse Within Youth-serving Organizations: Getting Started on Policies and Procedures," U.S. Department of Health and Human Services, Centers for Disease Control and Prevention (2007): 11.

Best Practice #3 - Off-Site Boundaries

1. David Finkelhor, Linda Meyer Williams, and Nanci Burns, *Nursery Crimes: Sexual Abuse in Day Care* (Newbury Park: Sage Publications, 1988), 60-61.

2. Carla van Dam, *Identifying Child Molesters: Preventing Child Sexual Abuse by Recognizing the Patterns of the Offender* (Binghamton: The Haworth Maltreatment and Trauma Press, 2001), 100.

3. Michele Elliott, Kevin Browne, and Jennifer Kilcoyne, "Child Sexual Abuse Prevention: What Offenders

Tell Us," *Child Abuse & Neglect* 19, no. 5 (1995): 585, doi:10.1016/0145-2134(95)00017-3.

4. Megan Chuchmach, Avni Patel, and Vic Walker, "USA Swimming Coach Pleads No Contest to Having Sex with Underage Swimmer," *ABC News,* April 23, 2010, accessed July 15, 2014, http://abcnews.go.com/Blotter/usa-swimming-coach-pleads-contest-sex-underage-swimmer/story?id=10460081.

5. Sandy K. Wurtele, "Preventing the Sexual Exploitation of Minors in Youth-serving Organizations," *Children and Youth Services Review* (2012): 2447, doi:10.1016/childyouth.2012.09.009.

Best Practice #3 - Off-Hours Boundaries

1. Janet Saul and Natalie C. Audage, "Preventing Child Sexual Abuse Within Youth-serving Organizations: Getting Started on Policies and Procedures," U.S. Department of Health and Human Services, Centers for Disease Control and Prevention (2007): 11.

2. Kenneth V. Lanning and Park Dietz, "Acquaintance Molestation and Youth-Serving Organizations," *J Interpers Violence* (May 2014): 18, doi:10.1177/0886260514532360.

3. Sandy K. Wurtele, "Preventing the Sexual Exploitation of Minors in Youth-serving Organizations," *Children and Youth Services Review* (2012): 2449, doi:10.1016/childyouth.2012.09.009.

4. Carla van Dam, *Identifying Child Molesters: Preventing Child Sexual Abuse by Recognizing the Patterns of the Offender* (Binghamton: The Haworth Maltreatment and Trauma Press, 2001), 146.

5. Michele Elliott, Kevin Browne, and Jennifer Kilcoyne, "Child Sexual Abuse Prevention: What Offenders Tell Us," *Child Abuse & Neglect* 19, no. 5 (1995): 581, doi:10.1016/0145-2134(95)00017-3.

6. Charol Shakeshaft, "Know the Warning Signs of Educator Sexual Misconduct," *Kappan Magazine* (February 2013): 12.

7. Howard N. Snyder, *Sexual Assault of Young Children as Reported to Law Enforcement: Victim, Incident, and Offender Characteristics*, A NIBRS Statistical Report, National Center for Juvenile Justice (2000): 11, NCJ-182-990.

8. Robin Sax, *Predators and Child Molesters: What Every Parent Needs to Know to Keep Kids Safe: A Sex Crimes DA Answers 100 of the Most Asked Questions* (Amherst: Prometheus Books, 2009), 86.

9. David Finkelhor, Heather Hammer, and Andrea J. Sedlak, *Sexually Assaulted Children: National Estimates and Characteristics*, NISMART, U.S. Department of Justice, Office of Juvenile Justice and Delinquency Prevention (August 2008): 7.

10. Sandy K. Wurtele, "Preventing the Sexual Exploitation of Minors in Youth-serving Organizations," *Children and Youth Services Review* (2012): 2447, doi:10.1016/childyouth.2012.09.009.

11. Dean G. Kilpatrick, Benjamin E. Saunders, and Daniel W. Smith, *Youth Victimization: Prevalence and Implication*, U.S. Department of Justice, Office of Justice Programs, National Institute of Justice (2003): 5.

12. Michele Elliott, Kevin Browne, and Jennifer Kilcoyne, "Child Sexual Abuse Prevention: What Offenders Tell Us," *Child Abuse & Neglect* 19, no. 5 (1995): 585, doi:10.1016/0145-2134(95)00017-3.

13. Howard N. Snyder, *Sexual Assault of Young Children as Reported to Law Enforcement: Victim, Incident, and Offender Characteristics*, A NIBRS Statistical Report, National Center for Juvenile Justice (2000): 11, NCJ-182-990.

14. Carla van Dam, *Identifying Child Molesters: Preventing Child Sexual Abuse by Recognizing the Patterns of the Offender*

(Binghamton: The Haworth Maltreatment and Trauma Press, 2001), 30-35.

15. Kenneth V. Lanning and Park Dietz, "Acquaintance Molestation and Youth-Serving Organizations," *J Interpers Violence* (May 2014): 15, doi:10.1177/0886260514532360.

16. Dominic Holden, "After Allegations of Sexual Abuse, Big Brothers Program Ends Sleepovers" *The Stranger*, February 20, 2012, accessed July 15, 2014, http://www.thestranger. com/slog/archives/2012/02/20/after-allegations-of-sexual-abuse-a-ban-on-sleepovers-for-big-brothers-and-little-brothersandview=comments.

17. Howard N. Snyder, *Sexual Assault of Young Children as Reported to Law Enforcement: Victim, Incident, and Offender Characteristics*, A NIBRS Statistical Report, National Center for Juvenile Justice (2000): 11, NCJ-182-990.

Best Practice #3 - Electronic Communication and Social Media Boundaries

1. "Is Social Networking Changing Childhood? A National Poll," Common Sense Media, accessed August 13, 2014, https://www.commonsensemedia.org/sites/default/files/uploads/pdfs/csm_teen_social_media_080609_final.pdf.

2. Mary Madden et al, "Teens and Technology 2013," PewResearch Internet Project, March 13, 2013, accessed August 13, 2014, http://www.pewinternet.org/2013/03/13/teens-and-technology-2013/.

3. Victoria J. Rideout, Ulla G. Foehr, and Donald F. Roberts, "Generation M2: Median in the Lives of 8– to 18–Year-Olds," The Henry J. Kaiser Family Foundation, January 2010, accessed August 13, 2014, http://files.eric.ed.gov/fulltext/ED527859.pdf.

4. Robin Sax, *Predators and Child Molesters: What Every Parent Needs to Know to Keep Kids Safe: A Sex Crimes DA Answers*

100 of the Most Asked Questions (Amherst: Prometheus Books, 2009), 86.

5.   Sandy K. Wurtele, "Preventing the Sexual Exploitation of Minors in Youth-serving Organizations," *Children and Youth Services Review* (2012): 2447, doi:10.1016/childyouth.2012.09.009.

6.   Kaitlin Lounsbury, Kimberly J. Mitchell, and David Finkelhor, "The True Prevalence of 'Sexting'," Crimes Against Children Research Center, University of New Hampshire, April 2011, http://www.unh.edu/ccrc/pdf/Sexting%20Fact%20Sheet%204_29_11.pdf.

7.   Mark Theoharis, "Teen Sexting: Learn the Details About Teen Sexting Laws and Penalties as Well as Information in Your State," CriminalDefenseLawyer.com, accessed August 13, 2014, http://www.criminaldefenselawyer.com/crime-penalties/juvenile/sexting.htm.

8.   Robin Sax, *Predators and Child Molesters: What Every Parent Needs to Know to Keep Kids Safe: A Sex Crimes DA Answers 100 of the Most Asked Questions* (Amherst: Prometheus Books, 2009), 86.

9.   Sandy K. Wurtele, "Preventing the Sexual Exploitation of Minors in Youth-serving Organizations," *Children and Youth Services Review* (2012): 2447, doi:10.1016/childyouth.2012.09.009.

10. Sandy K. Wurtele, "Preventing the Sexual Exploitation of Minors in Youth-serving Organizations," *Children and Youth Services Review* (2012): 2449, doi:10.1016/childyouth.2012.09.009.

11. David W. Chen and Patrick McGeehan, "Social Media Rules Limit New York Student-Teacher Contact," *The New York Times,* May 1, 2012, accessed August 11, 2014, http://www.nytimes.com/2012/05/02/nyregion/social-media-rules-for-nyc-school-staff-limits-contact-with-students.html?pagewanted=alland_r=0.

Best Practice #3 - Child-to-Child Boundaries

1. Cynthia Simpson, Rebecca K. Odor, and Saba Masho, *Childhood Sexual Assault Victimization in Virginia* (2004): 1.

2. David Finkelhor, Heather Hammer, and Andrea J. Sedlak, *Sexually Assaulted Children: National Estimates and Characteristics*, NISMART, U.S. Department of Justice, Office of Juvenile Justice and Delinquency Prevention (August 2008): 2.

3. David Finkelhor and Jennifer Dziuba-Leatherman, "Children as Victims of Violence: A National Survey," *Pediatrics* 94, no. 4 (October 1994): 414.

4. David Finkelhor, Linda Meyer Williams, and Nanci Burns, *Nursery Crimes: Sexual Abuse in Day Care* (Newbury Park: Sage Publications, 1988), 90.

5. Toni Cavanagh Johnson, *Helping Children with Sexual Behavior Problems: A Guidebook for Professionals and Caregivers* (San Diego: Institute on Violence, Abuse and Trauma, 2014).

6. David Finkelhor, Linda Meyer Williams, and Nanci Burns, *Nursery Crimes: Sexual Abuse in Day Care* (Newbury Park: Sage Publications, 1988), 87.

7. Cynthia Simpson, Rebecca K. Odor, and Saba Masho, *Childhood Sexual Assault Victimization in Virginia* (2004): 1.

8. David Finkelhor, Heather Hammer, and Andrea J. Sedlak, *Sexually Assaulted Children: National Estimates and Characteristics*, NISMART, U.S. Department of Justice, Office of Juvenile Justice and Delinquency Prevention (August 2008): 2.

9. David Finkelhor and Jennifer Dziuba-Leatherman, "Children as Victims of Violence: A National Survey," *Pediatrics* 94, no. 4 (October 1994): 414.

Best Practice #3 - Gift Boundaries

1.   Robin Sax, *Predators and Child Molesters: What Every Parent Needs to Know to Keep Kids Safe: A Sex Crimes DA Answers 100 of the Most Asked Questions* (Amherst: Prometheus Books, 2009), 86.

2.   Robin Sax, *It Happens Every Day: Inside the World of a Sex Crimes DA* (Amherst: Prometheus Books, 2010), 135.

3.   Kenneth V. Lanning and Park Dietz, "Acquaintance Molestation and Youth-Serving Organizations," *J Interpers Violence* (May 2014): 16, doi:10.1177/0886260514532360.

4.   Michele Elliott, Kevin Browne, and Jennifer Kilcoyne, "Child Sexual Abuse Prevention: What Offenders Tell Us," *Child Abuse & Neglect* 19, no. 5 (1995): 579, doi:10.1016/0145-2134(95)00017-3.

5.   "Sandusky Grand Jury Presentment," *ABC News,* accessed November 10, 2011, 2, http://abcnews.go.com/US/page/gerald-sandusky-grand-jury-presentment-14924522.

6.   Robin Sax, *Predators and Child Molesters: What Every Parent Needs to Know to Keep Kids Safe: A Sex Crimes DA Answers 100 of the Most Asked Questions* (Amherst: Prometheus Books, 2009), 86.

7.   Michele Elliott, Kevin Browne, and Jennifer Kilcoyne, "Child Sexual Abuse Prevention: What Offenders Tell Us," *Child Abuse & Neglect* 19, no. 5 (1995): 585, doi:10.1016/0145-2134(95)00017-3.

8.   Carla van Dam, *The Socially Skilled Child Molester: Differentiating the Guilty From the Falsely Accused* (Binghamton: The Haworth Press, Inc., 2006), 106.

Best Practice #4 - Regularly and Actively Assess Behaviors

1.   Carla van Dam, *The Socially Skilled Child Molester: Differentiating the Guilty From the Falsely Accused* (Binghamton: The Haworth Press, Inc., 2006), xi.

2. Carla van Dam, *The Socially Skilled Child Molester: Differentiating the Guilty From the Falsely Accused* (Binghamton: The Haworth Press, Inc., 2006), 39.

3. Carla van Dam, *The Socially Skilled Child Molester: Differentiating the Guilty From the Falsely Accused* (Binghamton: The Haworth Press, Inc., 2006), 98.

4. Michael Martinez and Paul Vercammen, "Attorneys to Release Confidential Boy Scouts Files on Alleged Child Sex Abusers," *CNN Justice*, October 18, 2012, accessed August 14, 2014, http://www.cnn.com/2012/10/17/justice/boys-scouts-sex-abuse/.

5. "Boy Scouts of America Provides Overview, Context to Youth Protection Program and Ineligible Volunteer Files," Boy Scouts of America Youth Protection, October 17, 2012, accessed June 14, 2014, http://www.scouting.org/BSAYouthProtection/Media_Center/IVFilesRelease.aspx.

6. David Crary, "Major Youth Groups Make Headway Against Sex Abuse," *Associated Press*, January 19, 2012, accessed October 28, 2014, http://www.mercurynews.com/ci_19791170.

7. Kenneth V. Lanning and Park Dietz, "Acquaintance Molestation and Youth-Serving Organizations," *J Interpers Violence* (May 2014): 16, 18, doi:10.1177/0886260514532360.

8. Charol Shakeshaft, *Educator Sexual Misconduct: A Synthesis of Existing Literature*, U.S. Department of Education, Office of the Under Secretary (2004): 49.

9. Sandy K. Wurtele, "Preventing the Sexual Exploitation of Minors in Youth-serving Organizations," *Children and Youth Services Review* (2012): 2447, doi:10.1016/childyouth.2012.09.009.

10. Carla van Dam, *The Socially Skilled Child Molester: Differentiating the Guilty From the Falsely Accused* (Binghamton: The Haworth Press, Inc., 2006), 39, 59, 60.

11. Cynthia Simpson, Rebecca K. Odor, and Saba Masho, *Childhood Sexual Assault Victimization in Virginia* (2004): 1.

12. Howard N. Snyder, *Sexual Assault of Young Children as Reported to Law Enforcement: Victim, Incident, and Offender Characteristics*, A NIBRS Statistical Report, National Center for Juvenile Justice (2000): 13, NCJ-182-990.

13. Carla van Dam, *The Socially Skilled Child Molester: Differentiating the Guilty From the Falsely Accused* (Binghamton: The Haworth Press, Inc., 2006).

14. Charol Shakeshaft, "Know the Warning Signs of Educator Sexual Misconduct," *Kappan Magazine* (February 2013): 12.

15. "Child Welfare: Federal Agencies Can Better Support State Efforts to Prevent and Respond to Sexual Abuse by School Personnel," Report to the Ranking Member, Committee on Education and the Workforce, House of Representatives, United States Government Accountability Office (2014): Abstract.

16. Charol Shakeshaft, *Educator Sexual Misconduct: A Synthesis of Existing Literature*, U.S. Department of Education, Office of the Under Secretary (2004): 48.

Best Practice #5 - Create an Accountability Team

1. Sandy K. Wurtele, "Preventing the Sexual Exploitation of Minors in Youth-serving Organizations," *Children and Youth Services Review* (2012): 2444, 2448, doi:10.1016/childyouth.2012.09.009.

2. Janet Saul and Natalie C. Audage, "Preventing Child Sexual Abuse Within Youth-serving Organizations: Getting Started on Policies and Procedures," U.S. Department of Health and Human Services, Centers for Disease Control and Prevention (2007): 22.

Best Practice #6 - Educate and Empower Children

1.   Sandy K. Wurtele, "Preventing the Sexual Exploitation of Minors in Youth-serving Organizations," *Children and Youth Services Review* (2012): 2444, 2448, doi:10.1016/childyouth.2012.09.009.

2.   Janet Saul and Natalie C. Audage, "Preventing Child Sexual Abuse Within Youth-serving Organizations: Getting Started on Policies and Procedures," U.S. Department of Health and Human Services, Centers for Disease Control and Prevention (2007): 22.

3.   Howard N. Snyder, *Sexual Assault of Young Children as Reported to Law Enforcement: Victim, Incident, and Offender Characteristics*, A NIBRS Statistical Report, National Center for Juvenile Justice (2000): 9, NCJ-182-990.

4.   Kenneth V. Lanning and Park Dietz, "Acquaintance Molestation and Youth-Serving Organizations," *J Interpers Violence* (May 2014): 7, doi:10.1177/0886260514532360.

5.   Kenneth V. Lanning and Park Dietz, "Acquaintance Molestation and Youth-Serving Organizations," *J Interpers Violence* (May 2014): 12, doi:10.1177/0886260514532360.

6.   Janis Wolak, Kimberly Mitchell, and David Finkelhor, "Online Victimization of Youth:5 Years Later," Crimes Against Children Research Center, University of New Hampshire, 2006, 15, http://www.unh.edu/ccrc/pdf/CV138.pdf.

7.   Shanta R. Dube et al, "Long-Term Consequences of Childhood Sexual Abuse by Gender of Victim," *Am J Prev Med* 28, no.5 (2005): 430, doi:10.1016/j.amepre.2005.01.015.

8.   Cynthia Simpson, Rebecca K. Odor, and Saba Masho, *Childhood Sexual Assault Victimization in Virginia* (2004): 1.

9.   Cynthia Simpson, Rebecca K. Odor, and Saba Masho, *Childhood Sexual Assault Victimization in Virginia* (2004): 1.

10. Howard N. Snyder, *Sexual Assault of Young Children as Reported to Law Enforcement: Victim, Incident, and Offender Characteristics*, A NIBRS Statistical Report, National Center for Juvenile Justice (2000): 15, NCJ-182-990.

11. Cynthia Simpson, Rebecca K. Odor, and Saba Masho, *Childhood Sexual Assault Victimization in Virginia* (2004): 10.

12. Howard N. Snyder, *Sexual Assault of Young Children as Reported to Law Enforcement: Victim, Incident, and Offender Characteristics*, A NIBRS Statistical Report, National Center for Juvenile Justice (2000): 15, NCJ-182-990.

13. Cynthia Simpson, Rebecca K. Odor, and Saba Masho, *Childhood Sexual Assault Victimization in Virginia* (2004): 1.

14. Howard N. Snyder, *Sexual Assault of Young Children as Reported to Law Enforcement: Victim, Incident, and Offender Characteristics*, A NIBRS Statistical Report, National Center for Juvenile Justice (2000): 13, NCJ-182-990.

15. Howard N. Snyder, *Sexual Assault of Young Children as Reported to Law Enforcement: Victim, Incident, and Offender Characteristics*, A NIBRS Statistical Report, National Center for Juvenile Justice (2000): 13, NCJ-182-990.

16. Cynthia Simpson, Rebecca K. Odor, and Saba Masho, *Childhood Sexual Assault Victimization in Virginia* (2004): 1.

17. Cynthia Simpson, Rebecca K. Odor, and Saba Masho, *Childhood Sexual Assault Victimization in Virginia* (2004): 11.

18. John Briere and Diana M. Elliott, "Prevalence and Psychological Sequelae of Self-Reported Childhood Physical and Sexual Abuse in a General Population Sample of Men and Women," *Child Abuse & Neglect* 27 (2003): 1210, doi:10.1016/j.chiabu.2003.09.008.

19. Julianna Pierce "Statistics on Female Abusers, Making Daughters Safe Again (MDSA), E-Mail to Diane Cranley dated December 28, 2011.

20. Dean G. Kilpatrick, Benjamin E. Saunders, and Daniel W. Smith, *Youth Victimization: Prevalence and Implication*, U.S. Department of Justice, Office of Justice Programs, National Institute of Justice (2003): 9.

21. Shanta R. Dube et al, "Long-Term Consequences of Childhood Sexual Abuse by Gender of Victim," *Am J Prev Med* 28, no.5 (2005): 430, doi:10.1016/j. amepre.2005.01.015.

22. Dean G. Kilpatrick, Benjamin E. Saunders, and Daniel W. Smith, *Youth Victimization: Prevalence and Implication*, U.S. Department of Justice, Office of Justice Programs, National Institute of Justice (2003): 10.

23. Dean G. Kilpatrick, Benjamin E. Saunders, and Daniel W. Smith, *Youth Victimization: Prevalence and Implication*, U.S. Department of Justice, Office of Justice Programs, National Institute of Justice (2003): 10.

24. Kenneth S. Kendler et al, "Childhood Sexual Abuse and Adult Psychiatric and Substance Use Disorders in Women An Epidemiological and Cotwin Control Analysis," *Arch Gen Psychiatry* 57 (October 2000): 953–959.

25. Stephen A. Wonderlich, Richard W. Wilsnack, Sharon C. Wilsnack, and T. Robert Harris "Childhood Sexual Abuse and Bulimic Behavior in a Nationally Representative Sample" *American Journal of Public Health* 86, no. 8 (August 1996): 1.

26. Nancy D. Kellogg, Thomas J. Hoffman, and Elizabeth R. Taylor, "Early Sexual Experiences Among Pregnant and Parenting Adolescents," *Adolescence* 34, no. 134 (Summer 1999): 293–303.

27. Jennie G. Noll, Penelope K. Trickett, and Frank W. Putnam, "A Prospective Investigation of the Impact of Childhood Sexual Abuse on the Development of Sexuality," *J Consult Clin Psychol* 71, no. 3 (June 2003): 575.

28. Elizabeth M. Saewyc, Lara Leanne Magee, and Sandra E. Pettingell, "Teenage Pregnancy and Associated Risk Behaviors," *Perspectives on Sexual and Reproductive Health* 36, no. 3 (2004): 101.

29. Debra Boyer and David Fine. "Sexual Abuse as a Factor in Adolescent Pregnancy and Child Maltreatment," *Family Planning Perspectives* 24, no. 4 (Jan-Feb 1992): 4.

30. Dean G. Kilpatrick, Benjamin E. Saunders, and Daniel W. Smith, *Youth Victimization: Prevalence and Implication*, U.S. Department of Justice, Office of Justice Programs, National Institute of Justice (2003): 10.

31. Richard Dembo et al, "The Role of Family Factors, Physical Abuse, and Sexual Victimization Experiences in High-Risk Youths' Alcohol and Other Drug Use and Delinquency: A Longitudinal Model," *Victims and Violence* 7, no. 3, (1992): 245-266, http://www.ingentaconnect.com/content/springer/vav/1992/00000007/00000003/art00005.

32. Vincent J. Felitti, "The Relation Between Adverse Childhood Experiences and Adult Health: Turning Gold into Lead," *The Permanente Journal* 6, no. 1 (Winter 2002): 45–47.

33. Vincent J. Felitti and Robert F. Anda, "The Relationship of Adverse Childhood Experiences to Adult Medical Disease, Psychiatric Disorders and Sexual Behavior: Implications for Healthcare," in *The Impact of Early Life Trauma on Health and Disease: The Hidden Epidemic*, eds. Ruth A. Lanius, Eric Vermetten, and Clare Pain, (Cambridge University Press, 2010): 77–87.

34. Shanta R. Dube et al, "Long-Term Consequences of Childhood Sexual Abuse by Gender of Victim," *Am J Prev Med* 28, no.5 (2005): 430, doi:10.1016/j.amepre.2005.01.015.

35. Shanta R. Dube et al, "Long-Term Consequences of Childhood Sexual Abuse by Gender of Victim,"

Am J Prev Med 28, no.5 (2005): 430, doi:10.1016/j. amepre.2005.01.015.

36.   Robert E. Longo, interview by Diane M. Cranley, *What We Should Tell Teens About Sex,* August 1, 2012.

37.   Cynthia Simpson, Rebecca K. Odor, and Saba Masho, *Childhood Sexual Assault Victimization in Virginia* (2004): 1.

38.   Howard N. Snyder, *Sexual Assault of Young Children as Reported to Law Enforcement: Victim, Incident, and Offender Characteristics,* A NIBRS Statistical Report, National Center for Juvenile Justice (2000): 13, NCJ-182-990.

39.   Michele Elliott, Kevin Browne, and Jennifer Kilcoyne, "Child Sexual Abuse Prevention: What Offenders Tell Us," *Child Abuse & Neglect* 19, no. 5 (1995): 582, doi:10.1016/0145-2134(95)00017-3.

40.   Michele Elliott, Kevin Browne, and Jennifer Kilcoyne, "Child Sexual Abuse Prevention: What Offenders Tell Us," *Child Abuse & Neglect* 19, no. 5 (1995): 582, doi:10.1016/0145-2134(95)00017-3.

Best Practice #7 - Pre-Establish Your Response
and Take Bold Action

1.   Toni Cavanagh Johnson, *Understanding Children's Sexual Behaviors - What's Natural and Healthy* (San Diego: 2013), 51. http://www.tcavjohn.com/products. php#Fundamentals.

2.   Colleen Curry, Beth Loyd, and Jim Avila, "Jerry Sandusky Witness Tells of Staring at Coach in the Showers With a Boy," *ABC News,* June 12, 2012, accessed May 10, 2014, http://abcnews.go.com/US/ jerry-sandusky-trial-hears-key-witness-mike-mcqueary/ story?id=16545142.

3.   Amy Davidson, "Screams in the Basement: Prosecutors Finish up in the Sandusky Trial," *The New Yorker,* June 15, 2012, accessed May 10, 2014, http://www.newyorker.

com/news/amy-davidson/screams-in-the-basement-
prosecutors-finish-up-in-the-sandusky-trial.

4.   Shakeshaft, Charol. "Know the warning signs of educator
sexual misconduct." *Kappan Magazine*, February 2013:
8–13. Charol Shakeshaft, "Know the Warning Signs of
Educator Sexual Misconduct," *Kappan Magazine* (February
2013): 13.

5.   Google Search, accessed August 5, 2014, https://www.
google.com/search?q=suspect+definitionandoq=suspect+d
efinitionandaqs=chrome.69i57.2763j0j7andsourceid=chro
meandes_sm=93andie=UTF-8.

6.   Robin Sax, *It Happens Every Day: Inside the World of a Sex
Crimes DA* (Amherst: Prometheus Books, 2010), 135.

7.   "Mandatory Reporters of Child Abuse and Neglect
(State Statutes Current Through November 2013)," Child
Welfare Information Gateway, U.S. Department of Health
and Human Services (2014): 1, https://www.childwelfare.
gov/systemwide/laws_policies/statutes/manda.cfm.

8.   "Mandatory Reporters of Child Abuse and Neglect
(State Statutes Current Through November 2013)," Child
Welfare Information Gateway, U.S. Department of Health
and Human Services (2014): 2, https://www.childwelfare.
gov/systemwide/laws_policies/statutes/manda.cfm.

9.   "Mandatory Reporters of Child Abuse and Neglect
(State Statutes Current Through November 2013)," Child
Welfare Information Gateway, U.S. Department of Health
and Human Services (2014): 2, https://www.childwelfare.
gov/systemwide/laws_policies/statutes/manda.cfm.

10.   Kenneth V. Lanning and Park Dietz, "Acquaintance
Molestation and Youth-Serving Organizations," *J Interpers
Violence* (May 2014): 18-19, doi:10.1177/0886260514532360.

11.   "Child Welfare: Federal Agencies Can Better Support
State Efforts to Prevent and Respond to Sexual Abuse
by School Personnel," Report to the Ranking Member,

Committee on Education and the Workforce, House of Representatives, United States Government Accountability Office (2014): 23.

12. "Penalties for Failure to Report and False Reporting of Child Abuse and Neglect," Child Welfare Information Gateway, U.S. Department of Health and Human Services (2014): 2, 3, accessed August 14, 2014, https://www.childwelfare.gov/systemwide/laws_policies/statutes/report.pdf#Page=2andview=Fit.

13. "Child Welfare: Federal Agencies Can Better Support State Efforts to Prevent and Respond to Sexual Abuse by School Personnel," Report to the Ranking Member, Committee on Education and the Workforce, House of Representatives, United States Government Accountability Office (2014): 29.

14. Carla van Dam, *The Socially Skilled Child Molester: Differentiating the Guilty From the Falsely Accused* (Binghamton: The Haworth Press, Inc., 2006), 96.

15. "Child Welfare: Federal Agencies Can Better Support State Efforts to Prevent and Respond to Sexual Abuse by School Personnel," Report to the Ranking Member, Committee on Education and the Workforce, House of Representatives, United States Government Accountability Office (2014): Abstract.

16. "Mandatory Reporters of Child Abuse and Neglect (State Statutes Current Through November 2013)," Child Welfare Information Gateway, U.S. Department of Health and Human Services (2014): 3, accessed August 14, 2014, https://www.childwelfare.gov/systemwide/laws_policies/statutes/manda.cfm.

17. "Child Welfare: Federal Agencies Can Better Support State Efforts to Prevent and Respond to Sexual Abuse by School Personnel," Report to the Ranking Member, Committee on Education and the Workforce, House of Representatives,

United States Government Accountability Office (2014): 26, 28.

18. Howard N. Snyder, *Sexual Assault of Young Children as Reported to Law Enforcement: Victim, Incident, and Offender Characteristics*, A NIBRS Statistical Report, National Center for Juvenile Justice (2000): 10, NCJ-182-990.

19. David Finkelhor, Heather Hammer, and Andrea J. Sedlak, *Sexually Assaulted Children: National Estimates and Characteristics*, NISMART, U.S. Department of Justice, Office of Juvenile Justice and Delinquency Prevention (August 2008): 7.

20. "Child Welfare: Federal Agencies Can Better Support State Efforts to Prevent and Respond to Sexual Abuse by School Personnel," Report to the Ranking Member, Committee on Education and the Workforce, House of Representatives, United States Government Accountability Office (2014): 34.

21. "Mandatory Reporters of Child Abuse and Neglect (State Statutes Current Through November 2013)," Child Welfare Information Gateway, U.S. Department of Health and Human Services (2014): 11, accessed August 14, 2014, https://www.childwelfare.gov/systemwide/laws_policies/statutes/manda.cfm.

22. Beth Barrett, "Mark Berndt's $40,000 Payoff," *LA Weekly*, February 16, 2012, accessed August 10, 2014, http://www.laweekly.com/2012-02-16/news/mark-berndt-miramonte-40000-payoff/.

23. Charol Shakeshaft, "Know the Warning Signs of Educator Sexual Misconduct," *Kappan Magazine* (February 2013): 12.

24. "Child Welfare: Federal Agencies Can Better Support State Efforts to Prevent and Respond to Sexual Abuse by School Personnel," Report to the Ranking Member, Committee on Education and the Workforce, House of

Representatives, United States Government Accountability Office (2014): 32.

25. Kenneth V. Lanning and Park Dietz, "Acquaintance Molestation and Youth-Serving Organizations," *J Interpers Violence* (May 2014): 21, doi:10.1177/0886260514532360.

26. Janet Saul and Natalie C. Audage, "Preventing Child Sexual Abuse Within Youth-serving Organizations: Getting Started on Policies and Procedures," U.S. Department of Health and Human Services, Centers for Disease Control and Prevention (2007): 19.

27. Carla van Dam, *The Socially Skilled Child Molester: Differentiating the Guilty From the Falsely Accused* (Binghamton: The Haworth Press, Inc., 2006).

28. Charol Shakeshaft, "Know the Warning Signs of Educator Sexual Misconduct," *Kappan Magazine* (February 2013): 10.

29. R.K. Oates et al, "Erroneous Concerns About Child Sexual Abuse," *Child Abuse & Neglect* 24, no. 1, (Jan 2000): Abstract.

30. David P. H. Jones and J. Melbourne McGraw, "Reliable and Fictitious Accounts of Sexual Abuse to Children," *Journal of Interpersonal Violence* 2, no. 1 (March 1987): 27–45.

31. Michele Elliott, Kevin Browne, and Jennifer Kilcoyne, "Child Sexual Abuse Prevention: What Offenders Tell Us," *Child Abuse & Neglect* 19, no. 5 (1995): 584, doi:10.1016/0145-2134(95)00017-3.

32. Charol Shakeshaft, "Know the Warning Signs of Educator Sexual Misconduct," *Kappan Magazine* (February 2013): 13.

33. Charol Shakeshaft, "Know the Warning Signs of Educator Sexual Misconduct," *Kappan Magazine* (February 2013): 12.

Best Practice #8 - Provide Support and Resource Referrals

1. Shanta R. Dube et al, "Long-Term Consequences of Childhood Sexual Abuse by Gender of Victim," *Am J Prev Med* 28, no.5 (2005): 430, doi:10.1016/j.amepre.2005.01.015.

2.	Cynthia Simpson, Rebecca K. Odor, and Saba Masho, *Childhood Sexual Assault Victimization in Virginia* (2004): 1.

3.	Seasonal Influenza (Flu), *Center for Disease Control and Prevention,* accessed August 5, 2014, http://www.cdc.gov/flu/about/qa/disease.htm.

4.	Shanta R. Dube et al, "Long-Term Consequences of Childhood Sexual Abuse by Gender of Victim," *Am J Prev Med* 28, no.5 (2005): 430, doi:10.1016/j.amepre.2005.01.015.

5.	Cynthia Simpson, Rebecca K. Odor, and Saba Masho, *Childhood Sexual Assault Victimization in Virginia* (2004): 1.

6.	Seasonal Influenza (Flu), *Center for Disease Control and Prevention,* accessed August 5, 2014, http://www.cdc.gov/flu/about/qa/disease.htm.

Next Steps

1.	Kenneth V. Lanning and Park Dietz, "Acquaintance Molestation and Youth-Serving Organizations," *J Interpers Violence* (May 2014): 5, doi:10.1177/0886260514532360.

Made in the USA
Las Vegas, NV
05 May 2022

48429526R00240